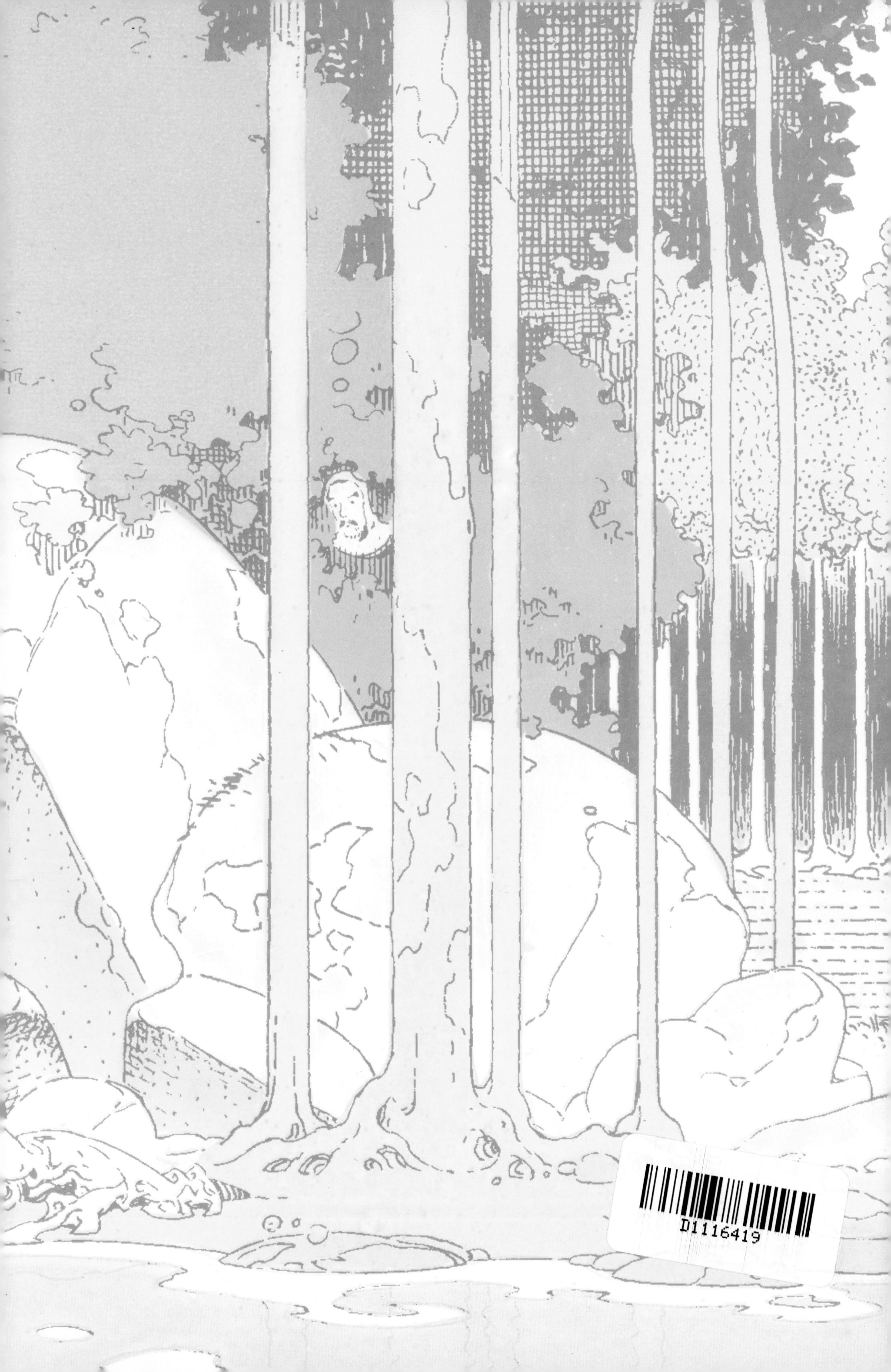

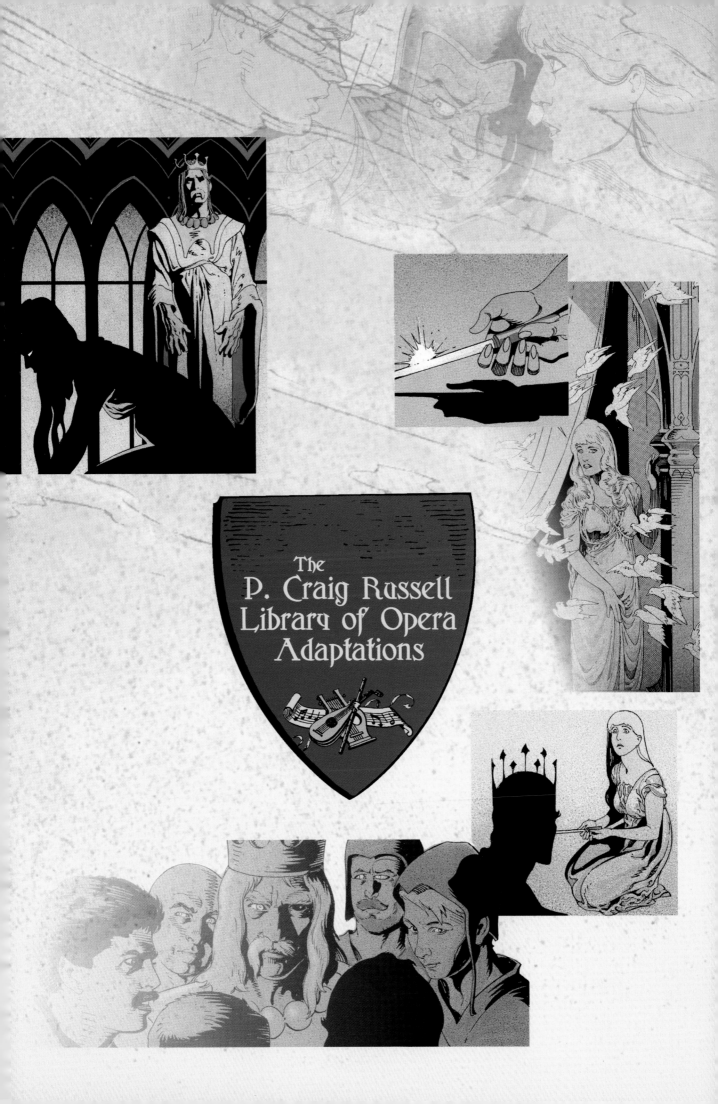

The
P. Craig Russell
Library of Opera
Adaptations

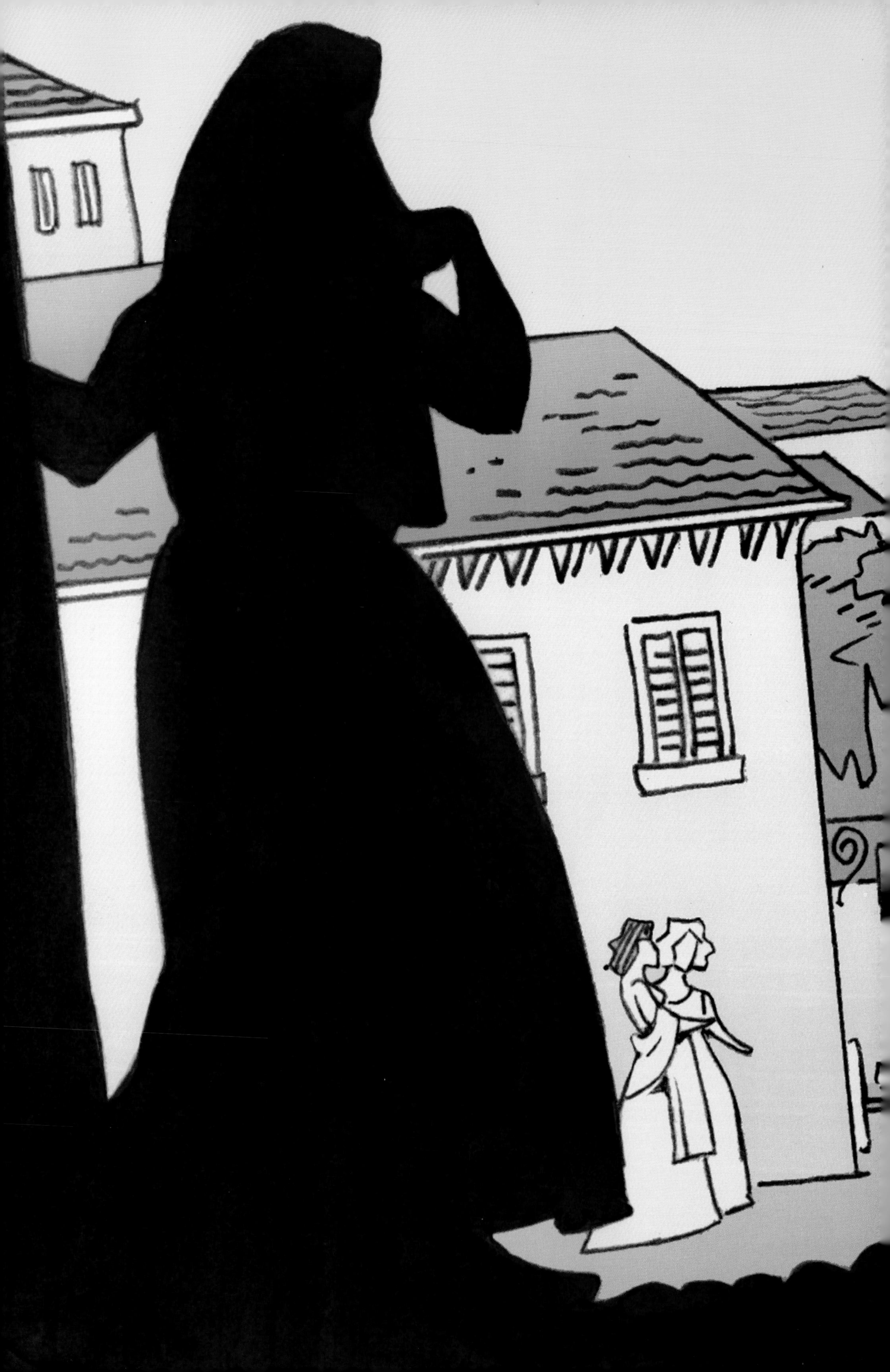

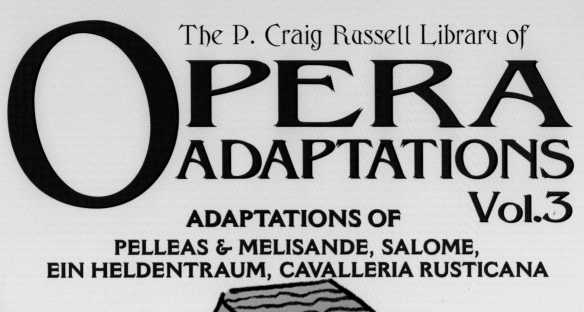

The P. Craig Russell Library of
OPERA ADAPTATIONS
Vol.3

ADAPTATIONS OF
PELLEAS & MELISANDE, SALOME,
EIN HELDENTRAUM, CAVALLERIA RUSTICANA

NBM

NANTIER · BEALL · MINOUSTCHINE

TABLE OF CONTENTS

ISBN 1-56163-388-7 cloth,
ISBN 1-56163-389-5 pb.
Pelleas & Melisande and Salome © 1984, 1986, 1990 P. Craig Russell
Ein Heldentraum and The Godfather's Code © 2004 P. Craig Russell
Printed in China

3   2   1

Colors for The Godfather's Code by Lovern Kindzierski.

Special thanks to the Ohio State University Cartoon
Research Library and its curator, Lucy Caswell, for archiv-
ing the materials in this series of books and making it available to the publisher. Most of P. Craig Russell's work is on
deposit at the library and is available to the public.

Library of Congress Cataloging-in-Publication Data

Russell, P. Craig
  [Selections. 2004]
  Pelleas & Melisande ; Salome ; Cavalleria rusticana / [adaptation by] P. Craig Russell.
    p. cm. -- (The P. Craig Russell library of opera adaptations ; v. 3)
  ISBN 1-56163-388-7 -- ISBN 1-56163-389-5 (pbk.)
    I. Title: Pellas &Melisande ; Salome ; Cavalleria rusticana. II. Title: Salome. III.
Title: Cavalleria rusticana. IV. Title: Pelleas et Melisande ; Salome ; Cavalleria rusticana.
V. Maeterlinck, Maurice, 1862-1949. Pelleas et Melisande. VI. Strauss, Richard,
1864-1949. Salone. VII. Mascagni, Pietro, 1863-1945. Cavalleria rusticana. VIII. Title:
Salome. IX. Title: Cavalleria rusticana. X. Title. XI. Russell, P. Craig Russell
library of opera adaptations ; v. 3.

PN6727.R85A6 2004
741.5'973--dc22
                                                    2004042679

PELLEAS & MELISANDE

INTRODUCTION

'**A** new indescribable power dominates this somnambulistic drama. All that is said therein at once hides and reveals the source of an unknown life.' So did Maurice Maeterlinck write of Ibsen's play *The Master Builder*, but the observation is remarkably true of his own work, which 'at once hides and reveals' its symbols, ideas, and characters.

Maurice Polydore-Marie-Bernard Maeterlinck was born in Ghent in 1862 and, though the greatest of all Belgian playwrights, he wrote in French. Indeed, his strongest influences were from the French Symbolist poets and his expression of the ideas of the Symbolists in drama is his great achievement. Though much admired in his own day for his poetry and philosophical prose as well as his many and varied works for the stage, it is a single play, *Pelléas and Melisande* (1892) by which he is known today. It is the undisputed masterpiece of both the author and the era.

Maeterlinck embodied some striking contradictions. A mystic who was involved in the occult in his early years, he was also an avid bicyclist and health enthusiast. (He died in 1949 at the age of 86). His philosophical pessimism is strangely offset by the constant suggestion throughout his work that man just may be able to understand himself and by such an appreciation even effect a change for the better in the human condition. But there is no clear ideology or plan set forth in his work – only speculation.

The Symbolists and especially Maeterlinck felt that the spoken word was somewhat impotent. Perhaps that is why Pelléas and Melisande is known primarily through Claude Debussy's sensitive musical setting. But if something is lacking in the words of this dream-play, it is only because something is lacking in language for Maeterlinck. The music of Debussy or the artwork of Russell may enunciate the action and meanings of the drama, but it remains a world of half-lives, ephemeral yet recognizable in some distracted corner of our minds.

Patrick C. Mason

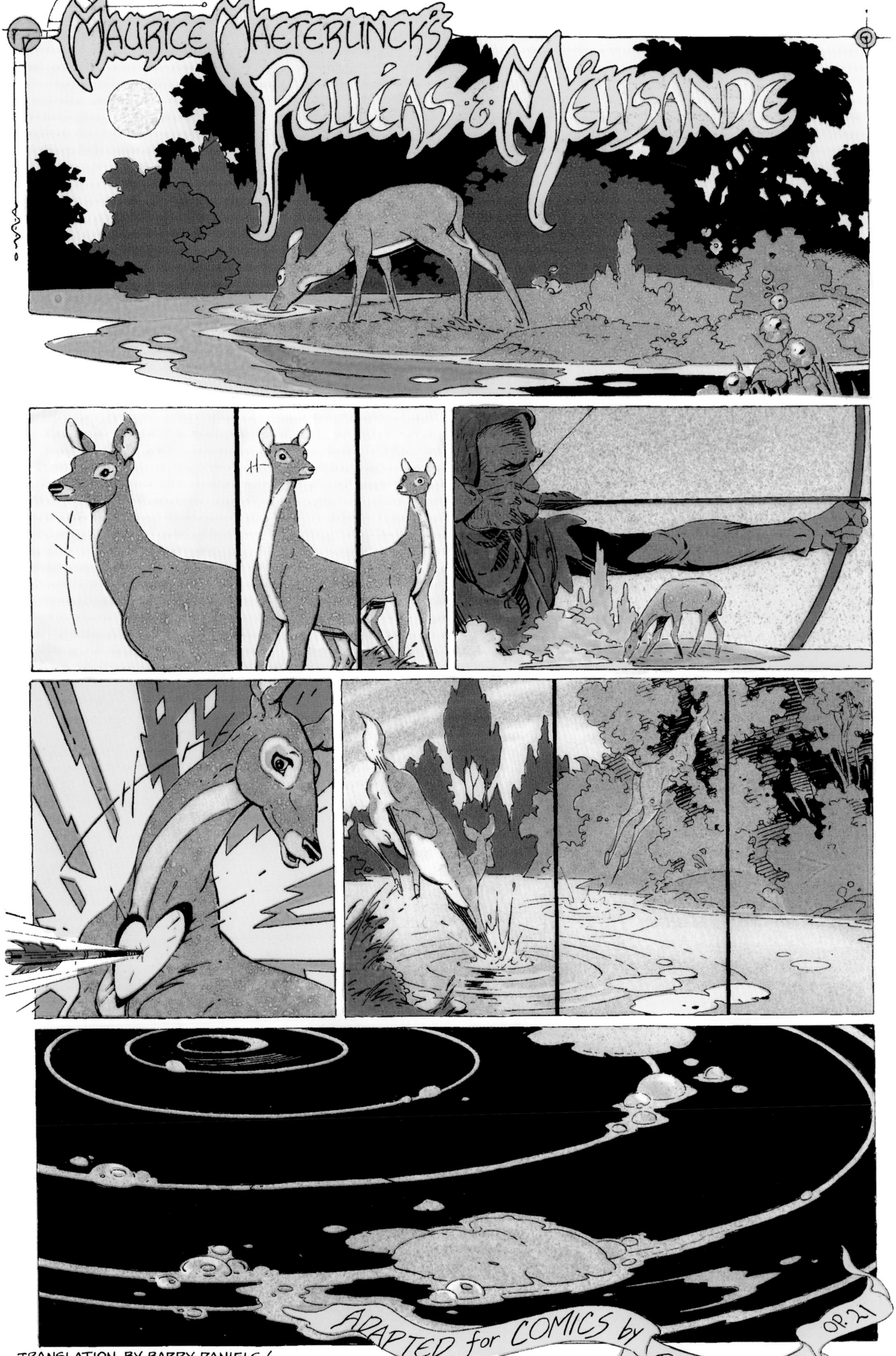
Maurice Maeterlinck's
Pelléas & Mélisande
Adapted for Comics by P. Craig Russell. Op. 21

TRANSLATION BY BARRY DANIELS/
LETTERING BY BILL PEARSON

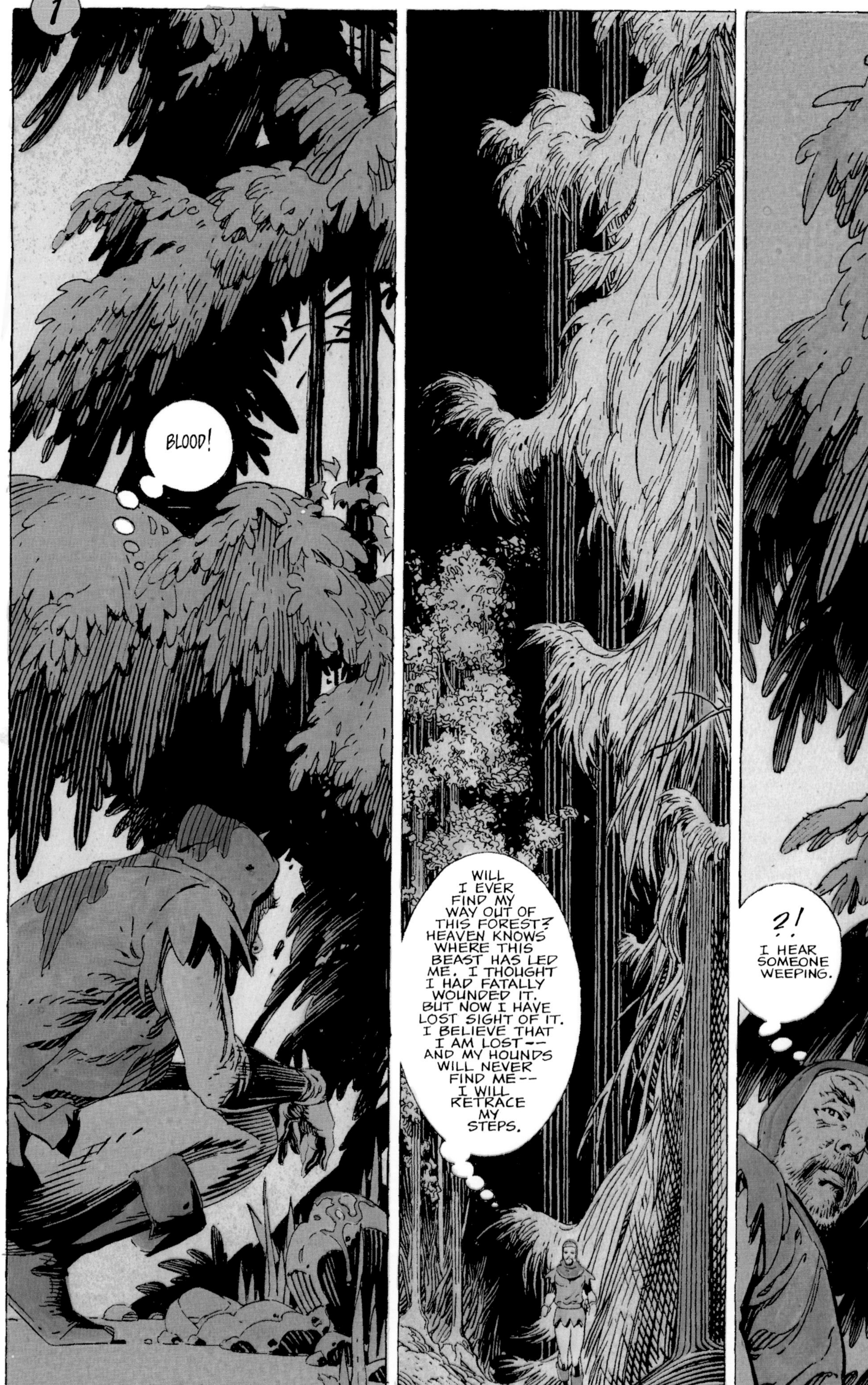
1
BLOOD!
WILL I EVER FIND MY WAY OUT OF THIS FOREST? HEAVEN KNOWS WHERE THIS BEAST HAS LED ME. I THOUGHT I HAD FATALLY WOUNDED IT. BUT NOW I HAVE LOST SIGHT OF IT. I BELIEVE THAT I AM LOST-- AND MY HOUNDS WILL NEVER FIND ME-- I WILL RETRACE MY STEPS.
?!
I HEAR SOMEONE WEEPING.

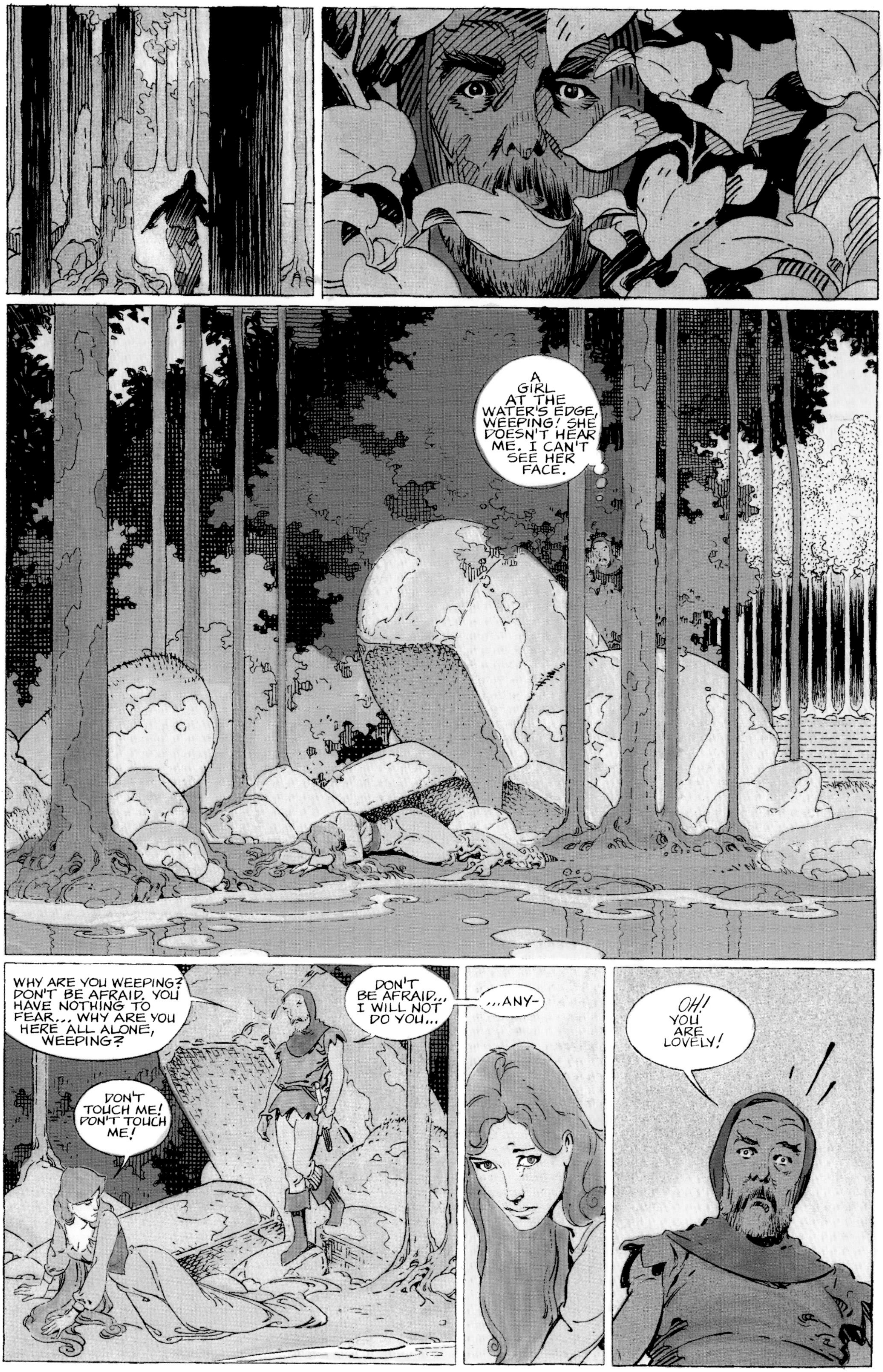
A GIRL AT THE WATER'S EDGE, WEEPING! SHE DOESN'T HEAR ME. I CAN'T SEE HER FACE.
WHY ARE YOU WEEPING? DON'T BE AFRAID. YOU HAVE NOTHING TO FEAR... WHY ARE YOU HERE ALL ALONE, WEEPING?
DON'T TOUCH ME! DON'T TOUCH ME!
DON'T BE AFRAID... I WILL NOT DO YOU...
...ANY-
OH! YOU ARE LOVELY!

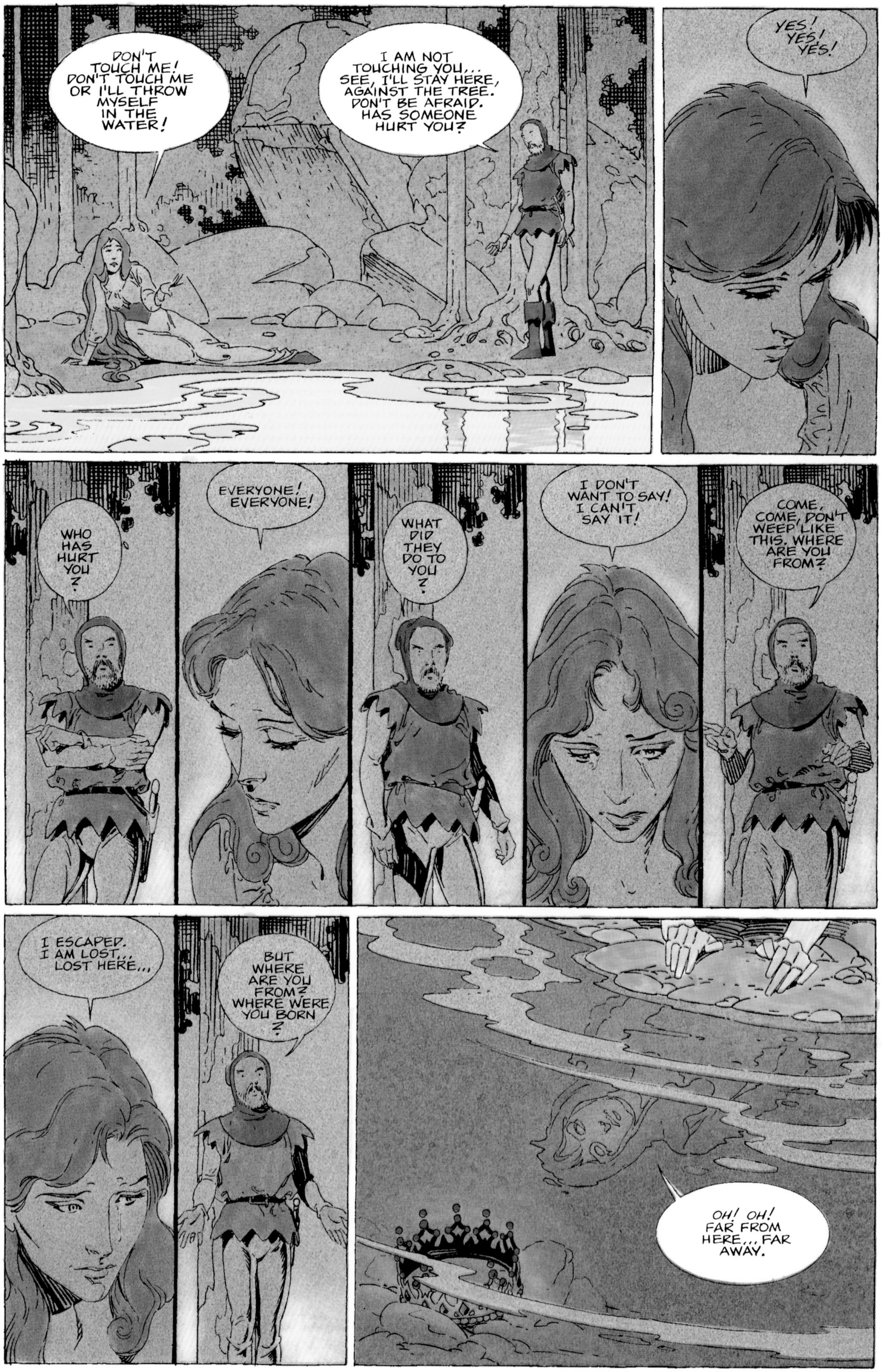
DON'T TOUCH ME! DON'T TOUCH ME OR I'LL THROW MYSELF IN THE WATER!
I AM NOT TOUCHING YOU... SEE, I'LL STAY HERE, AGAINST THE TREE. DON'T BE AFRAID. HAS SOMEONE HURT YOU?
YES! YES! YES!
WHO HAS HURT YOU?
EVERYONE! EVERYONE!
WHAT DID THEY DO TO YOU?
I DON'T WANT TO SAY! I CAN'T SAY IT!
COME, COME, DON'T WEEP LIKE THIS. WHERE ARE YOU FROM?
I ESCAPED. I AM LOST... LOST HERE...
BUT WHERE ARE YOU FROM? WHERE WERE YOU BORN?
OH! OH! FAR FROM HERE... FAR AWAY.

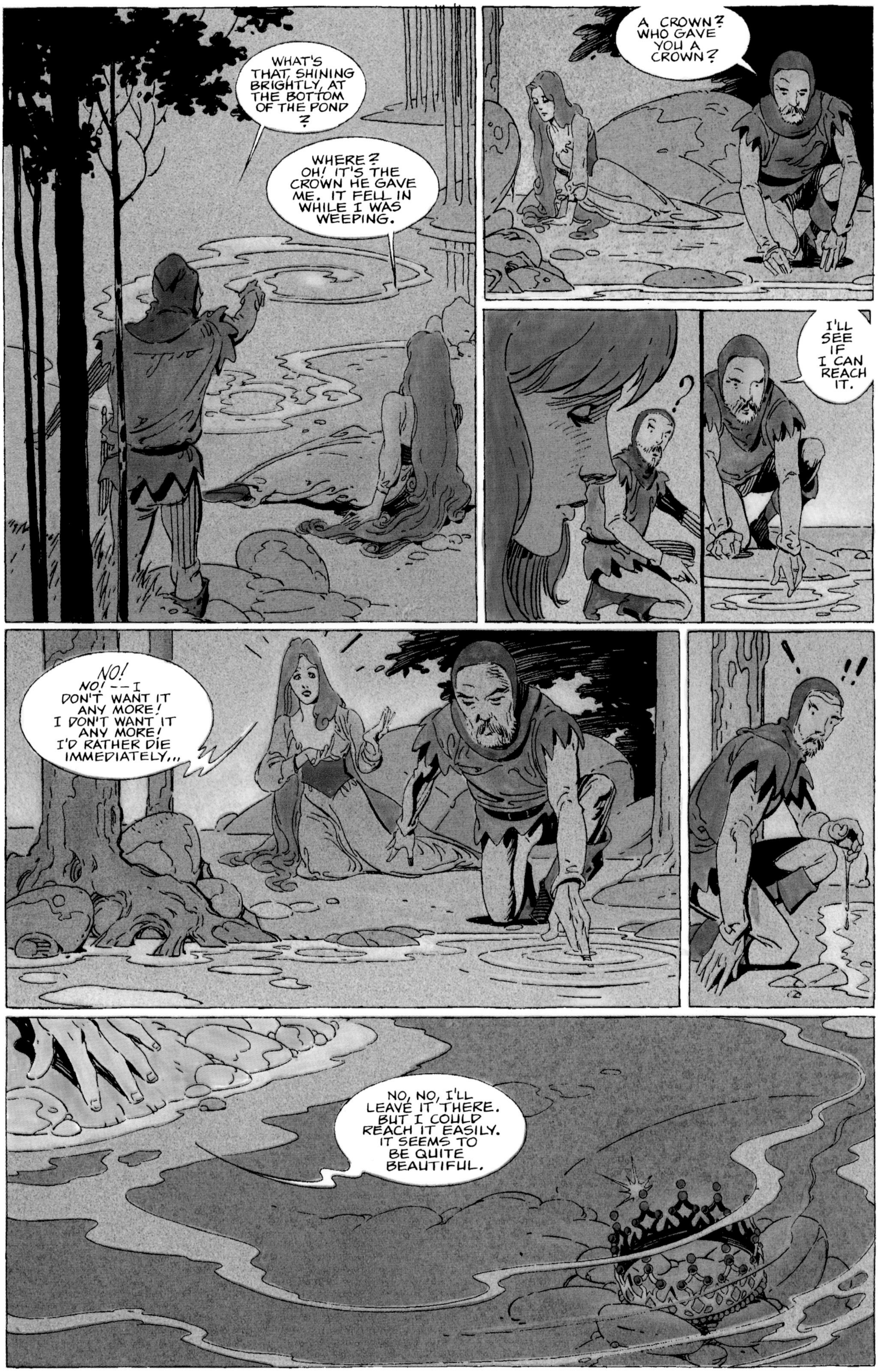
WHAT'S THAT, SHINING BRIGHTLY, AT THE BOTTOM OF THE POND ?
WHERE? OH! IT'S THE CROWN HE GAVE ME. IT FELL IN WHILE I WAS WEEPING.
A CROWN? WHO GAVE YOU A CROWN?
?
I'LL SEE IF I CAN REACH IT.
NO! NO! --I DON'T WANT IT ANY MORE! I DON'T WANT IT ANY MORE! I'D RATHER DIE IMMEDIATELY...
!!
NO, NO, I'LL LEAVE IT THERE. BUT I COULD REACH IT EASILY. IT SEEMS TO BE QUITE BEAUTIFUL.

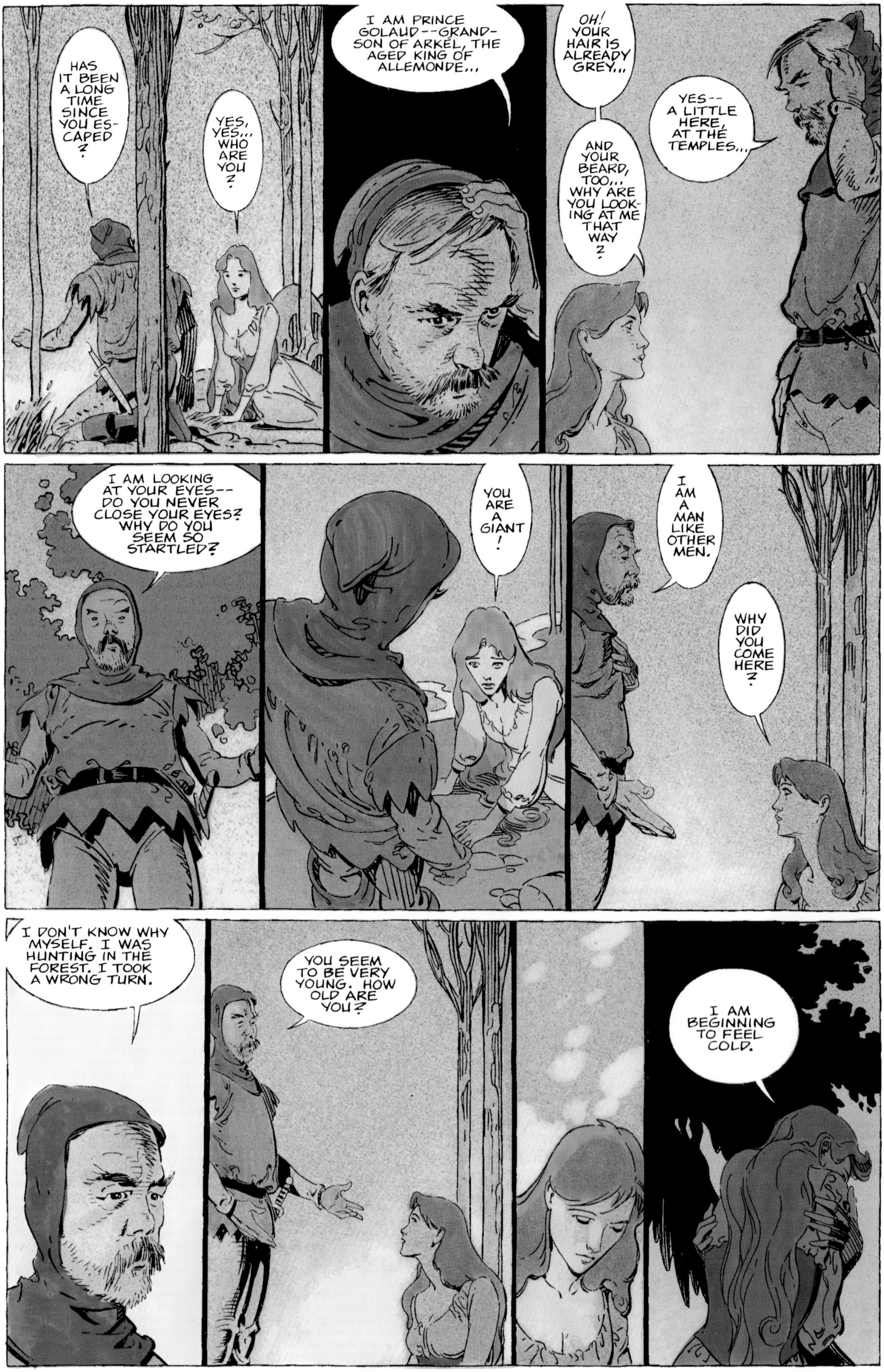
HAS IT BEEN A LONG TIME SINCE YOU ESCAPED?
YES, YES... WHO ARE YOU?
I AM PRINCE GOLAUD--GRANDSON OF ARKEL, THE AGED KING OF ALLEMONDE...
OH! YOUR HAIR IS ALREADY GREY...
AND YOUR BEARD, TOO... WHY ARE YOU LOOKING AT ME THAT WAY?
YES-- A LITTLE HERE, AT THE TEMPLES...
I AM LOOKING AT YOUR EYES-- DO YOU NEVER CLOSE YOUR EYES? WHY DO YOU SEEM SO STARTLED?
YOU ARE A GIANT!
I AM A MAN LIKE OTHER MEN.
WHY DID YOU COME HERE?
I DON'T KNOW WHY MYSELF. I WAS HUNTING IN THE FOREST. I TOOK A WRONG TURN.
YOU SEEM TO BE VERY YOUNG. HOW OLD ARE YOU?
I AM BEGINNING TO FEEL COLD.

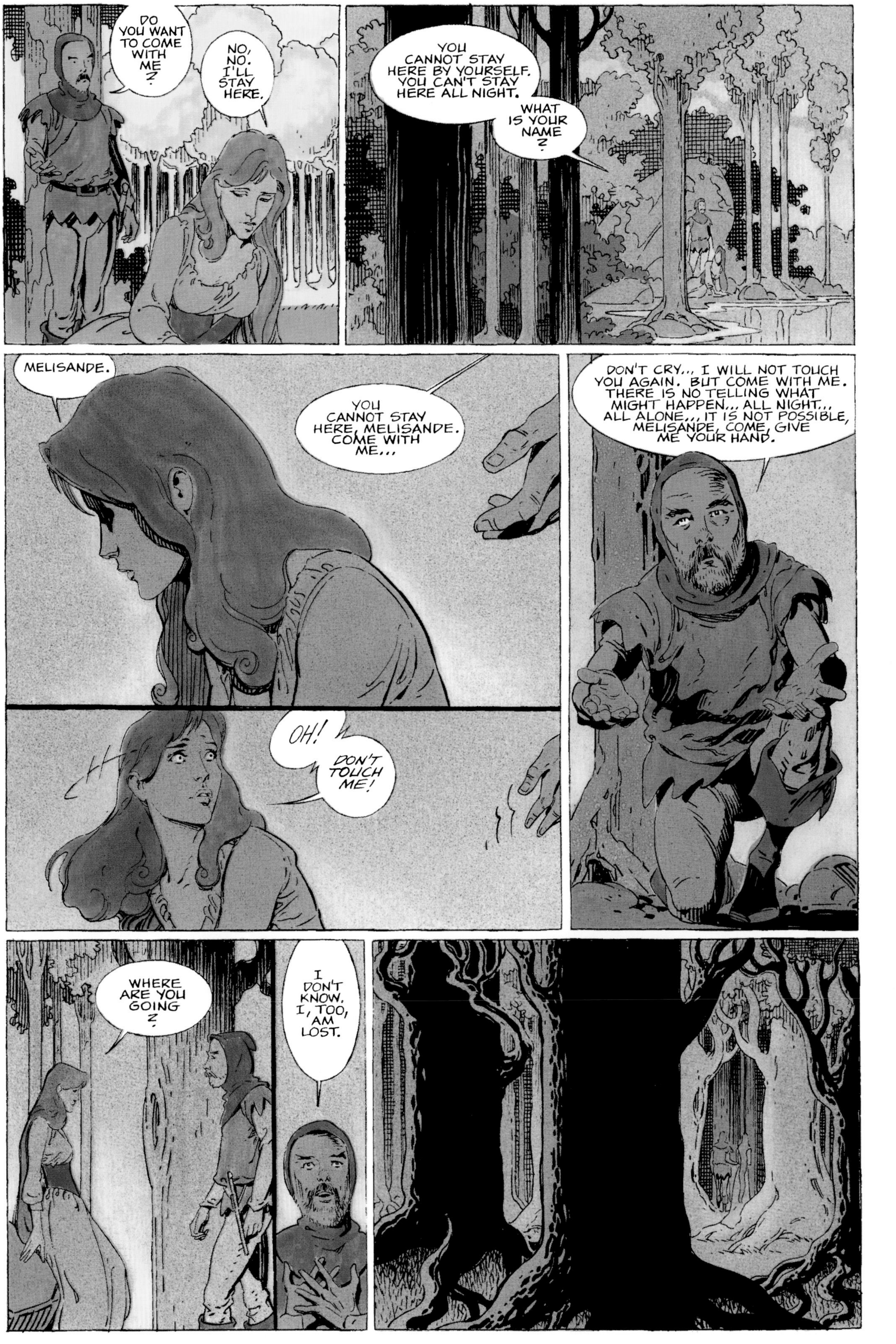
DO YOU WANT TO COME WITH ME ?
NO, NO. I'LL STAY HERE.
YOU CANNOT STAY HERE BY YOURSELF. YOU CAN'T STAY HERE ALL NIGHT.
WHAT IS YOUR NAME ?
MELISANDE.
YOU CANNOT STAY HERE, MELISANDE. COME WITH ME...
OH!
DON'T TOUCH ME!
DON'T CRY... I WILL NOT TOUCH YOU AGAIN. BUT COME WITH ME. THERE IS NO TELLING WHAT MIGHT HAPPEN... ALL NIGHT... ALL ALONE... IT IS NOT POSSIBLE, MELISANDE, COME, GIVE ME YOUR HAND.
WHERE ARE YOU GOING ?
I DON'T KNOW. I, TOO, AM LOST.

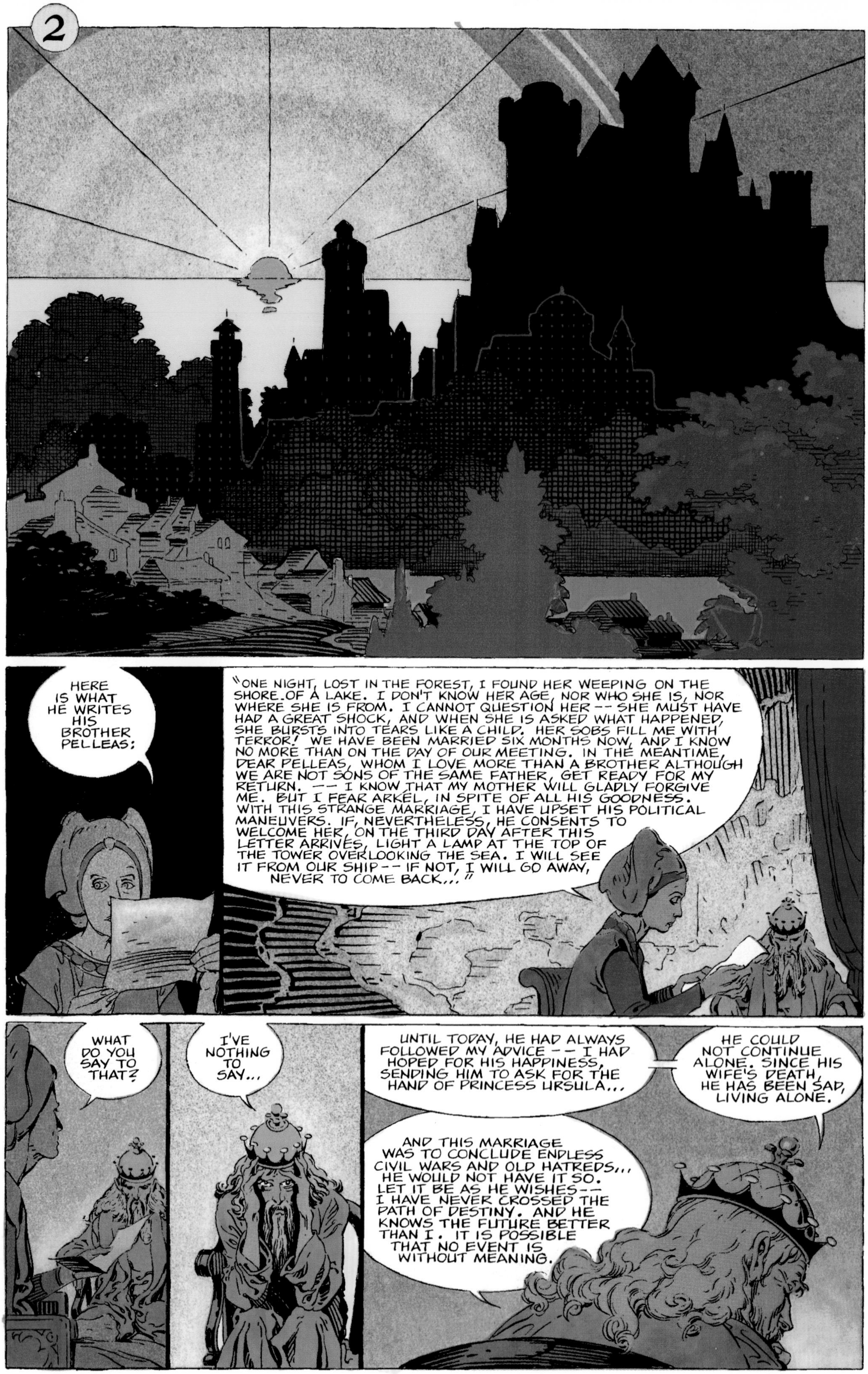
2
HERE IS WHAT HE WRITES HIS BROTHER PELLEAS:
"ONE NIGHT, LOST IN THE FOREST, I FOUND HER WEEPING ON THE SHORE OF A LAKE. I DON'T KNOW HER AGE, NOR WHO SHE IS, NOR WHERE SHE IS FROM. I CANNOT QUESTION HER -- SHE MUST HAVE HAD A GREAT SHOCK, AND WHEN SHE IS ASKED WHAT HAPPENED, SHE BURSTS INTO TEARS LIKE A CHILD. HER SOBS FILL ME WITH TERROR! WE HAVE BEEN MARRIED SIX MONTHS NOW, AND I KNOW NO MORE THAN ON THE DAY OF OUR MEETING. IN THE MEANTIME, DEAR PELLEAS, WHOM I LOVE MORE THAN A BROTHER ALTHOUGH WE ARE NOT SONS OF THE SAME FATHER, GET READY FOR MY RETURN. -- I KNOW THAT MY MOTHER WILL GLADLY FORGIVE ME. BUT I FEAR ARKËL, IN SPITE OF ALL HIS GOODNESS. WITH THIS STRANGE MARRIAGE, I HAVE UPSET HIS POLITICAL MANEUVERS. IF, NEVERTHELESS, HE CONSENTS TO WELCOME HER, ON THE THIRD DAY AFTER THIS LETTER ARRIVES, LIGHT A LAMP AT THE TOP OF THE TOWER OVERLOOKING THE SEA. I WILL SEE IT FROM OUR SHIP -- IF NOT, I WILL GO AWAY, NEVER TO COME BACK..."
WHAT DO YOU SAY TO THAT?
I'VE NOTHING TO SAY...
UNTIL TODAY, HE HAD ALWAYS FOLLOWED MY ADVICE -- I HAD HOPED FOR HIS HAPPINESS, SENDING HIM TO ASK FOR THE HAND OF PRINCESS URSULA...
HE COULD NOT CONTINUE ALONE. SINCE HIS WIFE'S DEATH, HE HAS BEEN SAD, LIVING ALONE.
AND THIS MARRIAGE WAS TO CONCLUDE ENDLESS CIVIL WARS AND OLD HATREDS... HE WOULD NOT HAVE IT SO. LET IT BE AS HE WISHES -- I HAVE NEVER CROSSED THE PATH OF DESTINY. AND HE KNOWS THE FUTURE BETTER THAN I. IT IS POSSIBLE THAT NO EVENT IS WITHOUT MEANING.

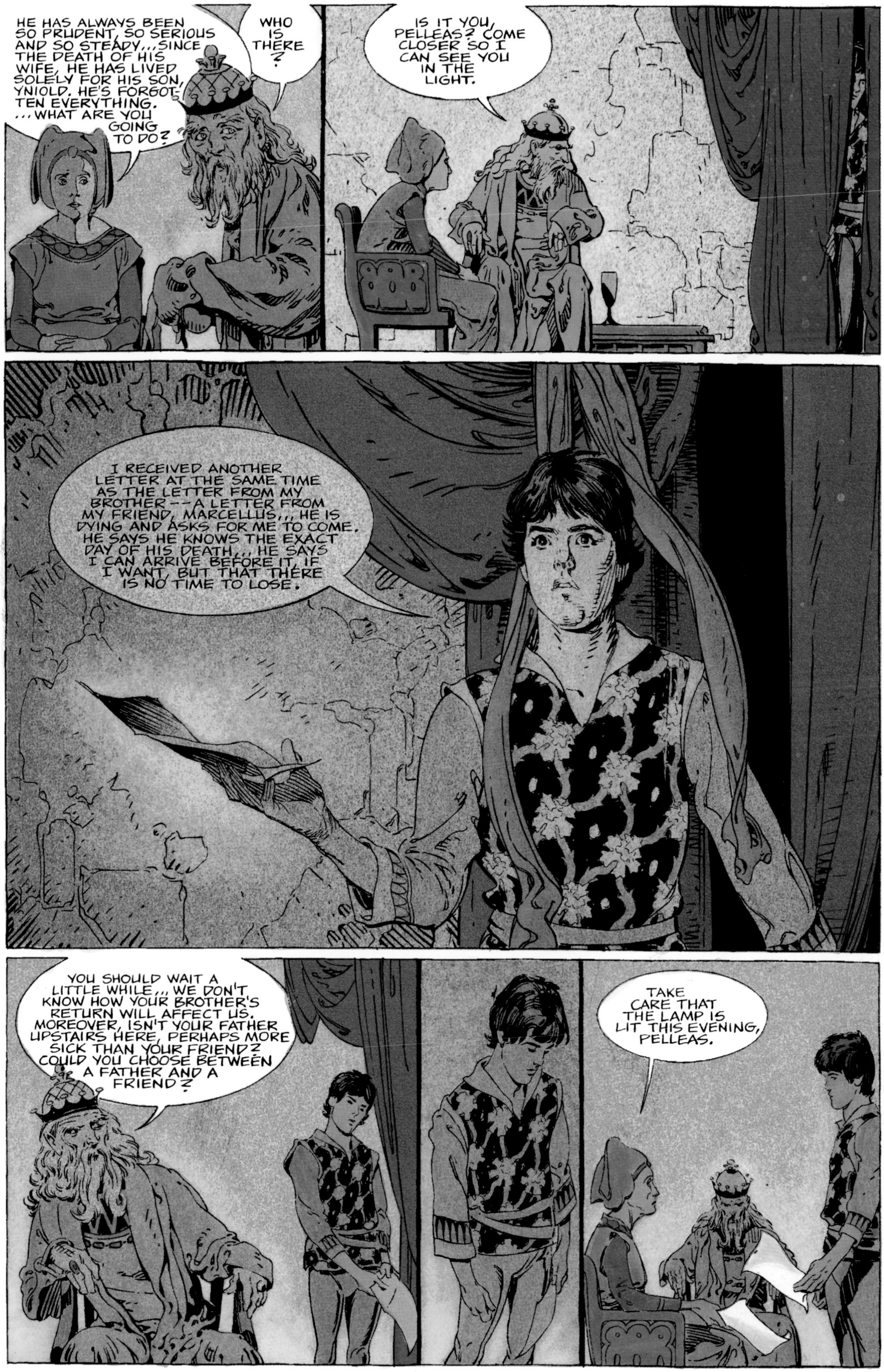
HE HAS ALWAYS BEEN SO PRUDENT, SO SERIOUS AND SO STEADY... SINCE THE DEATH OF HIS WIFE, HE HAS LIVED SOLELY FOR HIS SON, YNIOLD. HE'S FORGOTTEN EVERYTHING. ...WHAT ARE YOU GOING TO DO?
WHO IS THERE?
IS IT YOU, PELLEAS? COME CLOSER SO I CAN SEE YOU IN THE LIGHT.
I RECEIVED ANOTHER LETTER AT THE SAME TIME AS THE LETTER FROM MY BROTHER--A LETTER FROM MY FRIEND, MARCELLUS... HE IS DYING AND ASKS FOR ME TO COME. HE SAYS HE KNOWS THE EXACT DAY OF HIS DEATH... HE SAYS I CAN ARRIVE BEFORE IT, IF I WANT, BUT THAT THERE IS NO TIME TO LOSE.
YOU SHOULD WAIT A LITTLE WHILE... WE DON'T KNOW HOW YOUR BROTHER'S RETURN WILL AFFECT US. MOREOVER, ISN'T YOUR FATHER UPSTAIRS HERE, PERHAPS MORE SICK THAN YOUR FRIEND? COULD YOU CHOOSE BETWEEN A FATHER AND A FRIEND?
TAKE CARE THAT THE LAMP IS LIT THIS EVENING, PELLEAS.

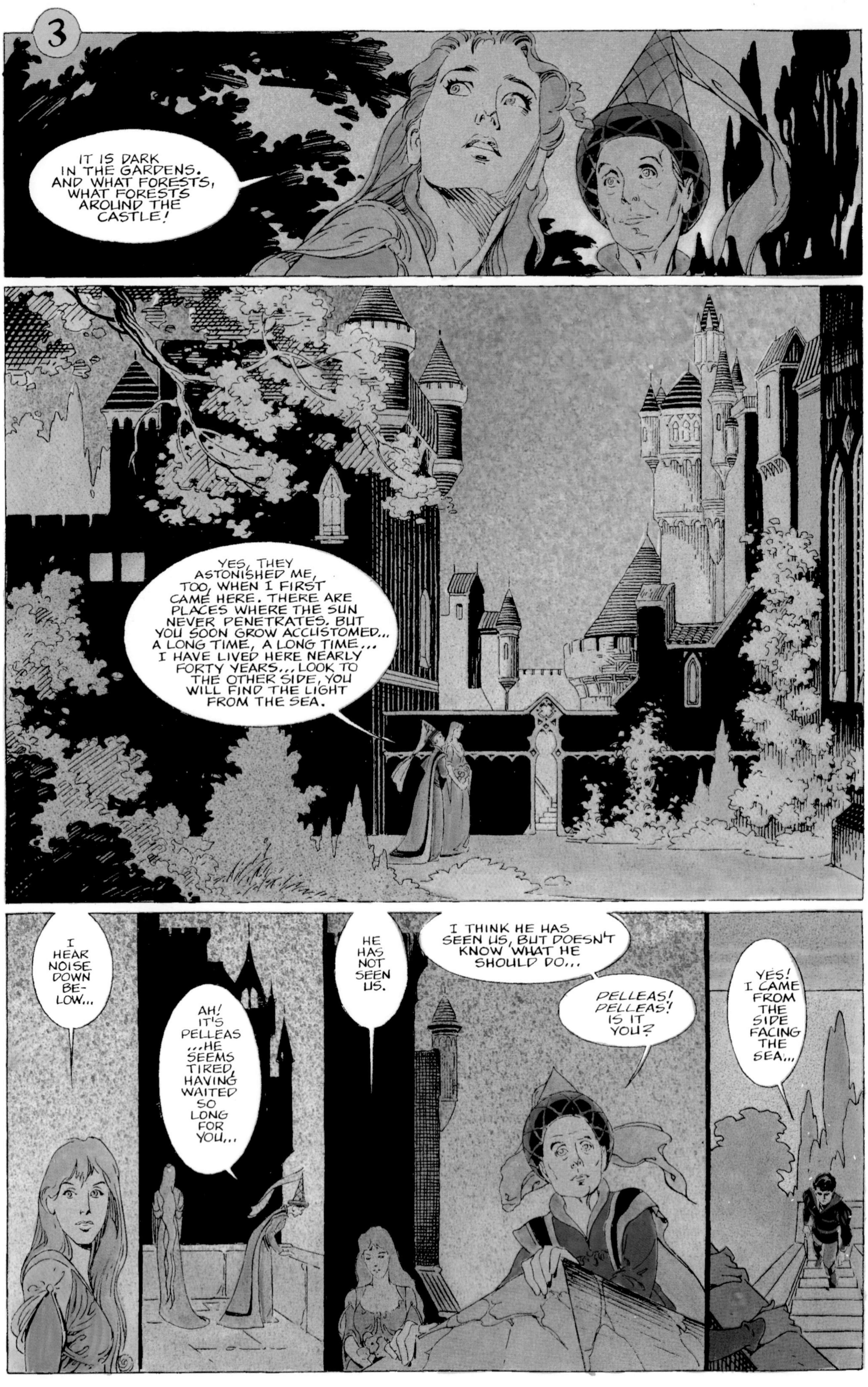
3
IT IS DARK IN THE GARDENS. AND WHAT FORESTS, WHAT FORESTS AROUND THE CASTLE!
YES, THEY ASTONISHED ME, TOO, WHEN I FIRST CAME HERE. THERE ARE PLACES WHERE THE SUN NEVER PENETRATES. BUT YOU SOON GROW ACCUSTOMED... A LONG TIME, A LONG TIME... I HAVE LIVED HERE NEARLY FORTY YEARS... LOOK TO THE OTHER SIDE, YOU WILL FIND THE LIGHT FROM THE SEA.
I HEAR NOISE DOWN BE-LOW...
AH! IT'S PELLEAS ...HE SEEMS TIRED, HAVING WAITED SO LONG FOR YOU...
HE HAS NOT SEEN US.
I THINK HE HAS SEEN US, BUT DOESN'T KNOW WHAT HE SHOULD DO...
PELLEAS! PELLEAS! IS IT YOU?
YES! I CAME FROM THE SIDE FACING THE SEA...

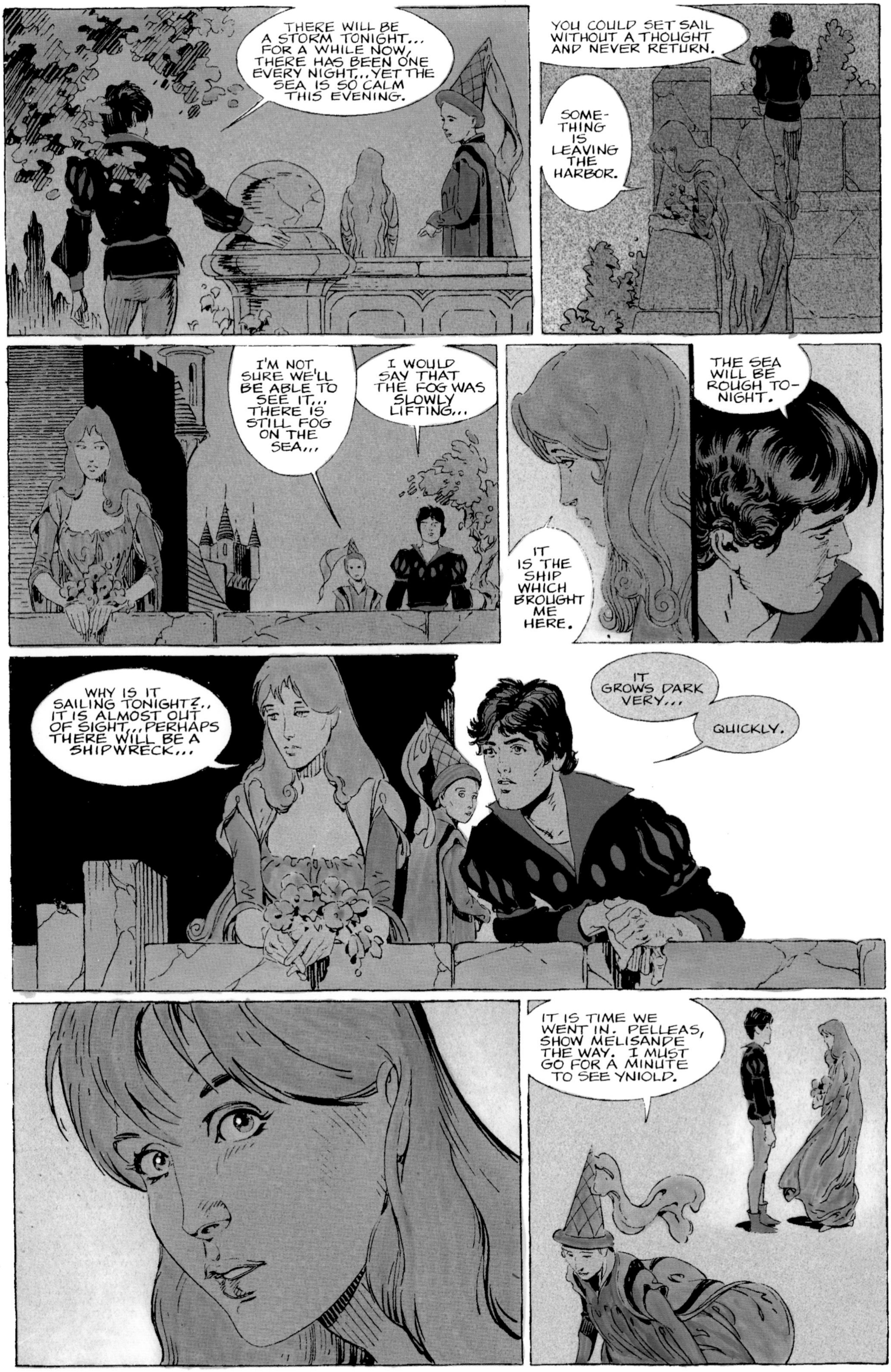
THERE WILL BE A STORM TONIGHT... FOR A WHILE NOW, THERE HAS BEEN ONE EVERY NIGHT... YET THE SEA IS SO CALM THIS EVENING.
YOU COULD SET SAIL WITHOUT A THOUGHT AND NEVER RETURN.
SOME-THING IS LEAVING THE HARBOR.
I'M NOT SURE WE'LL BE ABLE TO SEE IT... THERE IS STILL FOG ON THE SEA...
I WOULD SAY THAT THE FOG WAS SLOWLY LIFTING...
IT IS THE SHIP WHICH BROUGHT ME HERE.
THE SEA WILL BE ROUGH TO-NIGHT.
WHY IS IT SAILING TONIGHT?.. IT IS ALMOST OUT OF SIGHT... PERHAPS THERE WILL BE A SHIPWRECK...
IT GROWS DARK VERY...
QUICKLY.
IT IS TIME WE WENT IN. PELLEAS, SHOW MELISANDE THE WAY. I MUST GO FOR A MINUTE TO SEE YNIOLD.

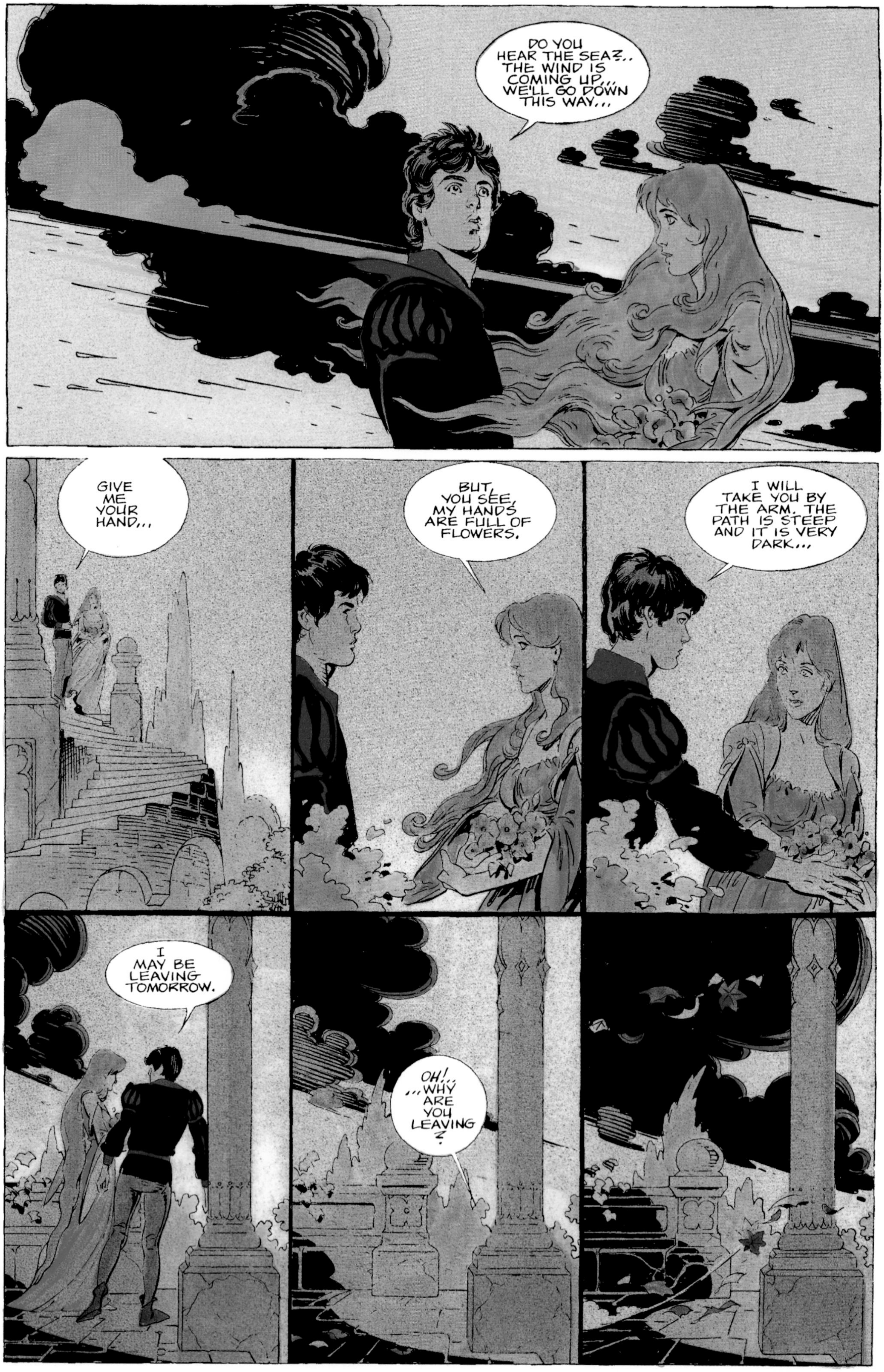
DO YOU HEAR THE SEA?.. THE WIND IS COMING UP... WE'LL GO DOWN THIS WAY...
GIVE ME YOUR HAND...
BUT, YOU SEE, MY HANDS ARE FULL OF FLOWERS.
I WILL TAKE YOU BY THE ARM. THE PATH IS STEEP AND IT IS VERY DARK...
I MAY BE LEAVING TOMORROW.
OH! ...WHY ARE YOU LEAVING ?

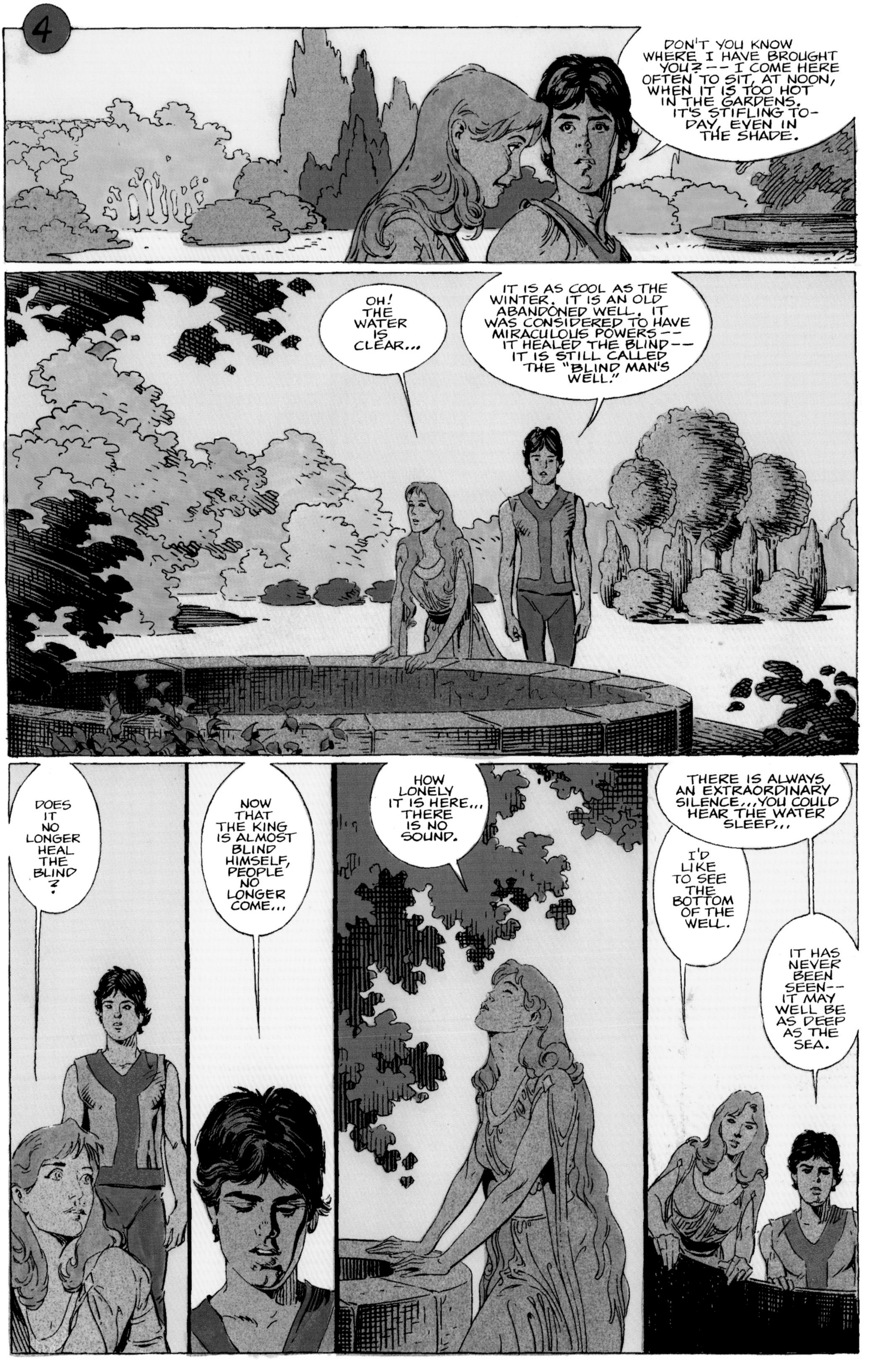
4
DON'T YOU KNOW WHERE I HAVE BROUGHT YOU? -- I COME HERE OFTEN TO SIT, AT NOON, WHEN IT IS TOO HOT IN THE GARDENS. IT'S STIFLING TO-DAY, EVEN IN THE SHADE.
OH! THE WATER IS CLEAR...
IT IS AS COOL AS THE WINTER. IT IS AN OLD ABANDONED WELL. IT WAS CONSIDERED TO HAVE MIRACULOUS POWERS -- IT HEALED THE BLIND -- IT IS STILL CALLED THE "BLIND MAN'S WELL."
DOES IT NO LONGER HEAL THE BLIND?
NOW THAT THE KING IS ALMOST BLIND HIMSELF, PEOPLE NO LONGER COME...
HOW LONELY IT IS HERE... THERE IS NO SOUND.
THERE IS ALWAYS AN EXTRAORDINARY SILENCE... YOU COULD HEAR THE WATER SLEEP...
I'D LIKE TO SEE THE BOTTOM OF THE WELL.
IT HAS NEVER BEEN SEEN-- IT MAY WELL BE AS DEEP AS THE SEA.

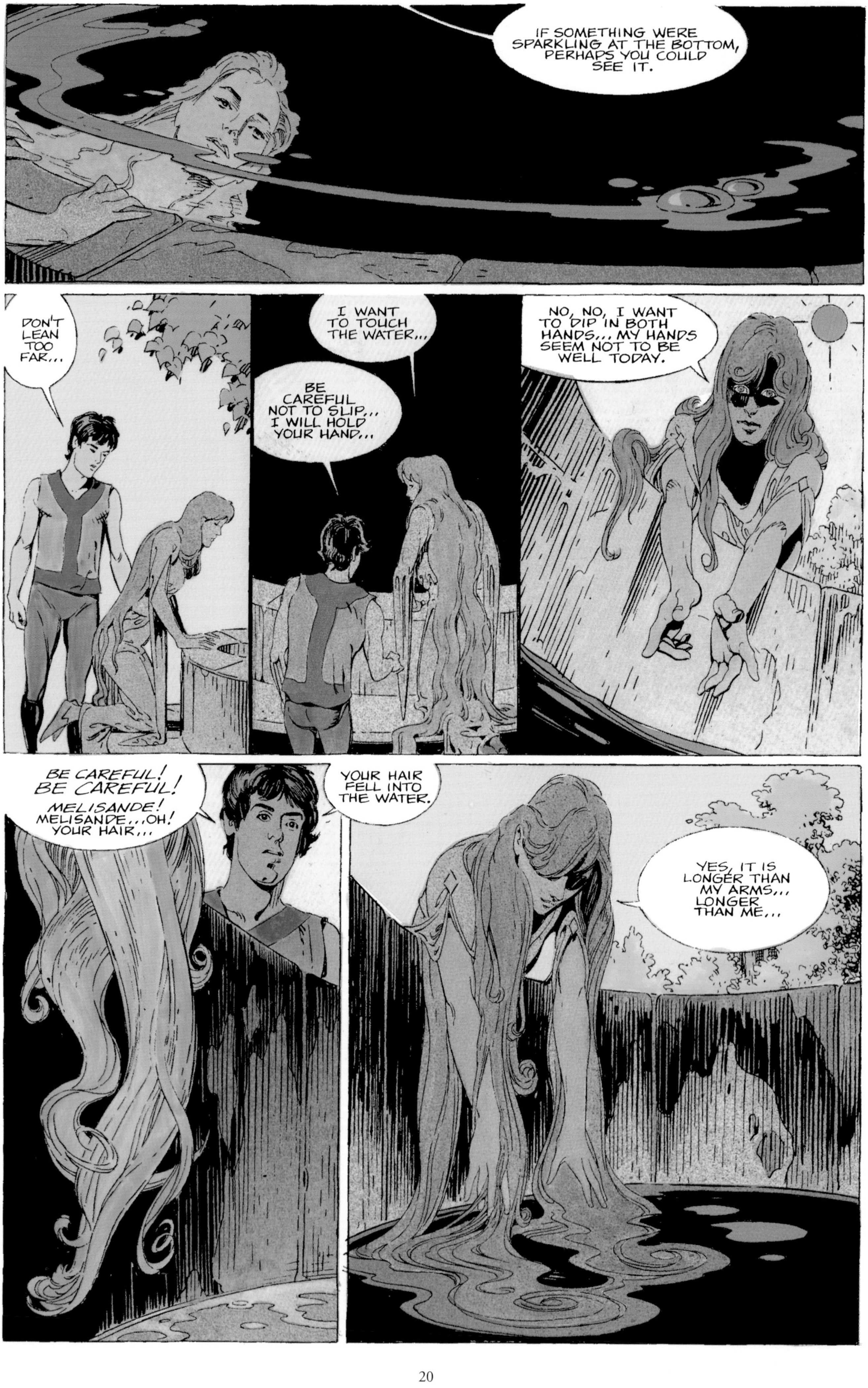
IF SOMETHING WERE SPARKLING AT THE BOTTOM, PERHAPS YOU COULD SEE IT.
DON'T LEAN TOO FAR...
I WANT TO TOUCH THE WATER...
BE CAREFUL NOT TO SLIP... I WILL HOLD YOUR HAND...
NO, NO, I WANT TO DIP IN BOTH HANDS... MY HANDS SEEM NOT TO BE WELL TODAY.
BE CAREFUL! BE CAREFUL! MELISANDE! MELISANDE...OH! YOUR HAIR...
YOUR HAIR FELL INTO THE WATER.
YES, IT IS LONGER THAN MY ARMS... LONGER THAN ME...

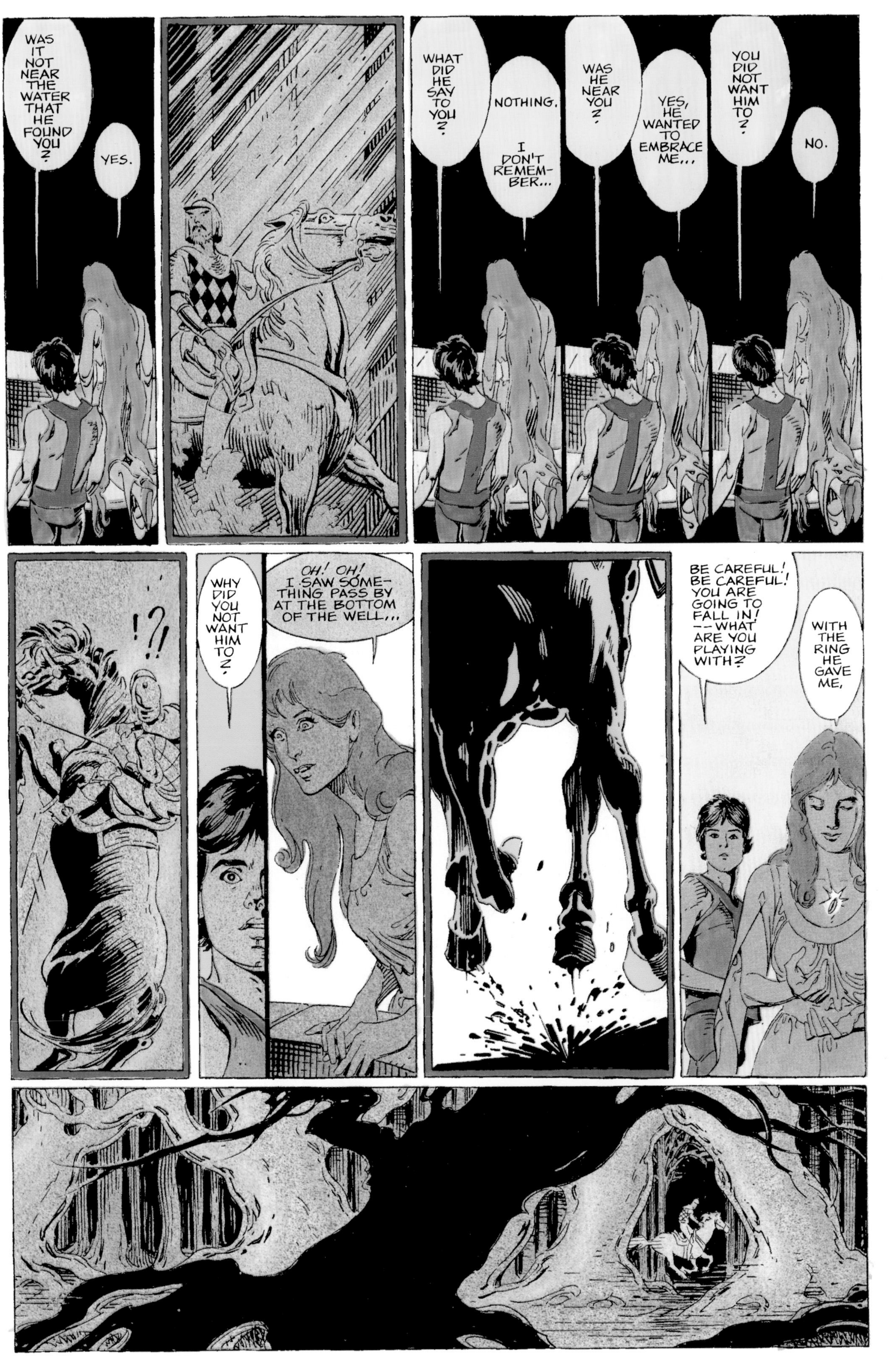
WAS IT NOT NEAR THE WATER THAT HE FOUND YOU?
YES.
WHAT DID HE SAY TO YOU?
NOTHING.
I DON'T REMEMBER...
WAS HE NEAR YOU?
YES, HE WANTED TO EMBRACE ME...
YOU DID NOT WANT HIM TO?
NO.
!?!
WHY DID YOU NOT WANT HIM TO?
OH! OH! I SAW SOMETHING PASS BY AT THE BOTTOM OF THE WELL...
BE CAREFUL! BE CAREFUL! YOU ARE GOING TO FALL IN! --WHAT ARE YOU PLAYING WITH?
WITH THE RING HE GAVE ME.

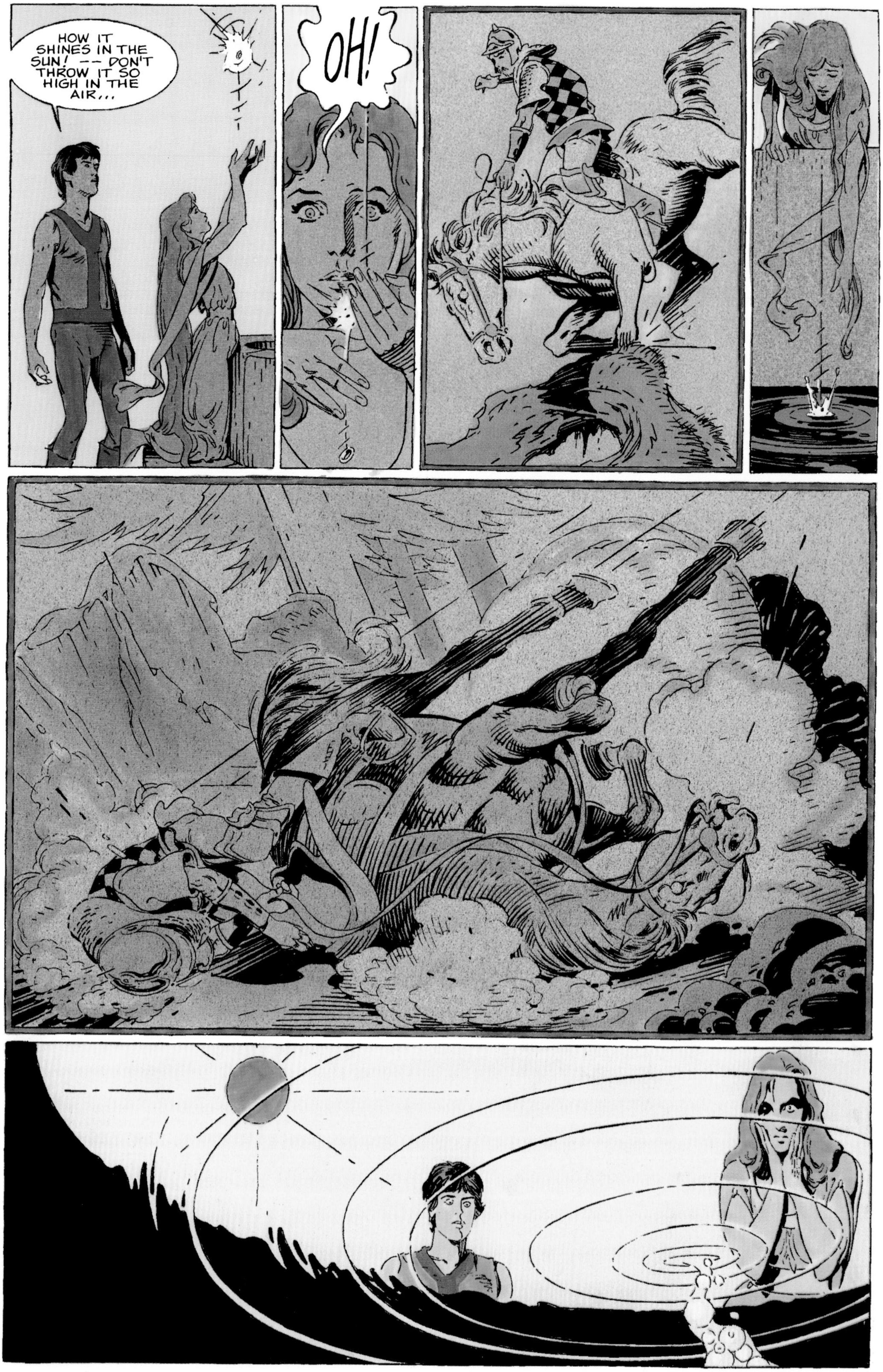
HOW IT SHINES IN THE SUN! -- DON'T THROW IT SO HIGH IN THE AIR...
OH!

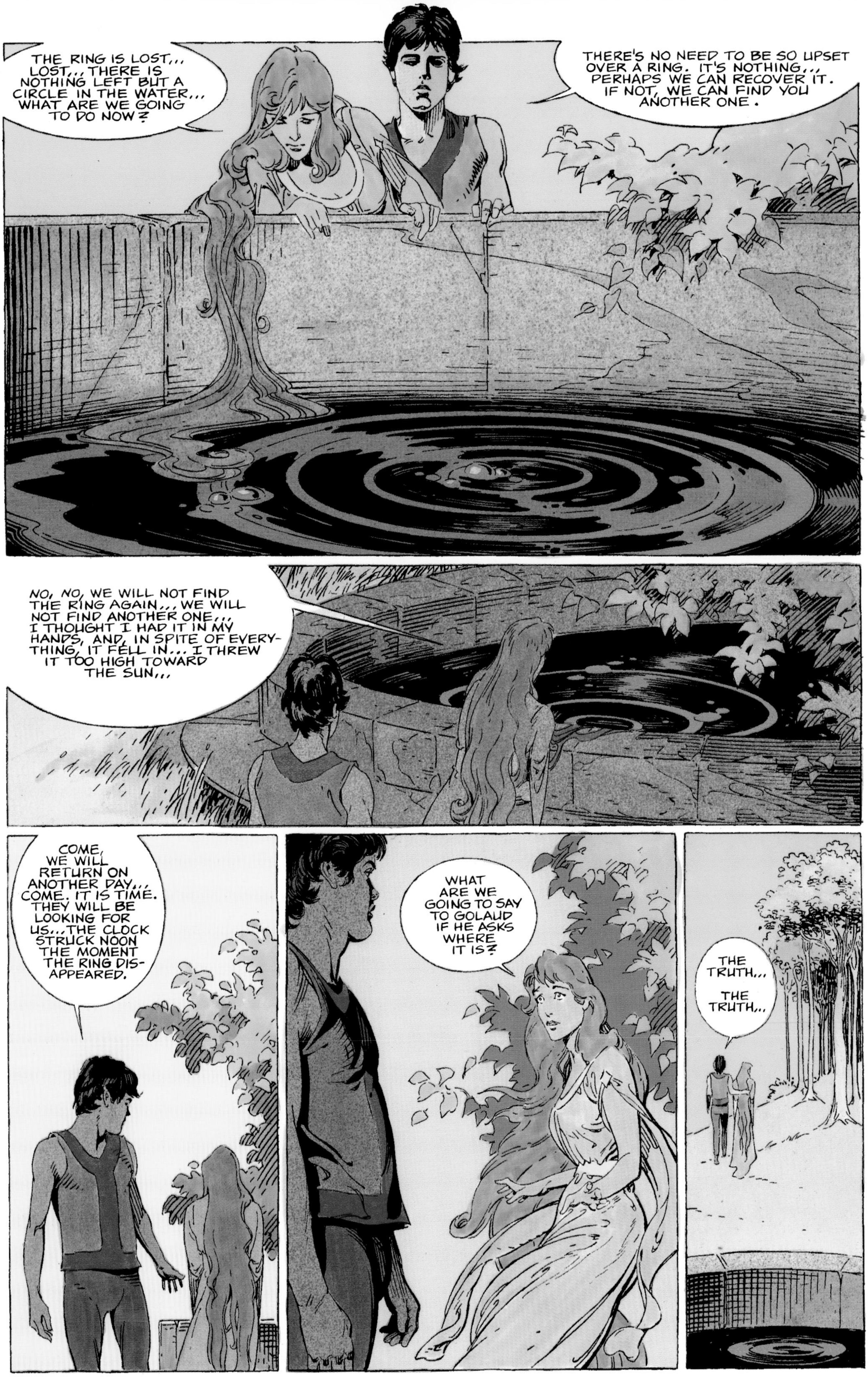
THE RING IS LOST,,, LOST,,, THERE IS NOTHING LEFT BUT A CIRCLE IN THE WATER,,, WHAT ARE WE GOING TO DO NOW?
THERE'S NO NEED TO BE SO UPSET OVER A RING. IT'S NOTHING,,, PERHAPS WE CAN RECOVER IT. IF NOT, WE CAN FIND YOU ANOTHER ONE.
NO, NO, WE WILL NOT FIND THE RING AGAIN,,, WE WILL NOT FIND ANOTHER ONE,,, I THOUGHT I HAD IT IN MY HANDS, AND, IN SPITE OF EVERYTHING, IT FELL IN... I THREW IT TOO HIGH TOWARD THE SUN,,,
COME, WE WILL RETURN ON ANOTHER DAY,,, COME. IT IS TIME. THEY WILL BE LOOKING FOR US... THE CLOCK STRUCK NOON THE MOMENT THE RING DISAPPEARED.
WHAT ARE WE GOING TO SAY TO GOLAUD IF HE ASKS WHERE IT IS?
THE TRUTH,,,
THE TRUTH,,,

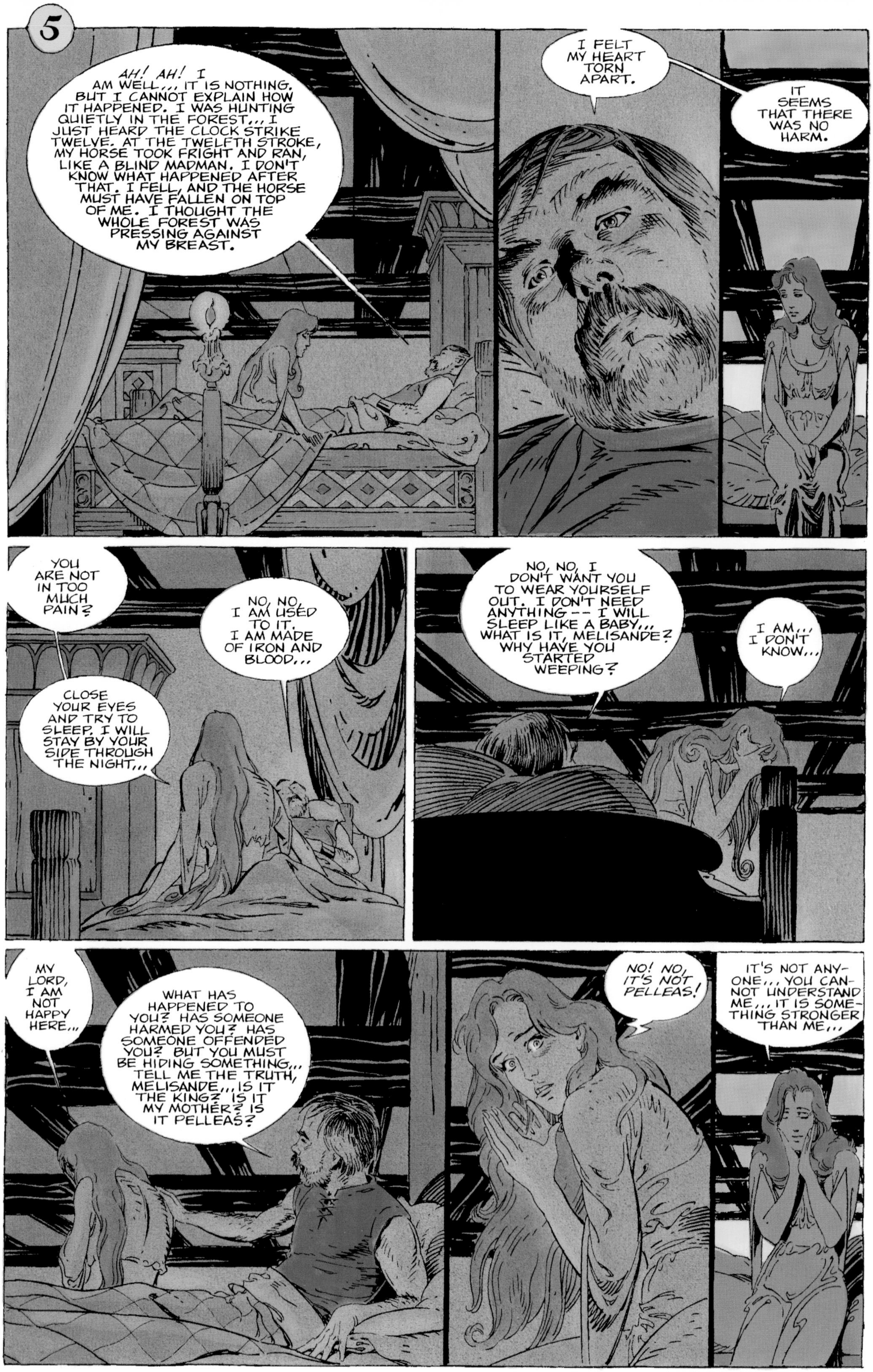
5
AH! AH! I AM WELL... IT IS NOTHING. BUT I CANNOT EXPLAIN HOW IT HAPPENED. I WAS HUNTING QUIETLY IN THE FOREST... I JUST HEARD THE CLOCK STRIKE TWELVE. AT THE TWELFTH STROKE, MY HORSE TOOK FRIGHT AND RAN, LIKE A BLIND MADMAN. I DON'T KNOW WHAT HAPPENED AFTER THAT. I FELL, AND THE HORSE MUST HAVE FALLEN ON TOP OF ME. I THOUGHT THE WHOLE FOREST WAS PRESSING AGAINST MY BREAST.
I FELT MY HEART TORN APART.
IT SEEMS THAT THERE WAS NO HARM.
YOU ARE NOT IN TOO MUCH PAIN?
NO, NO, I AM USED TO IT. I AM MADE OF IRON AND BLOOD...
CLOSE YOUR EYES AND TRY TO SLEEP. I WILL STAY BY YOUR SIDE THROUGH THE NIGHT...
NO, NO, I DON'T WANT YOU TO WEAR YOURSELF OUT. I DON'T NEED ANYTHING -- I WILL SLEEP LIKE A BABY... WHAT IS IT, MELISANDE? WHY HAVE YOU STARTED WEEPING?
I AM... I DON'T KNOW...
MY LORD, I AM NOT HAPPY HERE...
WHAT HAS HAPPENED TO YOU? HAS SOMEONE HARMED YOU? HAS SOMEONE OFFENDED YOU? BUT YOU MUST BE HIDING SOMETHING... TELL ME THE TRUTH, MELISANDE... IS IT THE KING? IS IT MY MOTHER? IS IT PELLEAS?
NO! NO, IT'S NOT PELLEAS!
IT'S NOT ANYONE... YOU CANNOT UNDERSTAND ME... IT IS SOMETHING STRONGER THAN ME...

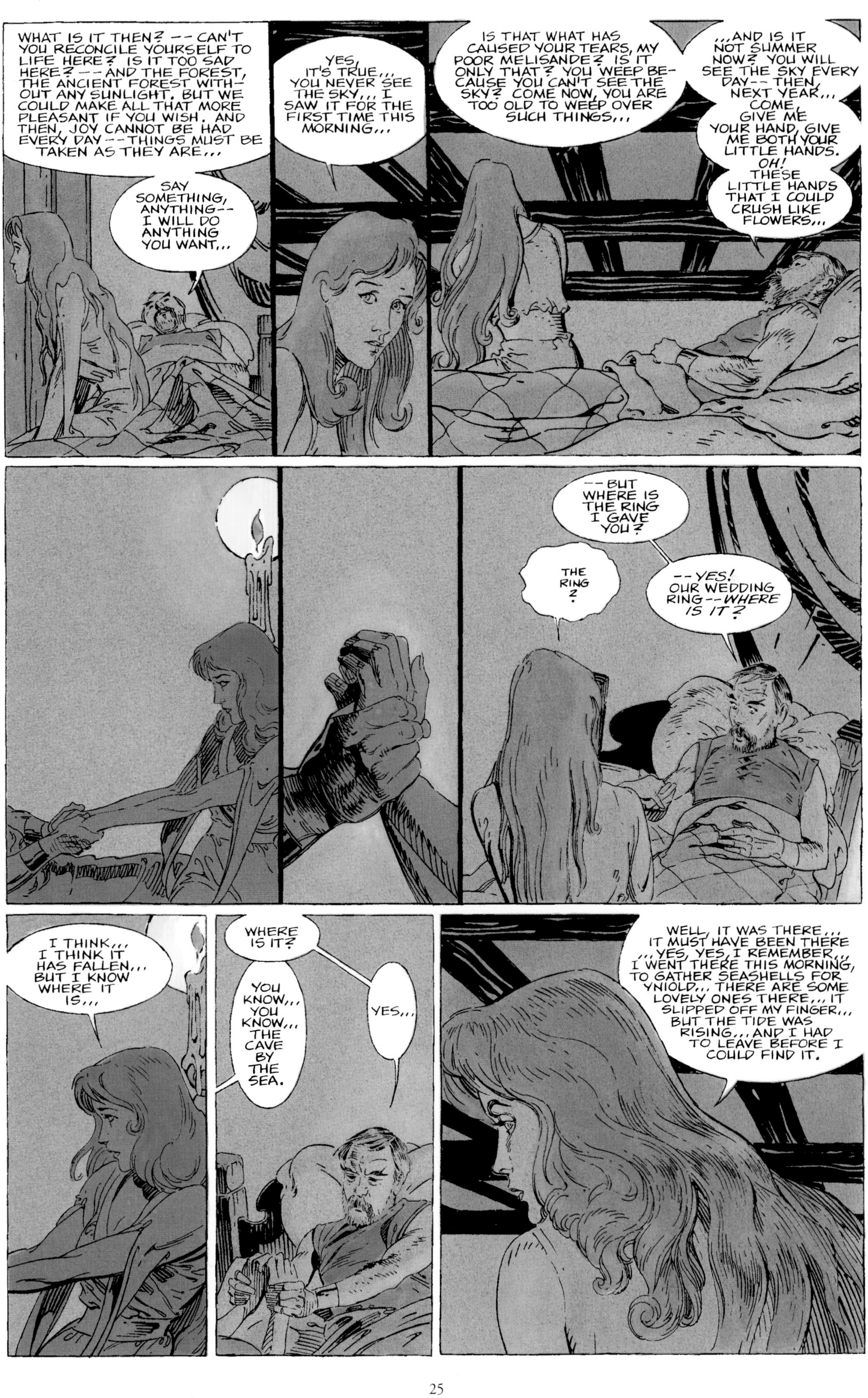
WHAT IS IT THEN? --CAN'T YOU RECONCILE YOURSELF TO LIFE HERE? IS IT TOO SAD HERE? --AND THE FOREST, THE ANCIENT FOREST WITHOUT ANY SUNLIGHT. BUT WE COULD MAKE ALL THAT MORE PLEASANT IF YOU WISH. AND THEN, JOY CANNOT BE HAD EVERY DAY--THINGS MUST BE TAKEN AS THEY ARE,,,
SAY SOMETHING, ANYTHING--I WILL DO ANYTHING YOU WANT,,,
YES, IT'S TRUE,,, YOU NEVER SEE THE SKY,,, I SAW IT FOR THE FIRST TIME THIS MORNING,,,
IS THAT WHAT HAS CAUSED YOUR TEARS, MY POOR MELISANDE? IS IT ONLY THAT? YOU WEEP BECAUSE YOU CAN'T SEE THE SKY? COME NOW, YOU ARE TOO OLD TO WEEP OVER SUCH THINGS,,,
,,,AND IS IT NOT SUMMER NOW? YOU WILL SEE THE SKY EVERY DAY--THEN, NEXT YEAR,,, COME, GIVE ME YOUR HAND, GIVE ME BOTH YOUR LITTLE HANDS. OH! THESE LITTLE HANDS THAT I COULD CRUSH LIKE FLOWERS,,,
--BUT WHERE IS THE RING I GAVE YOU?
THE RING?
--YES! OUR WEDDING RING--WHERE IS IT?
I THINK,,, I THINK IT HAS FALLEN,,, BUT I KNOW WHERE IT IS,,,
WHERE IS IT?
YOU KNOW,,, YOU KNOW,,, THE CAVE BY THE SEA.
YES,,,
WELL, IT WAS THERE,,, IT MUST HAVE BEEN THERE ,,,YES, YES, I REMEMBER,,, I WENT THERE THIS MORNING, TO GATHER SEASHELLS FOR YNIOLD,,, THERE ARE SOME LOVELY ONES THERE,,, IT SLIPPED OFF MY FINGER,,, BUT THE TIDE WAS RISING,,, AND I HAD TO LEAVE BEFORE I COULD FIND IT.

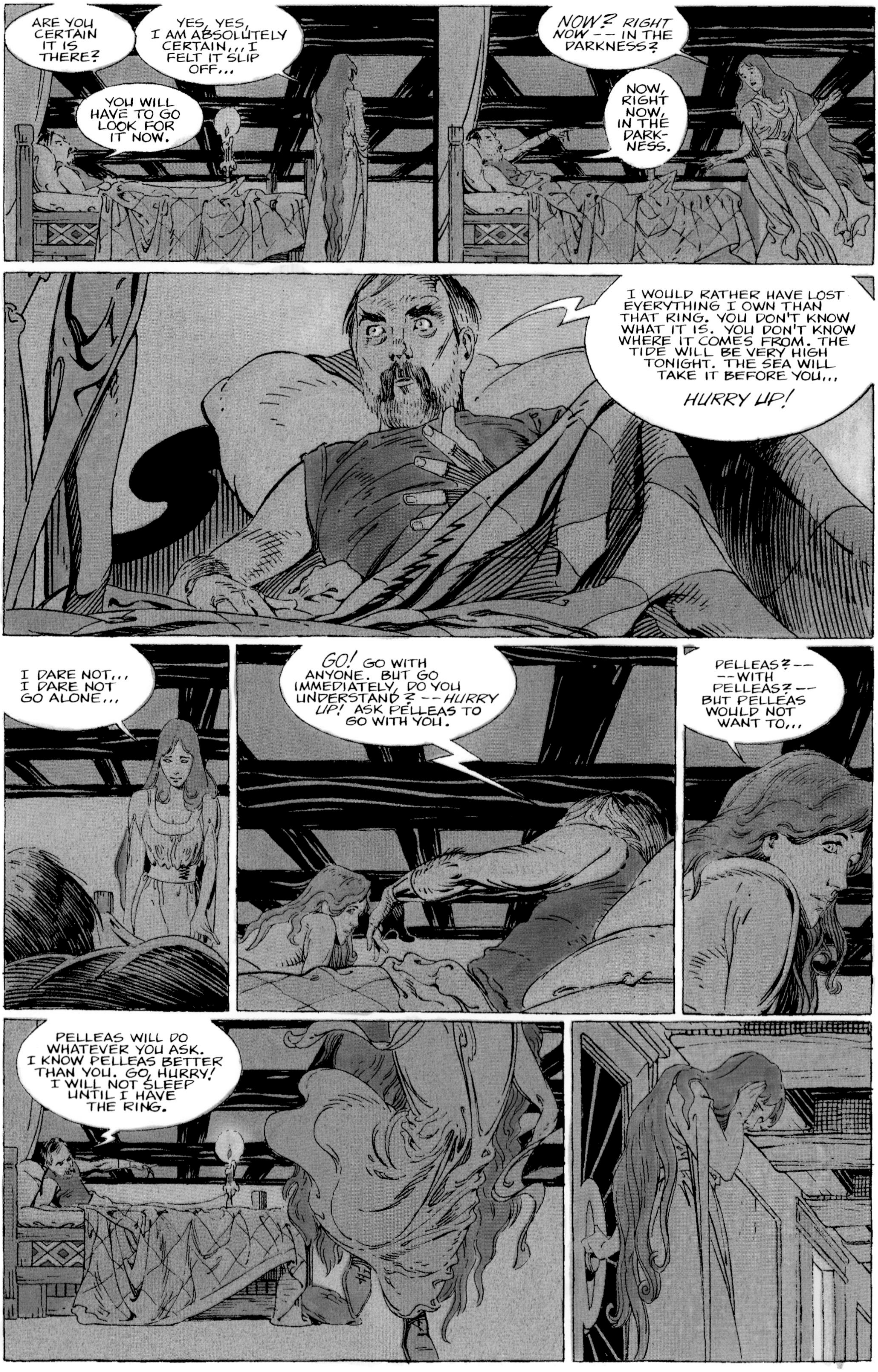
ARE YOU CERTAIN IT IS THERE?
YES, YES, I AM ABSOLUTELY CERTAIN,,, I FELT IT SLIP OFF...
YOU WILL HAVE TO GO LOOK FOR IT NOW.
NOW? RIGHT NOW -- IN THE DARKNESS?
NOW, RIGHT NOW, IN THE DARKNESS.
I WOULD RATHER HAVE LOST EVERYTHING I OWN THAN THAT RING. YOU DON'T KNOW WHAT IT IS. YOU DON'T KNOW WHERE IT COMES FROM. THE TIDE WILL BE VERY HIGH TONIGHT. THE SEA WILL TAKE IT BEFORE YOU,,, HURRY UP!
I DARE NOT,,, I DARE NOT GO ALONE,,,
GO! GO WITH ANYONE. BUT GO IMMEDIATELY, DO YOU UNDERSTAND? --HURRY UP! ASK PELLEAS TO GO WITH YOU.
PELLEAS? -- --WITH PELLEAS? -- BUT PELLEAS WOULD NOT WANT TO,,,
PELLEAS WILL DO WHATEVER YOU ASK. I KNOW PELLEAS BETTER THAN YOU. GO, HURRY! I WILL NOT SLEEP UNTIL I HAVE THE RING.

YOU HAVE NEVER BEEN INSIDE THIS CAVE?

NO...

WHEN YOU LIGHT A SMALL LAMP YOU WOULD SAY THE ROOF WAS COVERED WITH STARS, LIKE THE SKY.

THEN COME IN... YOU MUST BE ABLE TO DESCRIBE THE PLACE WHERE YOU LOST THE RING. IF HE QUESTIONS YOU... IT IS VERY LARGE, AND BEAUTIFUL. IT IS FILLED WITH BLUE SHADOWS.

GIVE ME YOUR HAND, DON'T TREMBLE, DON'T TREMBLE SO. THERE IS NO DANGER... DOES THE SOUND OF THE CAVE SCARE YOU? DO YOU HEAR THE SEA BEHIND US?--IT DOES NOT SEEM HAPPY TONIGHT...

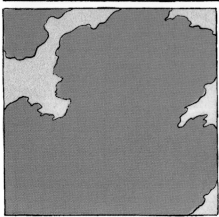

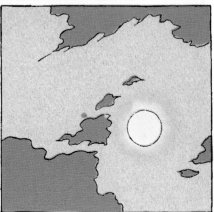

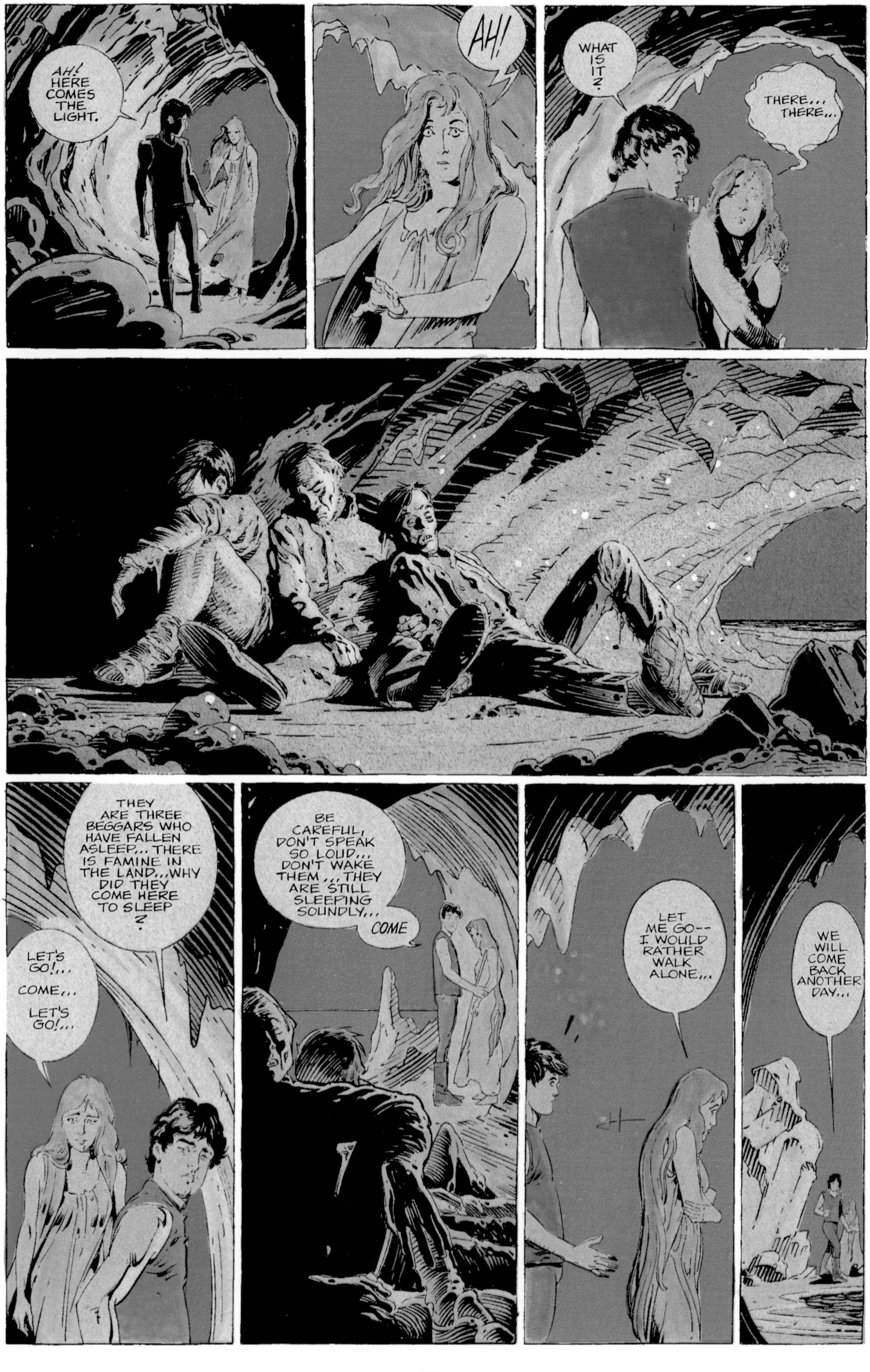
AH! HERE COMES THE LIGHT.
AH!
WHAT IS IT?
THERE... THERE...
THEY ARE THREE BEGGARS WHO HAVE FALLEN ASLEEP... THERE IS FAMINE IN THE LAND... WHY DID THEY COME HERE TO SLEEP?
LET'S GO!... COME... LET'S GO!...
BE CAREFUL, DON'T SPEAK SO LOUD... DON'T WAKE THEM... THEY ARE STILL SLEEPING SOUNDLY...
COME
LET ME GO-- I WOULD RATHER WALK ALONE...
WE WILL COME BACK ANOTHER DAY...

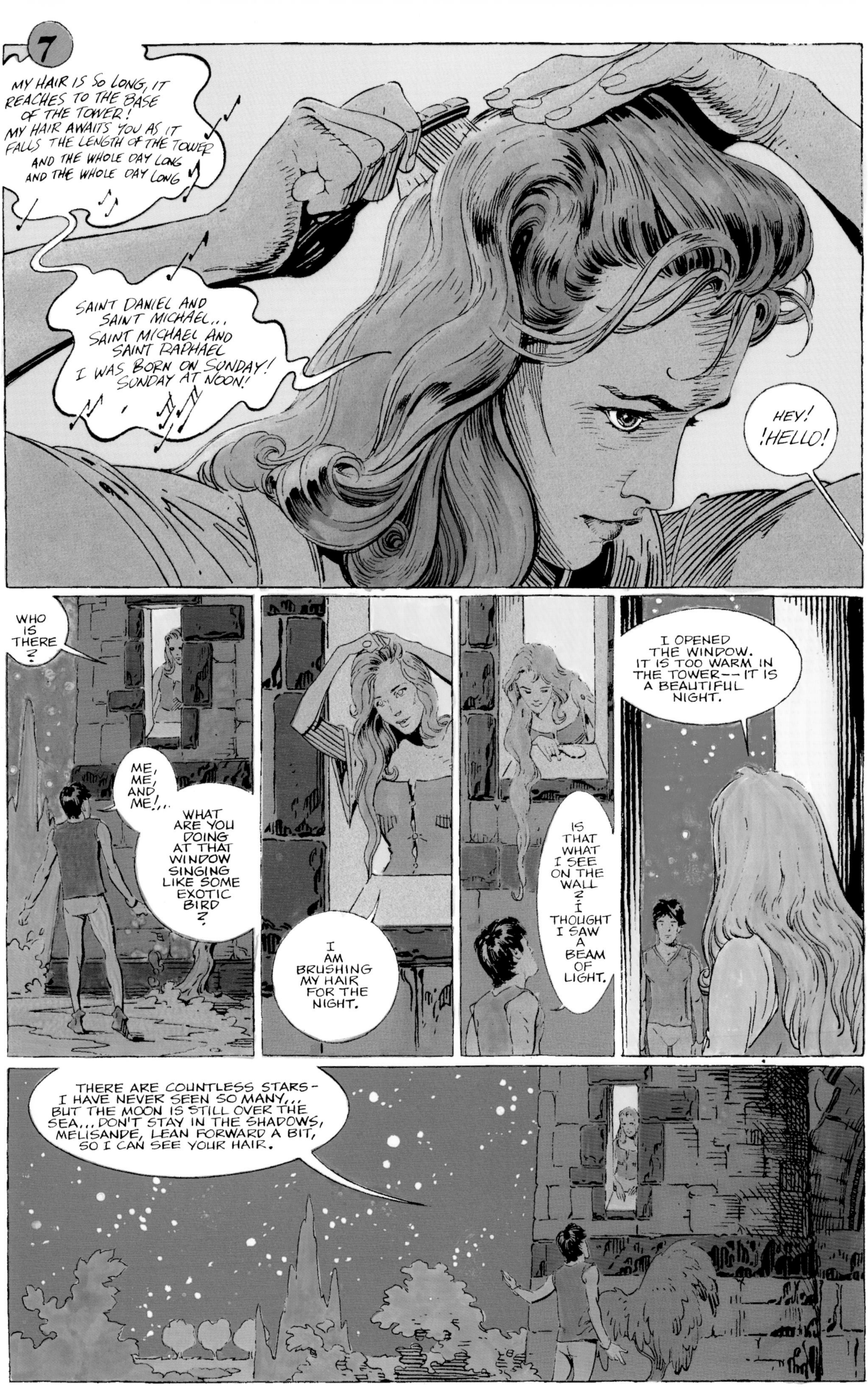
7
MY HAIR IS SO LONG, IT REACHES TO THE BASE OF THE TOWER! MY HAIR AWAITS YOU AS IT FALLS THE LENGTH OF THE TOWER AND THE WHOLE DAY LONG AND THE WHOLE DAY LONG
SAINT DANIEL AND SAINT MICHAEL... SAINT MICHAEL AND SAINT RAPHAEL I WAS BORN ON SUNDAY! SUNDAY AT NOON!
HEY! !HELLO!
WHO IS THERE ?
ME, ME, AND ME!..
WHAT ARE YOU DOING AT THAT WINDOW SINGING LIKE SOME EXOTIC BIRD ?
I AM BRUSHING MY HAIR FOR THE NIGHT.
IS THAT WHAT I SEE ON THE WALL ? I THOUGHT I SAW A BEAM OF LIGHT.
I OPENED THE WINDOW. IT IS TOO WARM IN THE TOWER-- IT IS A BEAUTIFUL NIGHT.
THERE ARE COUNTLESS STARS- I HAVE NEVER SEEN SO MANY... BUT THE MOON IS STILL OVER THE SEA... DON'T STAY IN THE SHADOWS, MELISANDE, LEAN FORWARD A BIT, SO I CAN SEE YOUR HAIR.

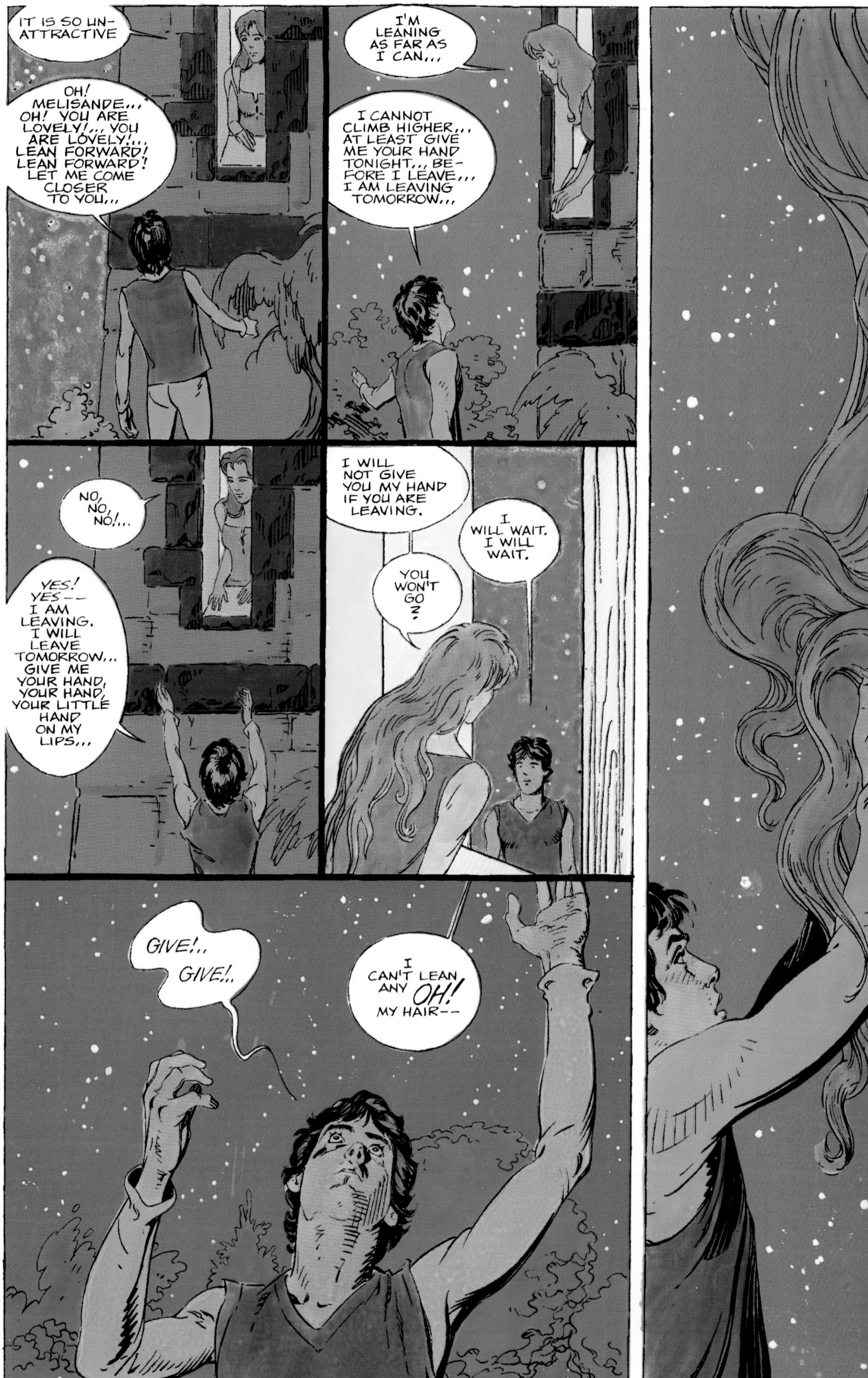
IT IS SO UN-ATTRACTIVE
OH! MELISANDE,,, OH! YOU ARE LOVELY!,,, YOU ARE LOVELY!,,, LEAN FORWARD! LEAN FORWARD! LET ME COME CLOSER TO YOU,,,
I'M LEANING AS FAR AS I CAN,,,
I CANNOT CLIMB HIGHER,,, AT LEAST GIVE ME YOUR HAND TONIGHT,,, BE-FORE I LEAVE,,, I AM LEAVING TOMORROW,,,
NO, NO, NO!,,,
YES! YES-- I AM LEAVING. I WILL LEAVE TOMORROW,,, GIVE ME YOUR HAND, YOUR HAND, YOUR LITTLE HAND ON MY LIPS,,,
I WILL NOT GIVE YOU MY HAND IF YOU ARE LEAVING.
YOU WON'T GO?
I WILL WAIT. I WILL WAIT.
GIVE!.. GIVE!..
I CAN'T LEAN ANY OH! MY HAIR--

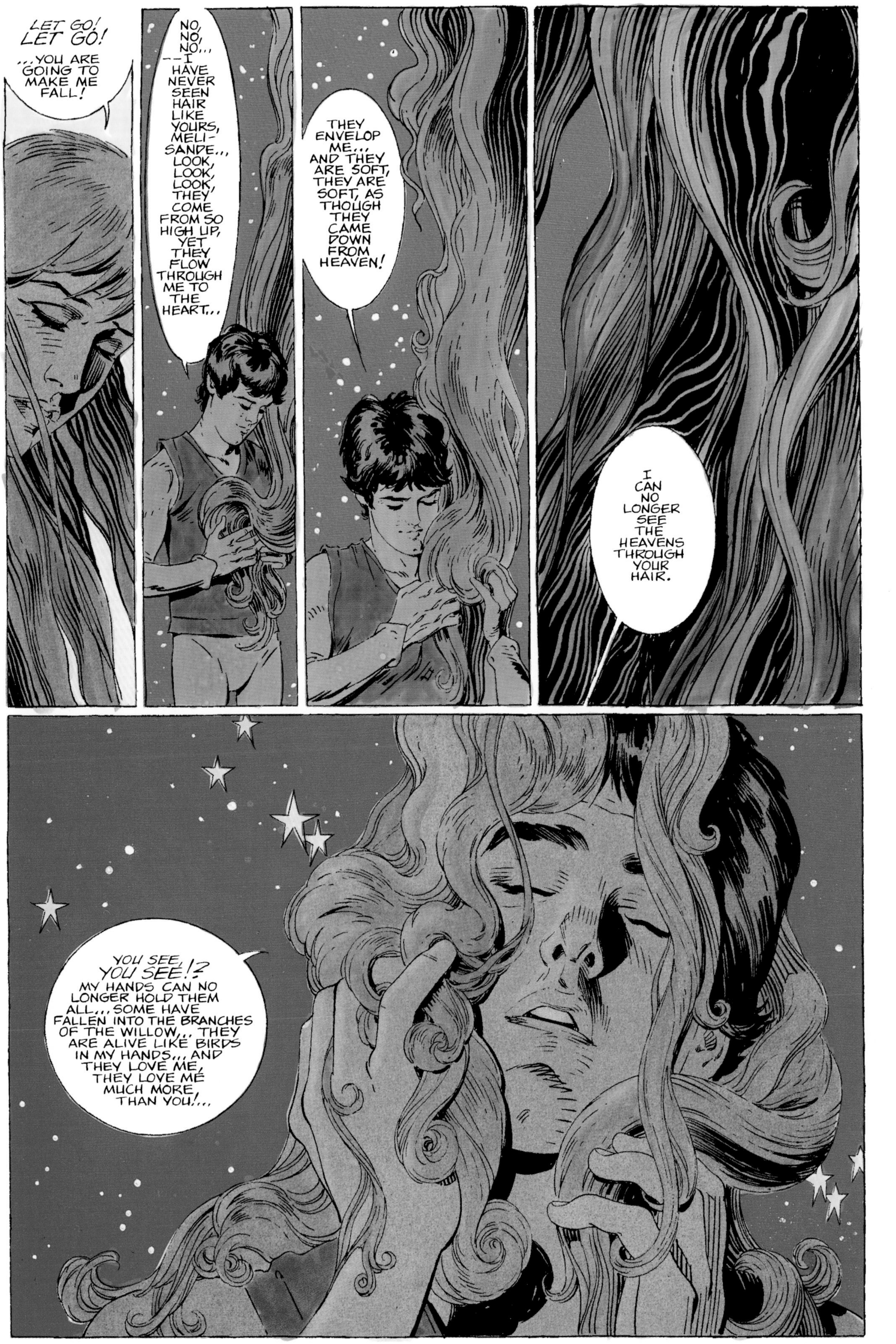
LET GO! LET GO! ...YOU ARE GOING TO MAKE ME FALL!
NO, NO, NO... --I HAVE NEVER SEEN HAIR LIKE YOURS, MELI-SANDE... LOOK, LOOK, LOOK, THEY COME FROM SO HIGH UP, YET THEY FLOW THROUGH ME TO THE HEART...
THEY ENVELOP ME... AND THEY ARE SOFT, THEY ARE SOFT, AS THOUGH THEY CAME DOWN FROM HEAVEN!
I CAN NO LONGER SEE THE HEAVENS THROUGH YOUR HAIR.
YOU SEE, YOU SEE!? MY HANDS CAN NO LONGER HOLD THEM ALL... SOME HAVE FALLEN INTO THE BRANCHES OF THE WILLOW... THEY ARE ALIVE LIKE BIRDS IN MY HANDS... AND THEY LOVE ME, THEY LOVE ME MUCH MORE THAN YOU!...

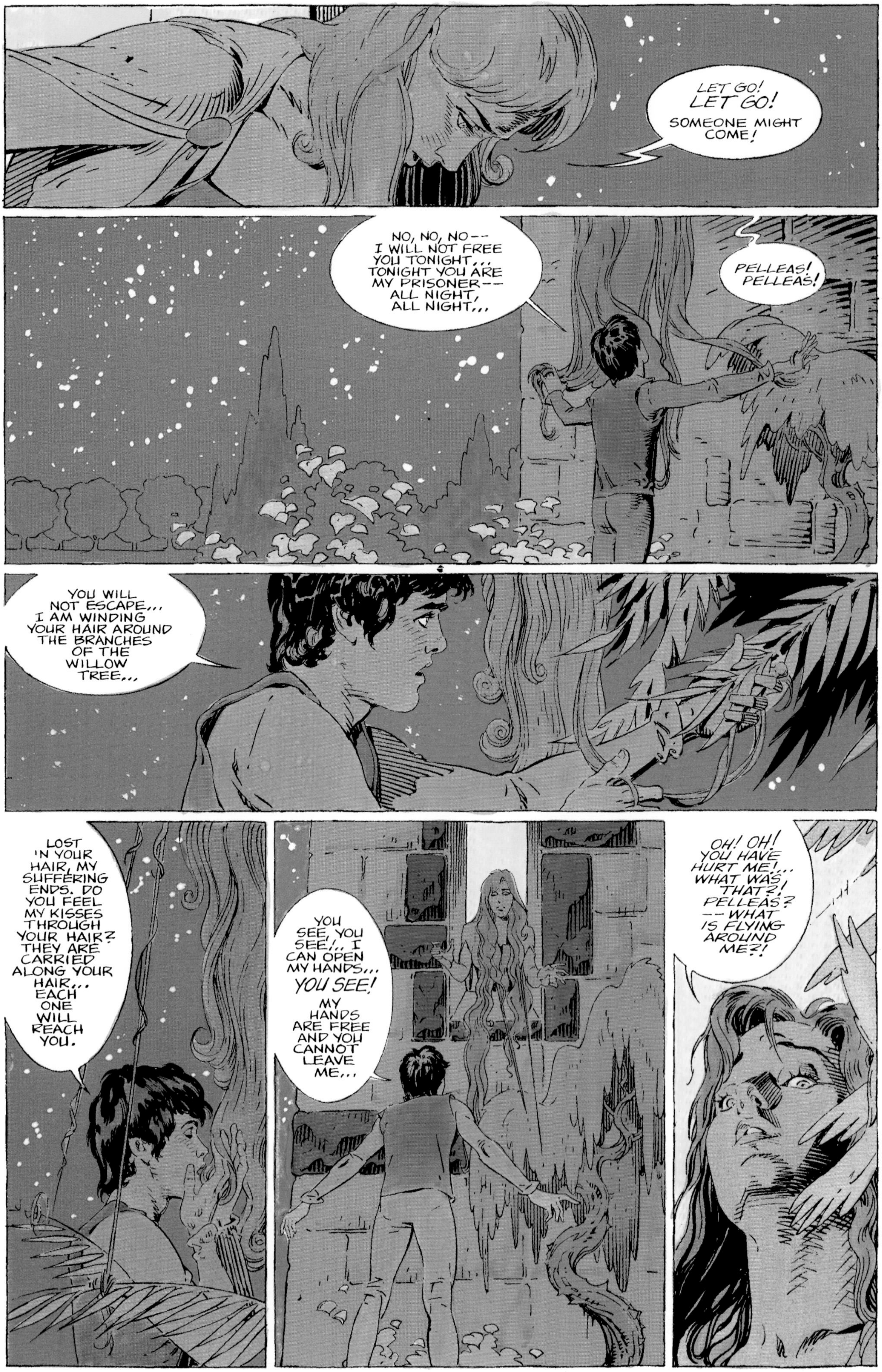
LET GO! LET GO! SOMEONE MIGHT COME!
NO, NO, NO-- I WILL NOT FREE YOU TONIGHT... TONIGHT YOU ARE MY PRISONER-- ALL NIGHT, ALL NIGHT...
PELLEAS! PELLEAS!
YOU WILL NOT ESCAPE... I AM WINDING YOUR HAIR AROUND THE BRANCHES OF THE WILLOW TREE...
LOST IN YOUR HAIR, MY SUFFERING ENDS. DO YOU FEEL MY KISSES THROUGH YOUR HAIR? THEY ARE CARRIED ALONG YOUR HAIR... EACH ONE WILL REACH YOU.
YOU SEE, YOU SEE!.. I CAN OPEN MY HANDS... YOU SEE! MY HANDS ARE FREE AND YOU CANNOT LEAVE ME...
OH! OH! YOU HAVE HURT ME!... WHAT WAS THAT?! PELLEAS? --WHAT IS FLYING AROUND ME?!

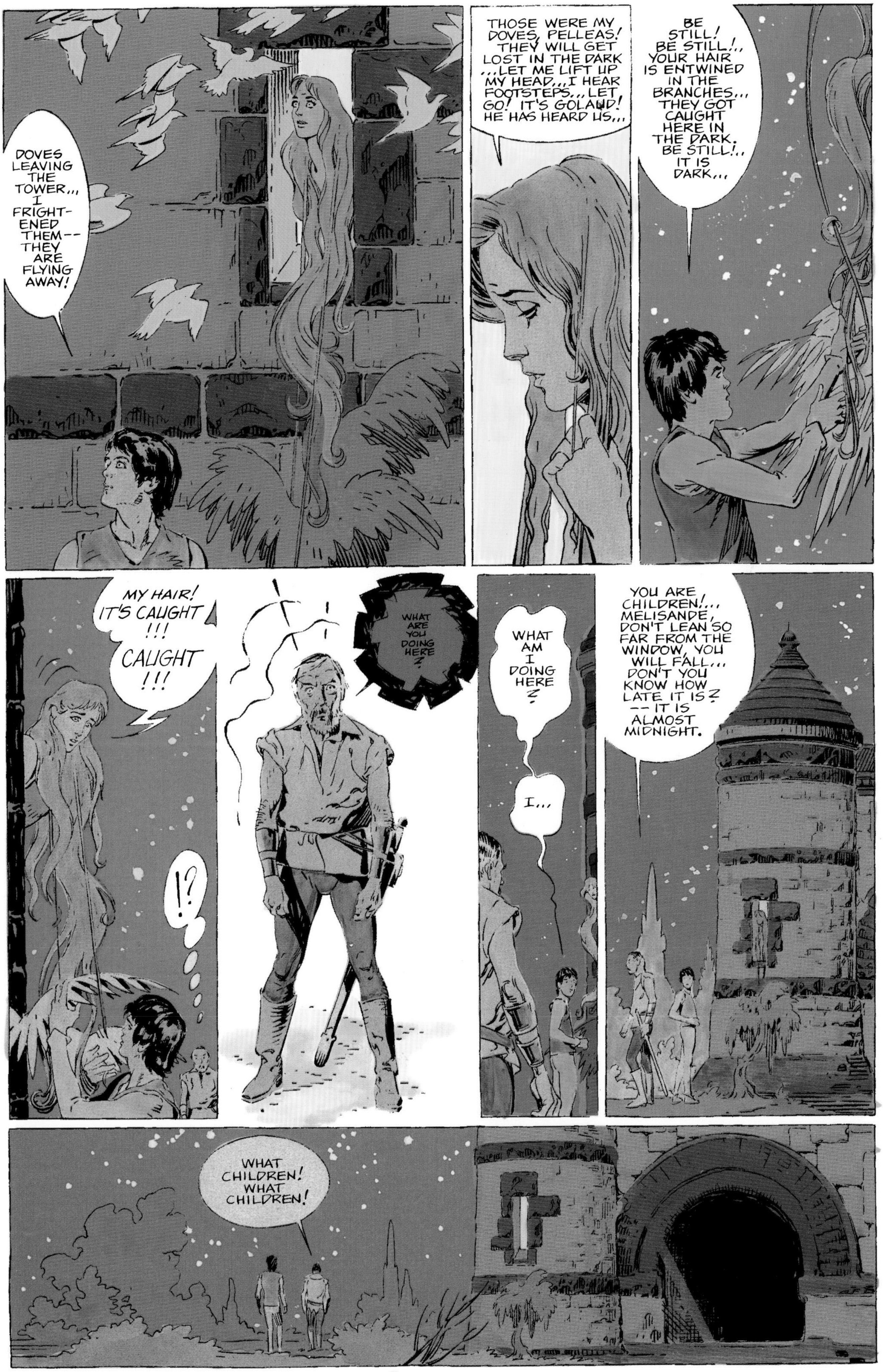
DOVES LEAVING THE TOWER... I FRIGHTENED THEM-- THEY ARE FLYING AWAY!
THOSE WERE MY DOVES, PELLEAS! THEY WILL GET LOST IN THE DARK ...LET ME LIFT UP MY HEAD... I HEAR FOOTSTEPS... LET GO! IT'S GOLAUD! HE HAS HEARD US...
BE STILL! BE STILL!.. YOUR HAIR IS ENTWINED IN THE BRANCHES... THEY GOT CAUGHT HERE IN THE DARK. BE STILL!.. IT IS DARK...
MY HAIR! IT'S CAUGHT !!! CAUGHT !!!
!?
WHAT ARE YOU DOING HERE?
WHAT AM I DOING HERE?
I...
YOU ARE CHILDREN!... MELISANDE, DON'T LEAN SO FAR FROM THE WINDOW, YOU WILL FALL... DON'T YOU KNOW HOW LATE IT IS? -- IT IS ALMOST MIDNIGHT.
WHAT CHILDREN! WHAT CHILDREN!

8

BE CAREFUL! THIS WAY! THIS WAY-- HAVE YOU NEVER DESCENDED INTO THESE VAULTS?

YES, ONCE, BUT THAT WAS LONG AGO.

WELL, HERE IS THE STAGNANT WATER I TOLD YOU ABOUT...

CAN YOU SMELL THE STENCH OF DEATH IN IT?

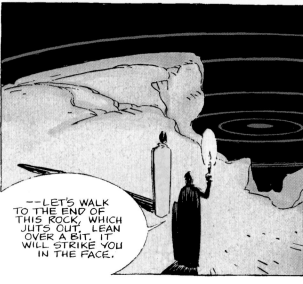

--LET'S WALK TO THE END OF THIS ROCK, WHICH JUTS OUT. LEAN OVER A BIT. IT WILL STRIKE YOU IN THE FACE.

LEAN OVER-- DON'T BE AFRAID...

I WILL HOLD YOU...

34

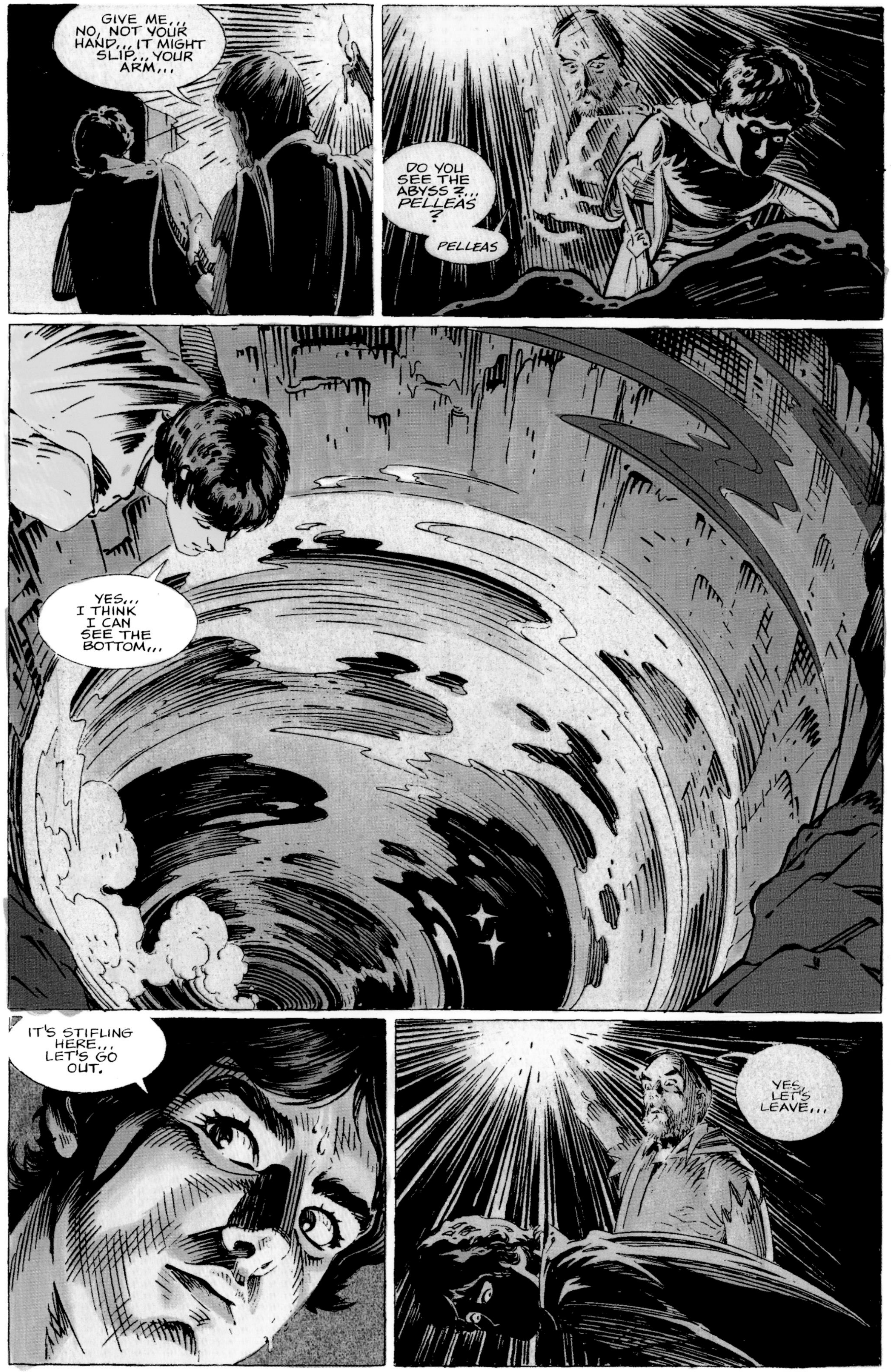
GIVE ME,,, NO, NOT YOUR HAND,,, IT MIGHT SLIP,,, YOUR ARM,,,
DO YOU SEE THE ABYSS ?,,, PELLEAS ?
PELLEAS
YES,,, I THINK I CAN SEE THE BOTTOM,,,
IT'S STIFLING HERE,,, LET'S GO OUT.
YES, LET'S LEAVE,,,

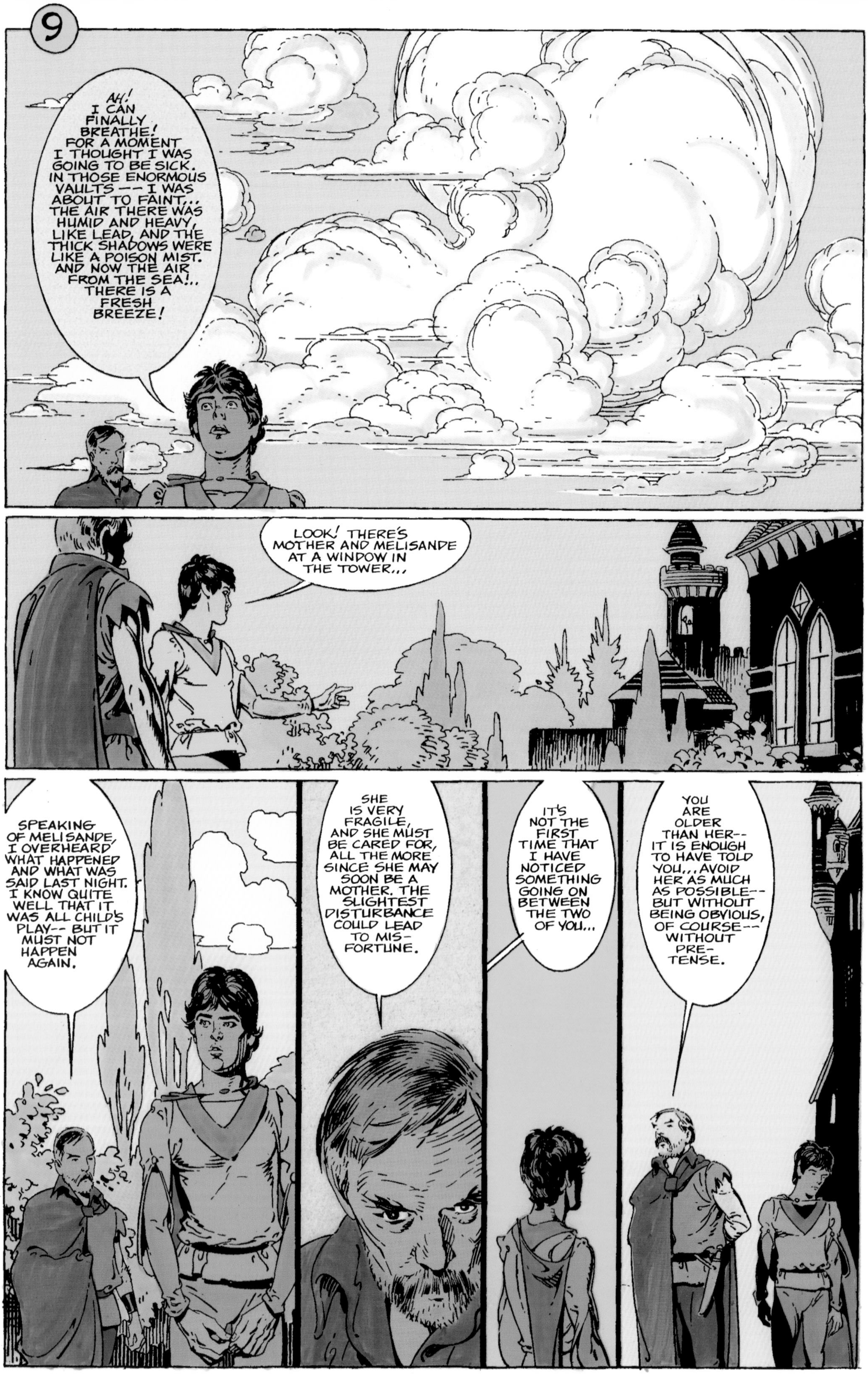
9
AH! I CAN FINALLY BREATHE! FOR A MOMENT I THOUGHT I WAS GOING TO BE SICK. IN THOSE ENORMOUS VAULTS -- I WAS ABOUT TO FAINT... THE AIR THERE WAS HUMID AND HEAVY, LIKE LEAD, AND THE THICK SHADOWS WERE LIKE A POISON MIST. AND NOW THE AIR FROM THE SEA!.. THERE IS A FRESH BREEZE!
LOOK! THERE'S MOTHER AND MELISANDE AT A WINDOW IN THE TOWER...
SPEAKING OF MELISANDE, I OVERHEARD WHAT HAPPENED AND WHAT WAS SAID LAST NIGHT. I KNOW QUITE WELL THAT IT WAS ALL CHILD'S PLAY-- BUT IT MUST NOT HAPPEN AGAIN.
SHE IS VERY FRAGILE, AND SHE MUST BE CARED FOR, ALL THE MORE SINCE SHE MAY SOON BE A MOTHER. THE SLIGHTEST DISTURBANCE COULD LEAD TO MIS-FORTUNE.
IT'S NOT THE FIRST TIME THAT I HAVE NOTICED SOMETHING GOING ON BETWEEN THE TWO OF YOU...
YOU ARE OLDER THAN HER-- IT IS ENOUGH TO HAVE TOLD YOU... AVOID HER AS MUCH AS POSSIBLE-- BUT WITHOUT BEING OBVIOUS, OF COURSE-- WITHOUT PRE-TENSE.

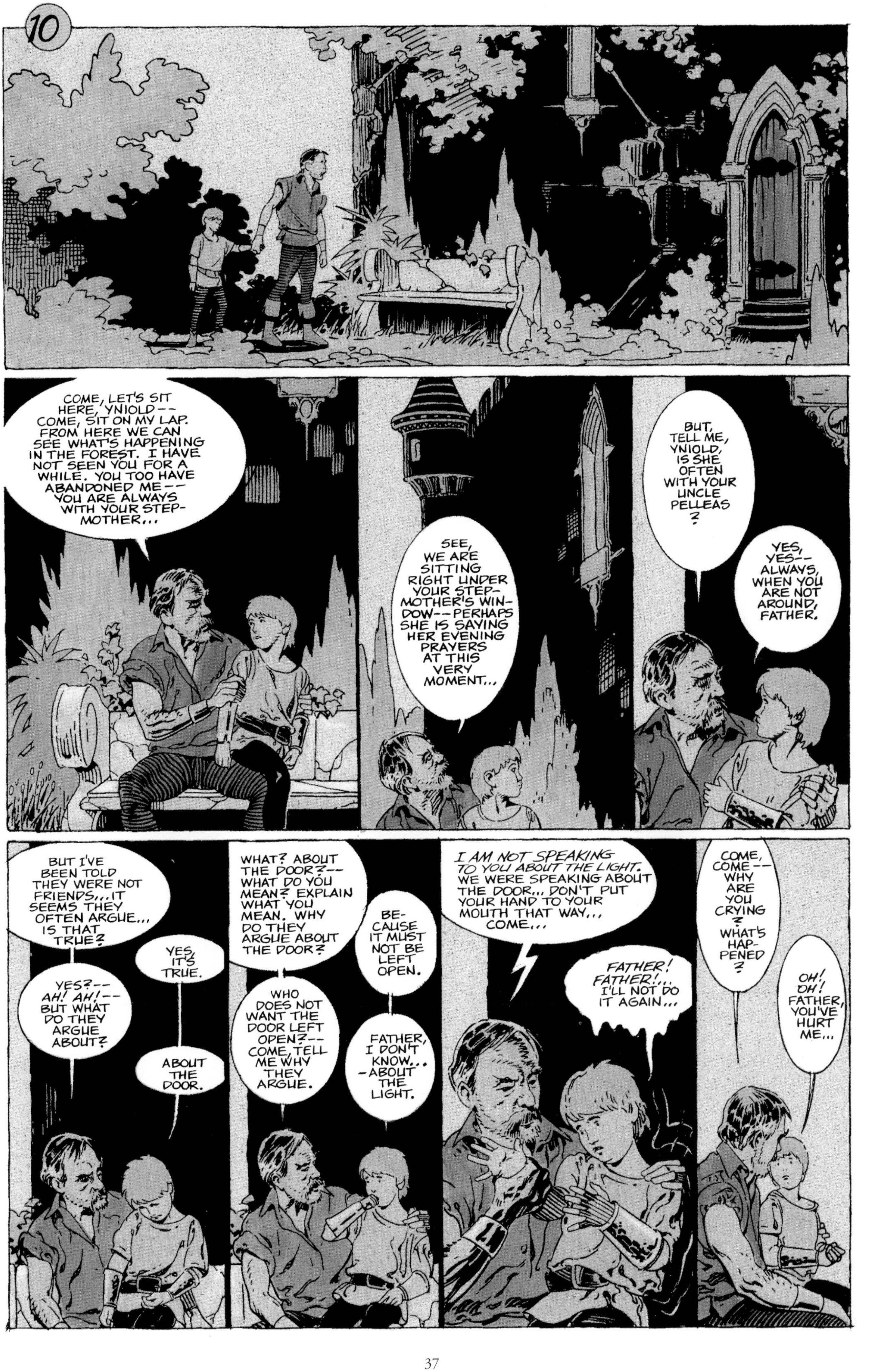
10
COME, LET'S SIT HERE, YNIOLD-- COME, SIT ON MY LAP. FROM HERE WE CAN SEE WHAT'S HAPPENING IN THE FOREST. I HAVE NOT SEEN YOU FOR A WHILE. YOU TOO HAVE ABANDONED ME-- YOU ARE ALWAYS WITH YOUR STEP-MOTHER...
SEE, WE ARE SITTING RIGHT UNDER YOUR STEP-MOTHER'S WIN-DOW--PERHAPS SHE IS SAYING HER EVENING PRAYERS AT THIS VERY MOMENT...
BUT, TELL ME, YNIOLD, IS SHE OFTEN WITH YOUR UNCLE PELLEAS?
YES, YES-- ALWAYS, WHEN YOU ARE NOT AROUND, FATHER.
BUT I'VE BEEN TOLD THEY WERE NOT FRIENDS... IT SEEMS THEY OFTEN ARGUE... IS THAT TRUE?
YES, IT'S TRUE.
YES?-- AH! AH!-- BUT WHAT DO THEY ARGUE ABOUT?
ABOUT THE DOOR.
WHAT? ABOUT THE DOOR?-- WHAT DO YOU MEAN? EXPLAIN WHAT YOU MEAN. WHY DO THEY ARGUE ABOUT THE DOOR?
BE-CAUSE IT MUST NOT BE LEFT OPEN.
WHO DOES NOT WANT THE DOOR LEFT OPEN?-- COME, TELL ME WHY THEY ARGUE.
FATHER, I DON'T KNOW... -ABOUT THE LIGHT.
I AM NOT SPEAKING TO YOU ABOUT THE LIGHT. WE WERE SPEAKING ABOUT THE DOOR... DON'T PUT YOUR HAND TO YOUR MOUTH THAT WAY... COME...
FATHER! FATHER!... I'LL NOT DO IT AGAIN...
COME, COME-- WHY ARE YOU CRYING? WHAT'S HAP-PENED?
OH! OH! FATHER, YOU'VE HURT ME...

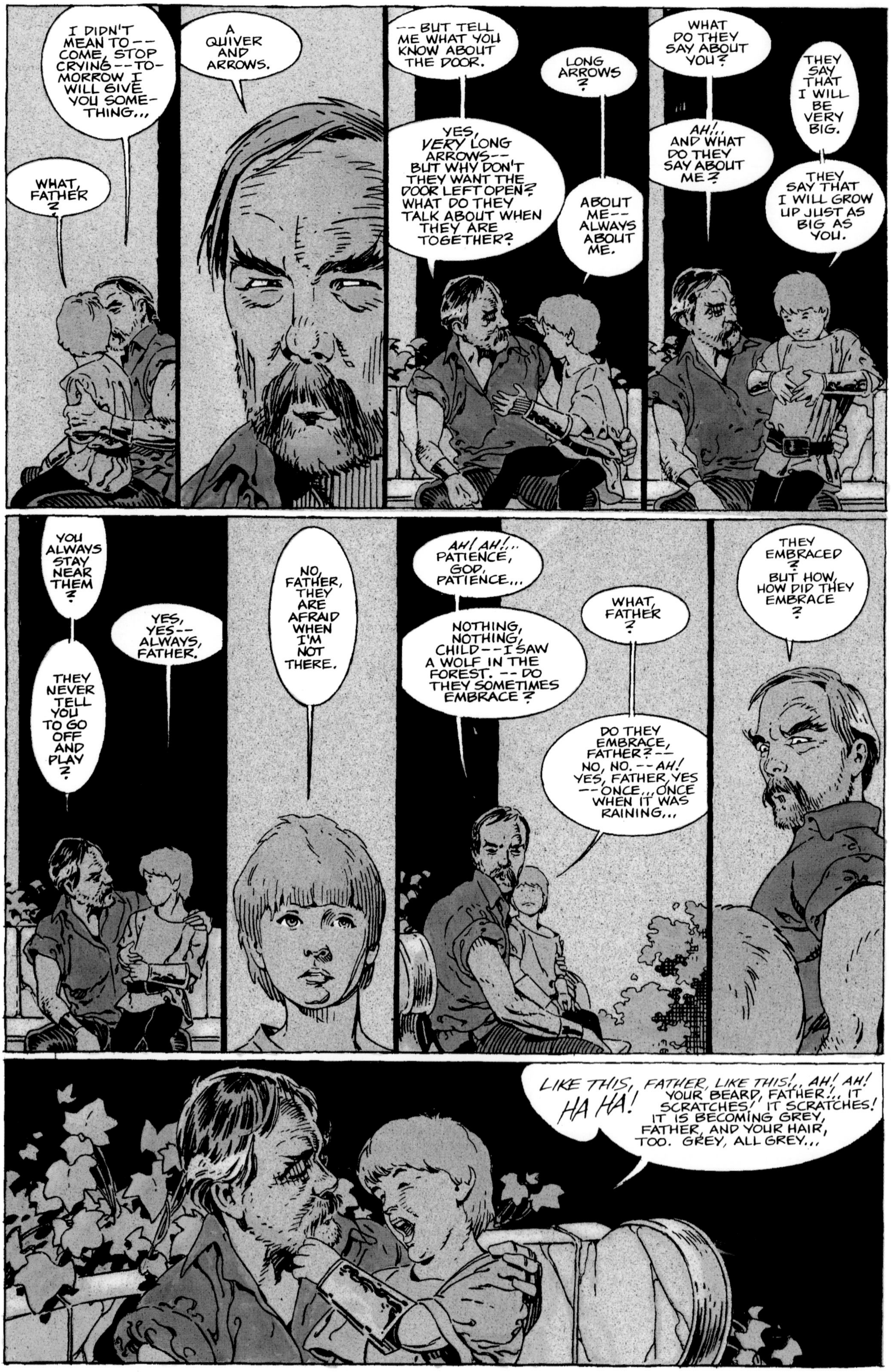

I DIDN'T MEAN TO-- COME, STOP CRYING--TO-MORROW I WILL GIVE YOU SOME-THING...
WHAT, FATHER?
A QUIVER AND ARROWS.
--BUT TELL ME WHAT YOU KNOW ABOUT THE DOOR.
LONG ARROWS?
YES, VERY LONG ARROWS-- BUT WHY DON'T THEY WANT THE DOOR LEFT OPEN? WHAT DO THEY TALK ABOUT WHEN THEY ARE TOGETHER?
ABOUT ME-- ALWAYS ABOUT ME.
WHAT DO THEY SAY ABOUT YOU?
THEY SAY THAT I WILL BE VERY BIG.
AH!, AND WHAT DO THEY SAY ABOUT ME?
THEY SAY THAT I WILL GROW UP JUST AS BIG AS YOU.
YOU ALWAYS STAY NEAR THEM?
YES, YES-- ALWAYS, FATHER.
THEY NEVER TELL YOU TO GO OFF AND PLAY?
NO, FATHER, THEY ARE AFRAID WHEN I'M NOT THERE.
AH! AH!.. PATIENCE, GOD, PATIENCE...
NOTHING, NOTHING, CHILD--I SAW A WOLF IN THE FOREST. --DO THEY SOMETIMES EMBRACE?
WHAT, FATHER?
DO THEY EMBRACE, FATHER?-- NO, NO.--AH! YES, FATHER, YES --ONCE... ONCE WHEN IT WAS RAINING...
THEY EMBRACED? BUT HOW, HOW DID THEY EMBRACE?
LIKE THIS, FATHER, LIKE THIS!.. AH! AH! HA HA! YOUR BEARD, FATHER!.. IT SCRATCHES! IT SCRATCHES! IT IS BECOMING GREY, FATHER, AND YOUR HAIR, TOO. GREY, ALL GREY...

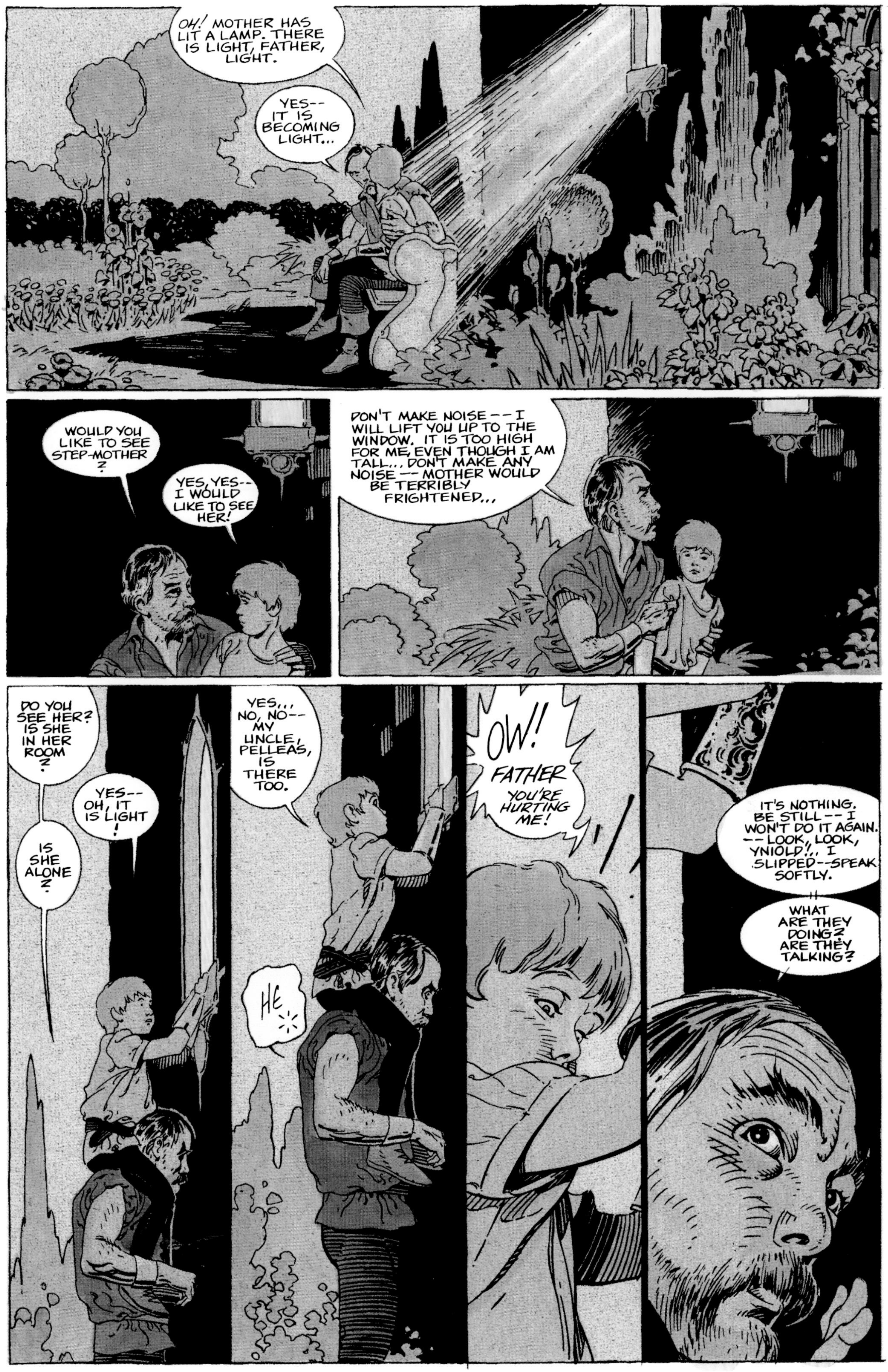
OH! MOTHER HAS LIT A LAMP. THERE IS LIGHT, FATHER, LIGHT.
YES-- IT IS BECOMING LIGHT...
WOULD YOU LIKE TO SEE STEP-MOTHER?
YES, YES-- I WOULD LIKE TO SEE HER!
DON'T MAKE NOISE -- I WILL LIFT YOU UP TO THE WINDOW. IT IS TOO HIGH FOR ME, EVEN THOUGH I AM TALL... DON'T MAKE ANY NOISE -- MOTHER WOULD BE TERRIBLY FRIGHTENED...
DO YOU SEE HER? IS SHE IN HER ROOM?
YES-- OH, IT IS LIGHT!
IS SHE ALONE?
YES... NO, NO-- MY UNCLE, PELLEAS, IS THERE TOO.
HE
OW! FATHER YOU'RE HURTING ME!
IT'S NOTHING. BE STILL -- I WON'T DO IT AGAIN. -- LOOK, LOOK, YNIOLD!... I SLIPPED--SPEAK SOFTLY.
WHAT ARE THEY DOING? ARE THEY TALKING?

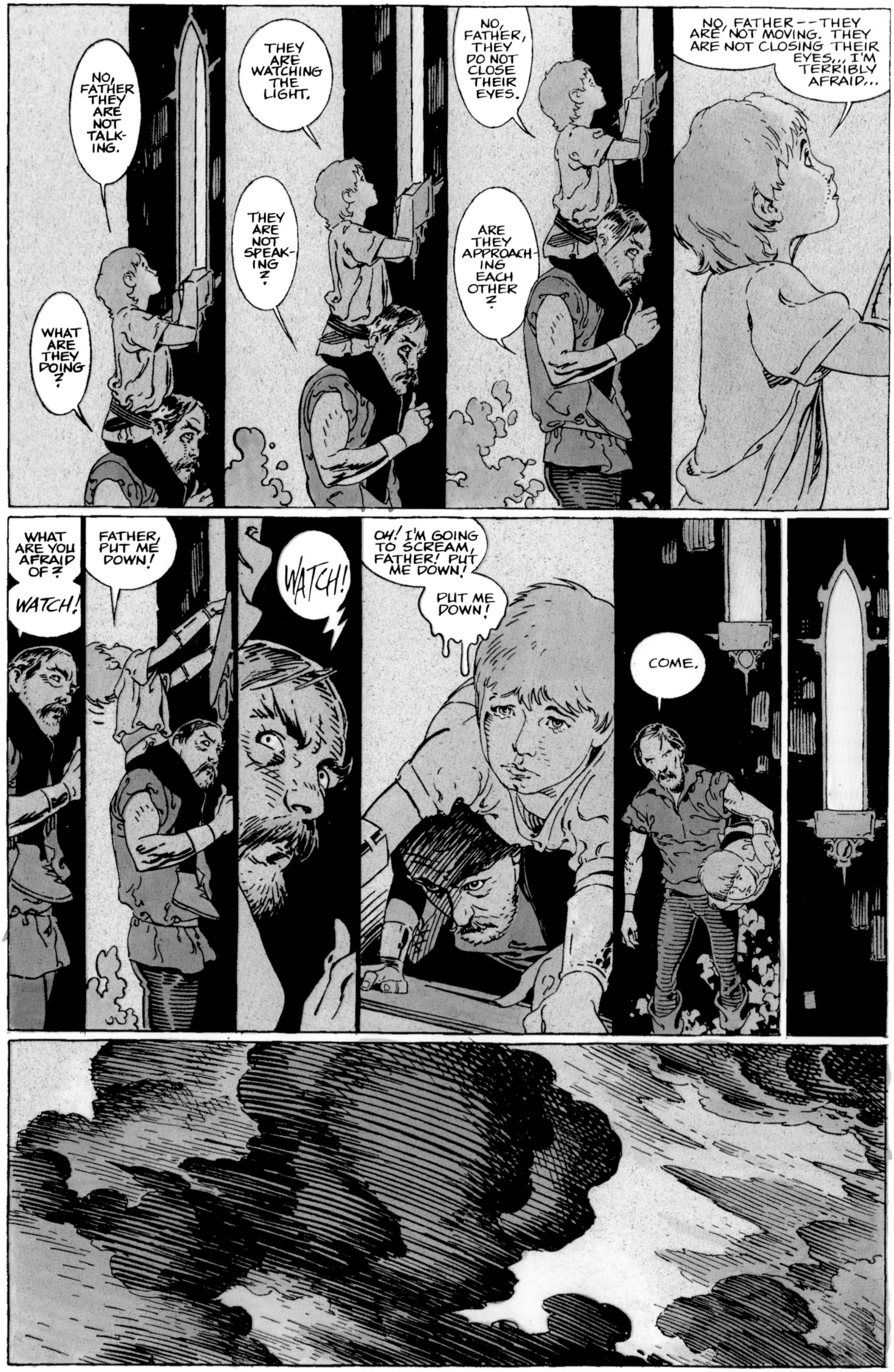

NO, FATHER THEY ARE NOT TALK-ING.
WHAT ARE THEY DOING?
THEY ARE WATCHING THE LIGHT.
THEY ARE NOT SPEAK-ING?
NO, FATHER, THEY DO NOT CLOSE THEIR EYES.
ARE THEY APPROACH-ING EACH OTHER?
NO, FATHER--THEY ARE NOT MOVING. THEY ARE NOT CLOSING THEIR EYES... I'M TERRIBLY AFRAID...
WHAT ARE YOU AFRAID OF?
WATCH!
FATHER, PUT ME DOWN!
WATCH!
OH! I'M GOING TO SCREAM, FATHER! PUT ME DOWN!
PUT ME DOWN!
COME.

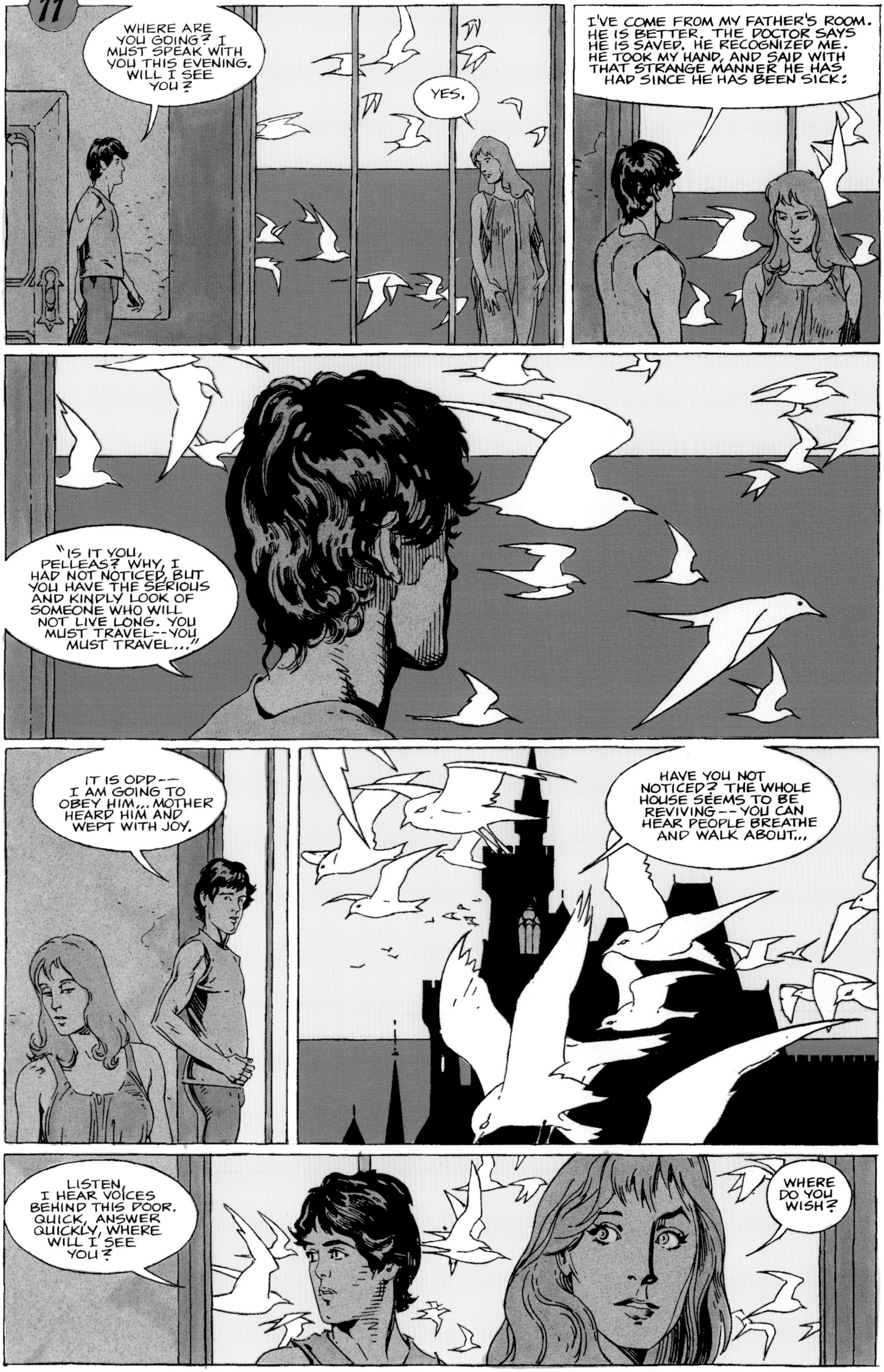
11
WHERE ARE YOU GOING? I MUST SPEAK WITH YOU THIS EVENING. WILL I SEE YOU?
YES.
I'VE COME FROM MY FATHER'S ROOM. HE IS BETTER. THE DOCTOR SAYS HE IS SAVED. HE RECOGNIZED ME. HE TOOK MY HAND, AND SAID WITH THAT STRANGE MANNER HE HAS HAD SINCE HE HAS BEEN SICK:
"IS IT YOU, PELLEAS? WHY, I HAD NOT NOTICED, BUT YOU HAVE THE SERIOUS AND KINDLY LOOK OF SOMEONE WHO WILL NOT LIVE LONG. YOU MUST TRAVEL--YOU MUST TRAVEL..."
IT IS ODD-- I AM GOING TO OBEY HIM... MOTHER HEARD HIM AND WEPT WITH JOY.
HAVE YOU NOT NOTICED? THE WHOLE HOUSE SEEMS TO BE REVIVING--YOU CAN HEAR PEOPLE BREATHE AND WALK ABOUT...
LISTEN, I HEAR VOICES BEHIND THIS DOOR. QUICK, ANSWER QUICKLY, WHERE WILL I SEE YOU?
WHERE DO YOU WISH?

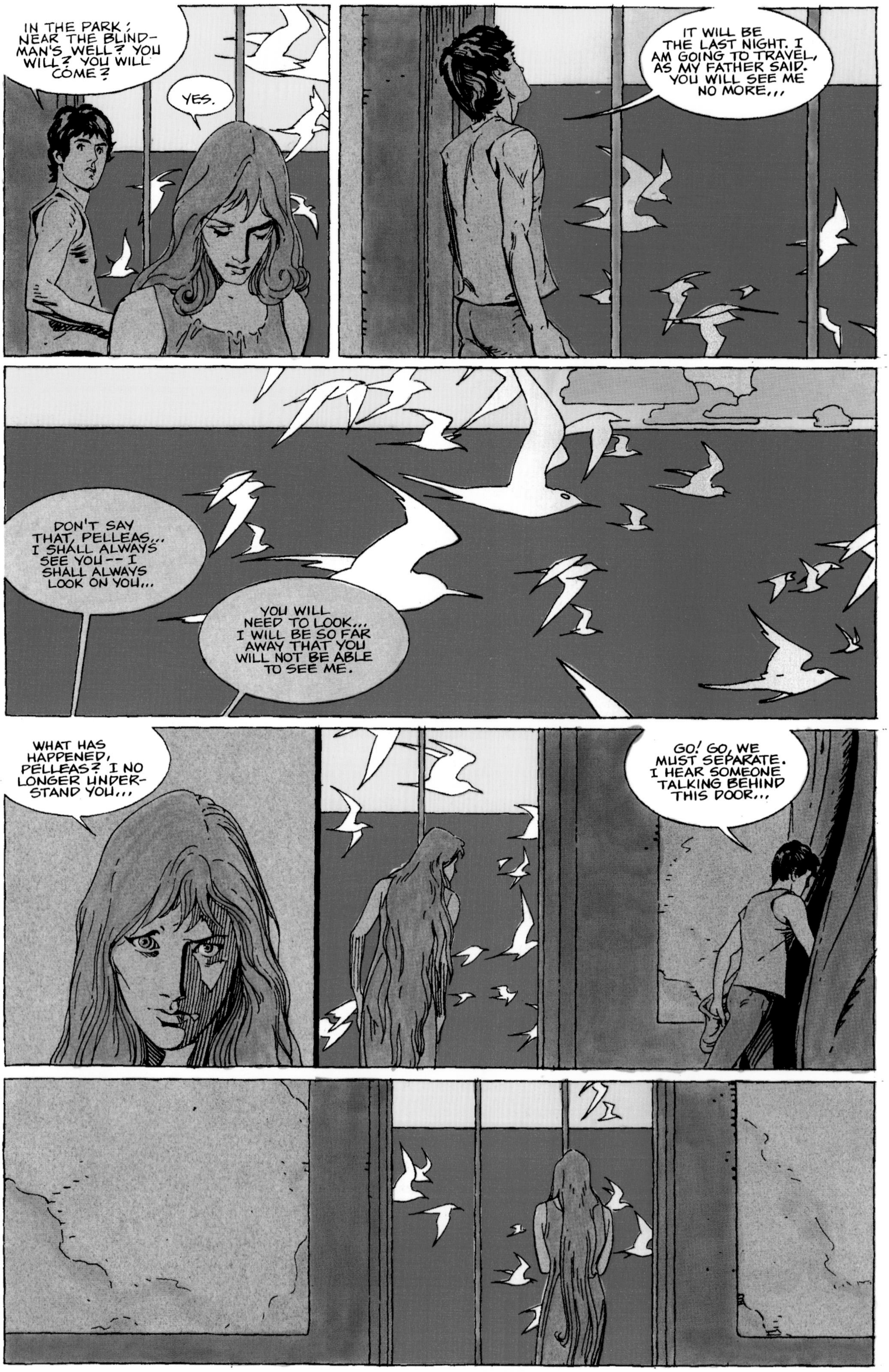
IN THE PARK; NEAR THE BLIND-MAN'S WELL? YOU WILL? YOU WILL COME?
YES.
IT WILL BE THE LAST NIGHT. I AM GOING TO TRAVEL, AS MY FATHER SAID. YOU WILL SEE ME NO MORE...
DON'T SAY THAT, PELLEAS... I SHALL ALWAYS SEE YOU-- I SHALL ALWAYS LOOK ON YOU...
YOU WILL NEED TO LOOK... I WILL BE SO FAR AWAY THAT YOU WILL NOT BE ABLE TO SEE ME.
WHAT HAS HAPPENED, PELLEAS? I NO LONGER UNDER-STAND YOU...
GO! GO, WE MUST SEPARATE. I HEAR SOMEONE TALKING BEHIND THIS DOOR...

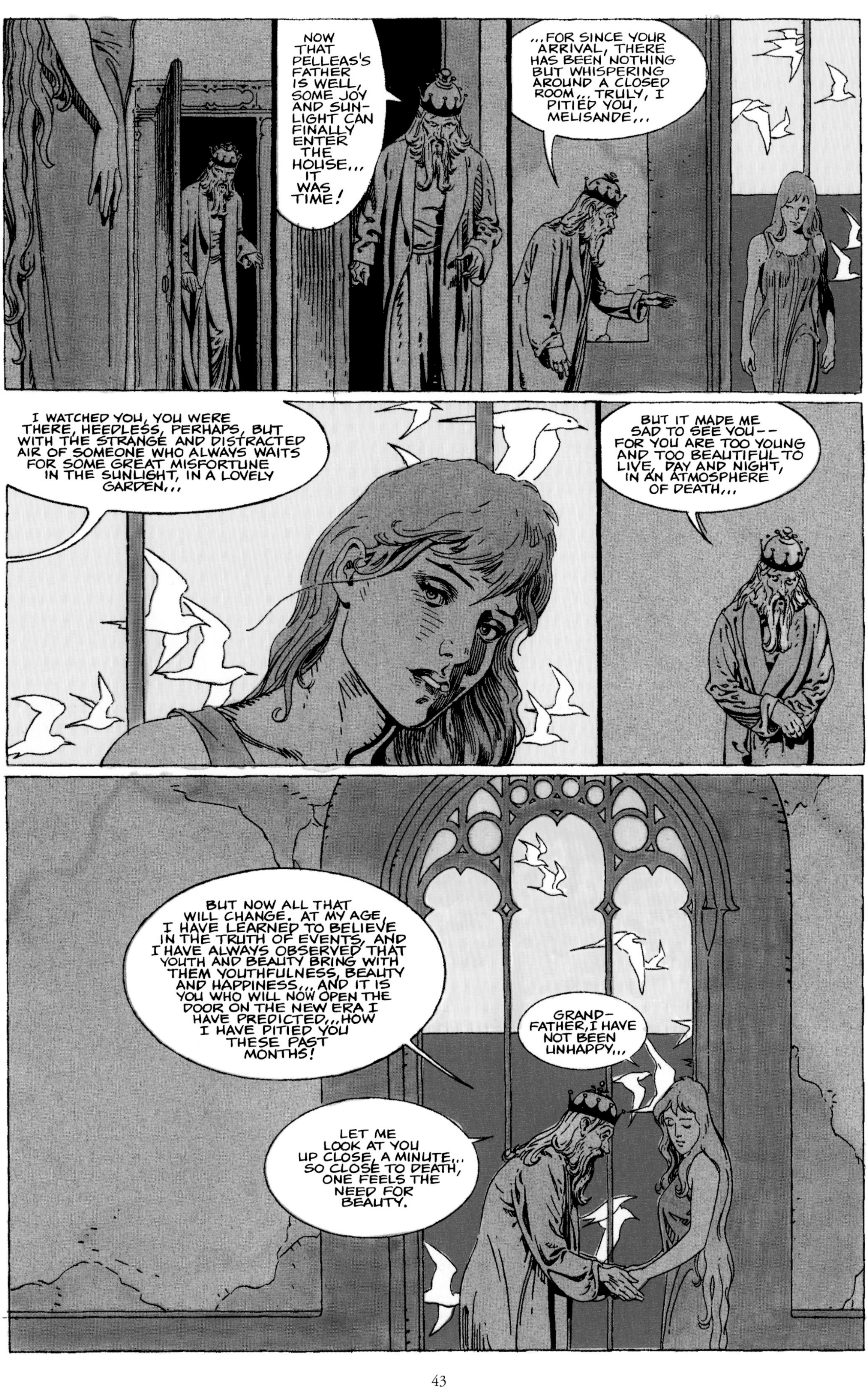
NOW THAT PELLEAS'S FATHER IS WELL, SOME JOY AND SUNLIGHT CAN FINALLY ENTER THE HOUSE... IT WAS TIME!
...FOR SINCE YOUR ARRIVAL, THERE HAS BEEN NOTHING BUT WHISPERING AROUND A CLOSED ROOM... TRULY, I PITIED YOU, MELISANDE...
I WATCHED YOU, YOU WERE THERE, HEEDLESS, PERHAPS, BUT WITH THE STRANGE AND DISTRACTED AIR OF SOMEONE WHO ALWAYS WAITS FOR SOME GREAT MISFORTUNE IN THE SUNLIGHT, IN A LOVELY GARDEN...
BUT IT MADE ME SAD TO SEE YOU-- FOR YOU ARE TOO YOUNG AND TOO BEAUTIFUL TO LIVE, DAY AND NIGHT, IN AN ATMOSPHERE OF DEATH...
BUT NOW ALL THAT WILL CHANGE. AT MY AGE, I HAVE LEARNED TO BELIEVE IN THE TRUTH OF EVENTS, AND I HAVE ALWAYS OBSERVED THAT YOUTH AND BEAUTY BRING WITH THEM YOUTHFULNESS, BEAUTY AND HAPPINESS... AND IT IS YOU WHO WILL NOW OPEN THE DOOR ON THE NEW ERA I HAVE PREDICTED... HOW I HAVE PITIED YOU THESE PAST MONTHS!
GRAND-FATHER, I HAVE NOT BEEN UNHAPPY...
LET ME LOOK AT YOU UP CLOSE, A MINUTE... SO CLOSE TO DEATH, ONE FEELS THE NEED FOR BEAUTY.

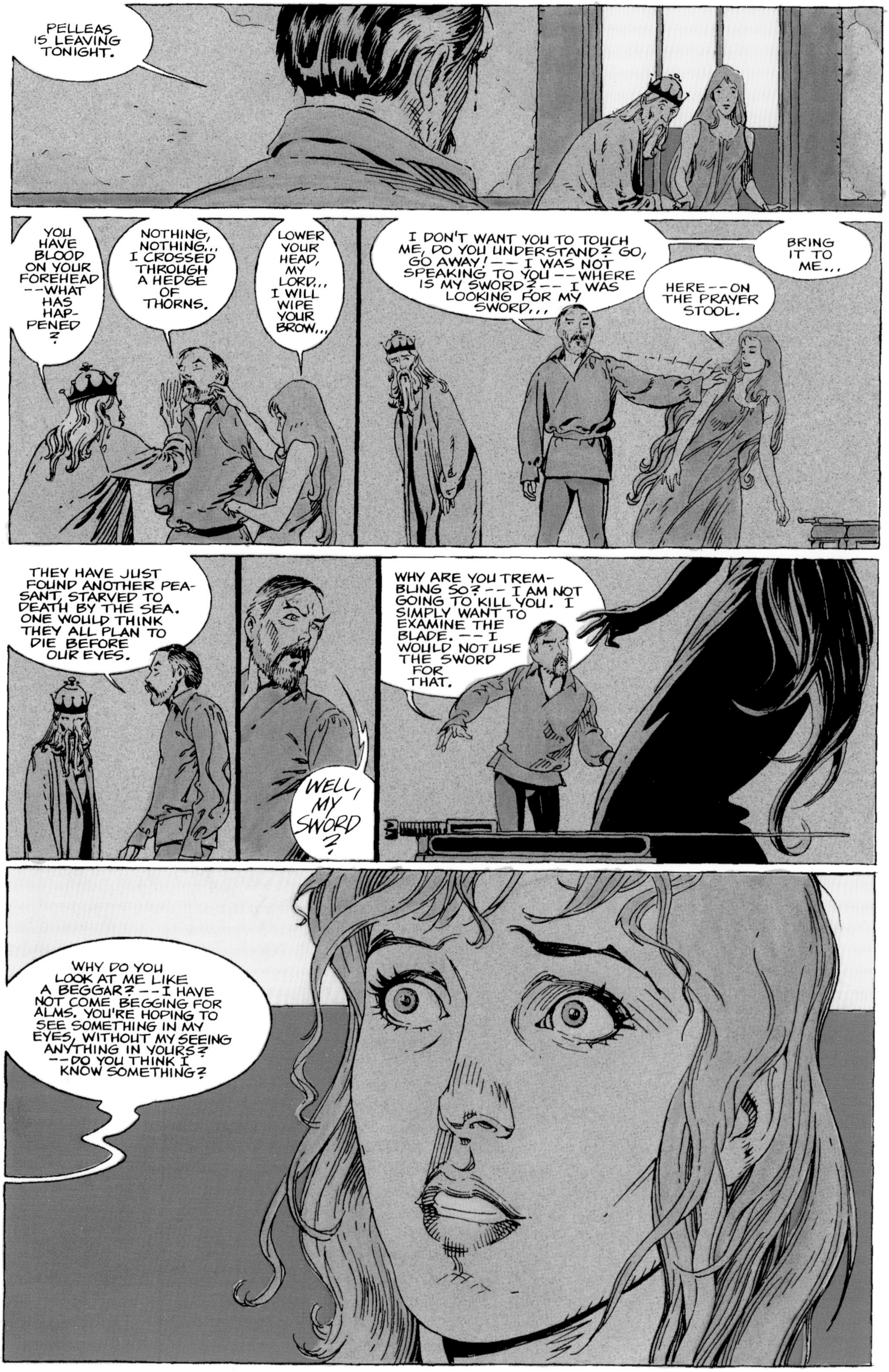
PELLEAS IS LEAVING TONIGHT.
YOU HAVE BLOOD ON YOUR FOREHEAD --WHAT HAS HAP-PENED?
NOTHING, NOTHING... I CROSSED THROUGH A HEDGE OF THORNS.
LOWER YOUR HEAD, MY LORD... I WILL WIPE YOUR BROW...
I DON'T WANT YOU TO TOUCH ME, DO YOU UNDERSTAND? GO, GO AWAY! -- I WAS NOT SPEAKING TO YOU --WHERE IS MY SWORD? -- I WAS LOOKING FOR MY SWORD...
BRING IT TO ME...
HERE --ON THE PRAYER STOOL.
THEY HAVE JUST FOUND ANOTHER PEA-SANT, STARVED TO DEATH BY THE SEA. ONE WOULD THINK THEY ALL PLAN TO DIE BEFORE OUR EYES.
WELL, MY SWORD?
WHY ARE YOU TREM-BLING SO? -- I AM NOT GOING TO KILL YOU. I SIMPLY WANT TO EXAMINE THE BLADE. -- I WOULD NOT USE THE SWORD FOR THAT.
WHY DO YOU LOOK AT ME LIKE A BEGGAR? --I HAVE NOT COME BEGGING FOR ALMS. YOU'RE HOPING TO SEE SOMETHING IN MY EYES, WITHOUT MY SEEING ANYTHING IN YOURS? --DO YOU THINK I KNOW SOMETHING?

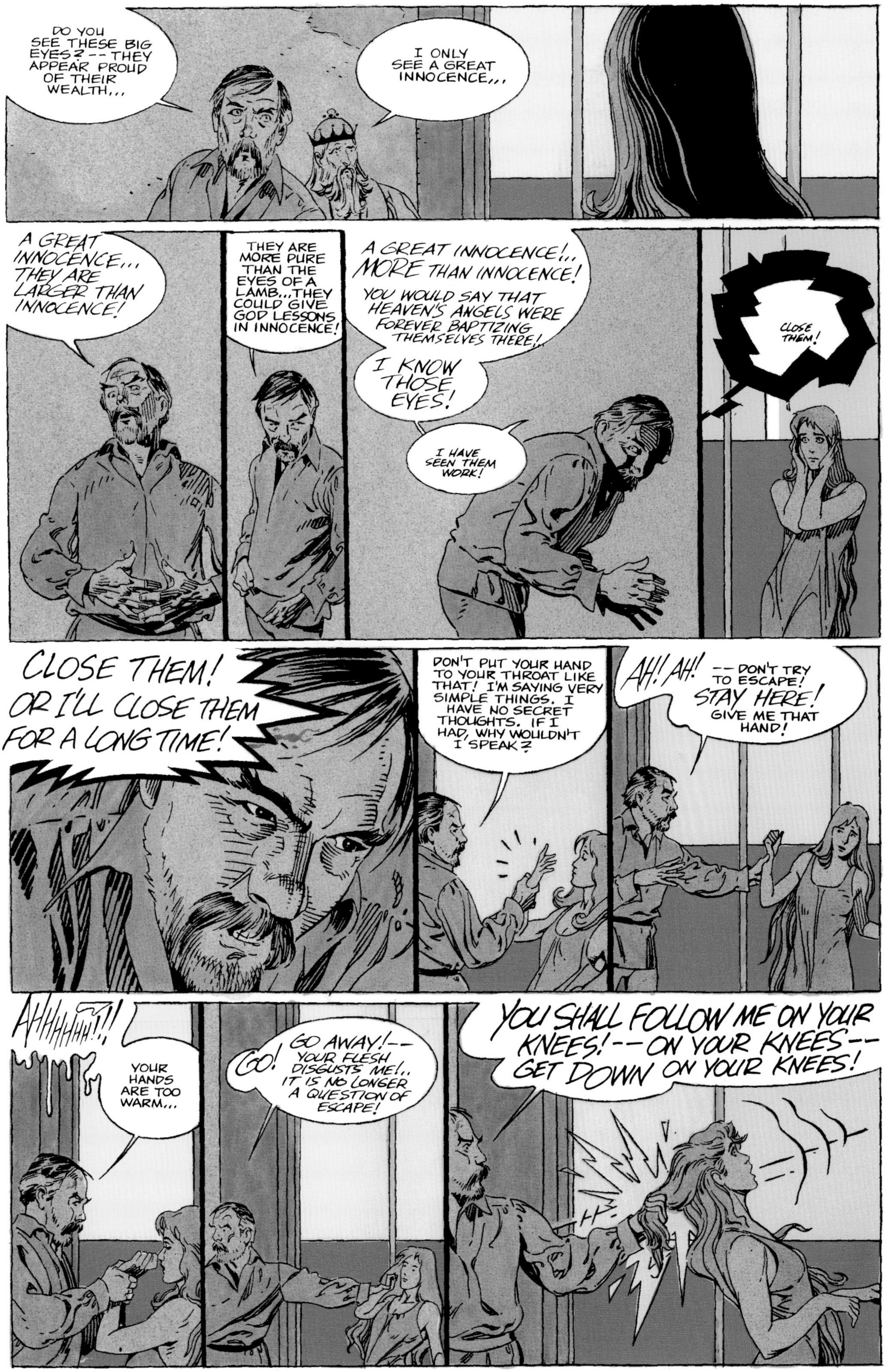

DO YOU SEE THESE BIG EYES? -- THEY APPEAR PROUD OF THEIR WEALTH,,,
I ONLY SEE A GREAT INNOCENCE,,,
A GREAT INNOCENCE,,, THEY ARE LARGER THAN INNOCENCE!
THEY ARE MORE PURE THAN THE EYES OF A LAMB,,THEY COULD GIVE GOD LESSONS IN INNOCENCE!
A GREAT INNOCENCE!,, MORE THAN INNOCENCE!
YOU WOULD SAY THAT HEAVEN'S ANGELS WERE FOREVER BAPTIZING THEMSELVES THERE!,
I KNOW THOSE EYES!
I HAVE SEEN THEM WORK!
CLOSE THEM!
CLOSE THEM! OR I'LL CLOSE THEM FOR A LONG TIME!
DON'T PUT YOUR HAND TO YOUR THROAT LIKE THAT! I'M SAYING VERY SIMPLE THINGS. I HAVE NO SECRET THOUGHTS. IF I HAD, WHY WOULDN'T I SPEAK?
AH! AH!
-- DON'T TRY TO ESCAPE! STAY HERE! GIVE ME THAT HAND!
AHHHHHH!!!!
YOUR HANDS ARE TOO WARM,,,
GO!
GO AWAY!-- YOUR FLESH DISGUSTS ME!,, IT IS NO LONGER A QUESTION OF ESCAPE!
YOU SHALL FOLLOW ME ON YOUR KNEES!--ON YOUR KNEES-- GET DOWN ON YOUR KNEES!

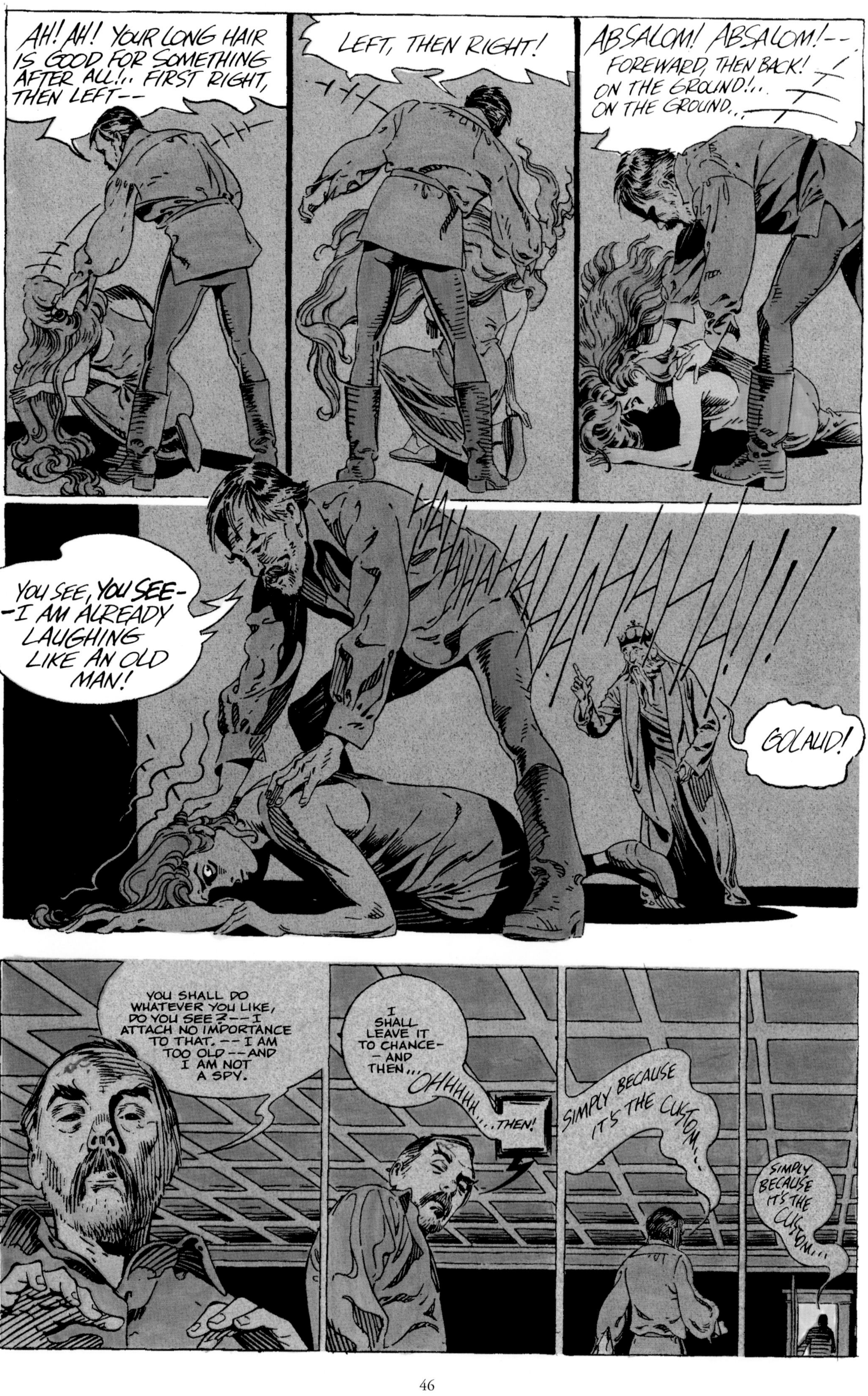
AH! AH! YOUR LONG HAIR IS GOOD FOR SOMETHING AFTER ALL!.. FIRST RIGHT, THEN LEFT--
LEFT, THEN RIGHT!
ABSALOM! ABSALOM!-- FOREWARD, THEN BACK! ON THE GROUND!.. ON THE GROUND..
YOU SEE, YOU SEE--I AM ALREADY LAUGHING LIKE AN OLD MAN!
HAHAHAHAHAHAHAHA!!
GOLAUD!
YOU SHALL DO WHATEVER YOU LIKE, DO YOU SEE?--I ATTACH NO IMPORTANCE TO THAT. --I AM TOO OLD--AND I AM NOT A SPY.
I SHALL LEAVE IT TO CHANCE--AND THEN...
OHHHHH...THEN!
SIMPLY BECAUSE IT'S THE CUSTOM...
SIMPLY BECAUSE IT'S THE CUSTOM...

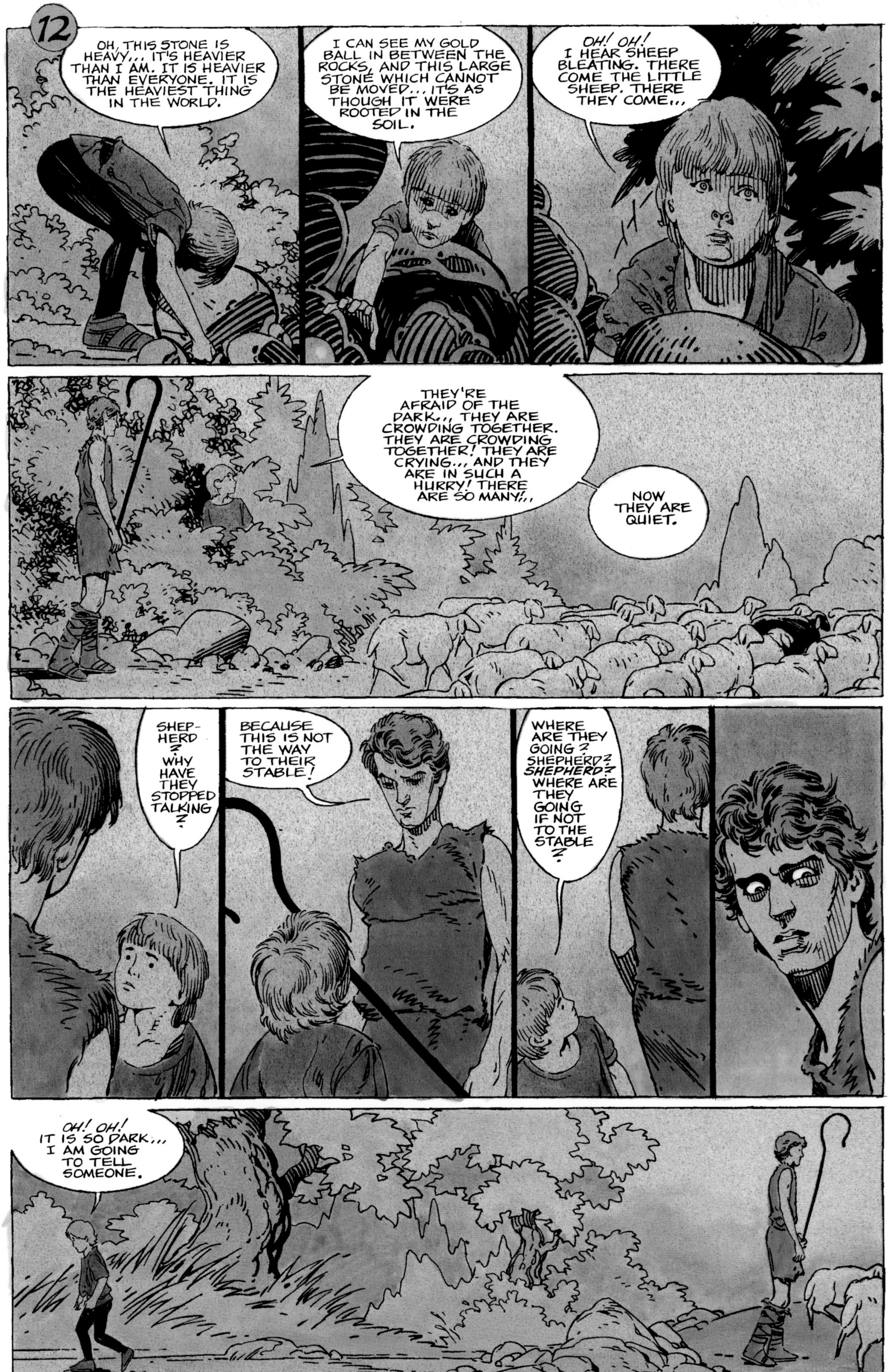
12
OH, THIS STONE IS HEAVY... IT'S HEAVIER THAN I AM. IT IS HEAVIER THAN EVERYONE. IT IS THE HEAVIEST THING IN THE WORLD.
I CAN SEE MY GOLD BALL IN BETWEEN THE ROCKS, AND THIS LARGE STONE WHICH CANNOT BE MOVED... IT'S AS THOUGH IT WERE ROOTED IN THE SOIL.
OH! OH! I HEAR SHEEP BLEATING. THERE COME THE LITTLE SHEEP. THERE THEY COME...
THEY'RE AFRAID OF THE DARK... THEY ARE CROWDING TOGETHER. THEY ARE CROWDING TOGETHER! THEY ARE CRYING... AND THEY ARE IN SUCH A HURRY! THERE ARE SO MANY!..
NOW THEY ARE QUIET.
SHEPHERD? WHY HAVE THEY STOPPED TALKING?
BECAUSE THIS IS NOT THE WAY TO THEIR STABLE!
WHERE ARE THEY GOING? SHEPHERD? SHEPHERD? WHERE ARE THEY GOING IF NOT TO THE STABLE?
OH! OH! IT IS SO DARK... I AM GOING TO TELL SOMEONE.

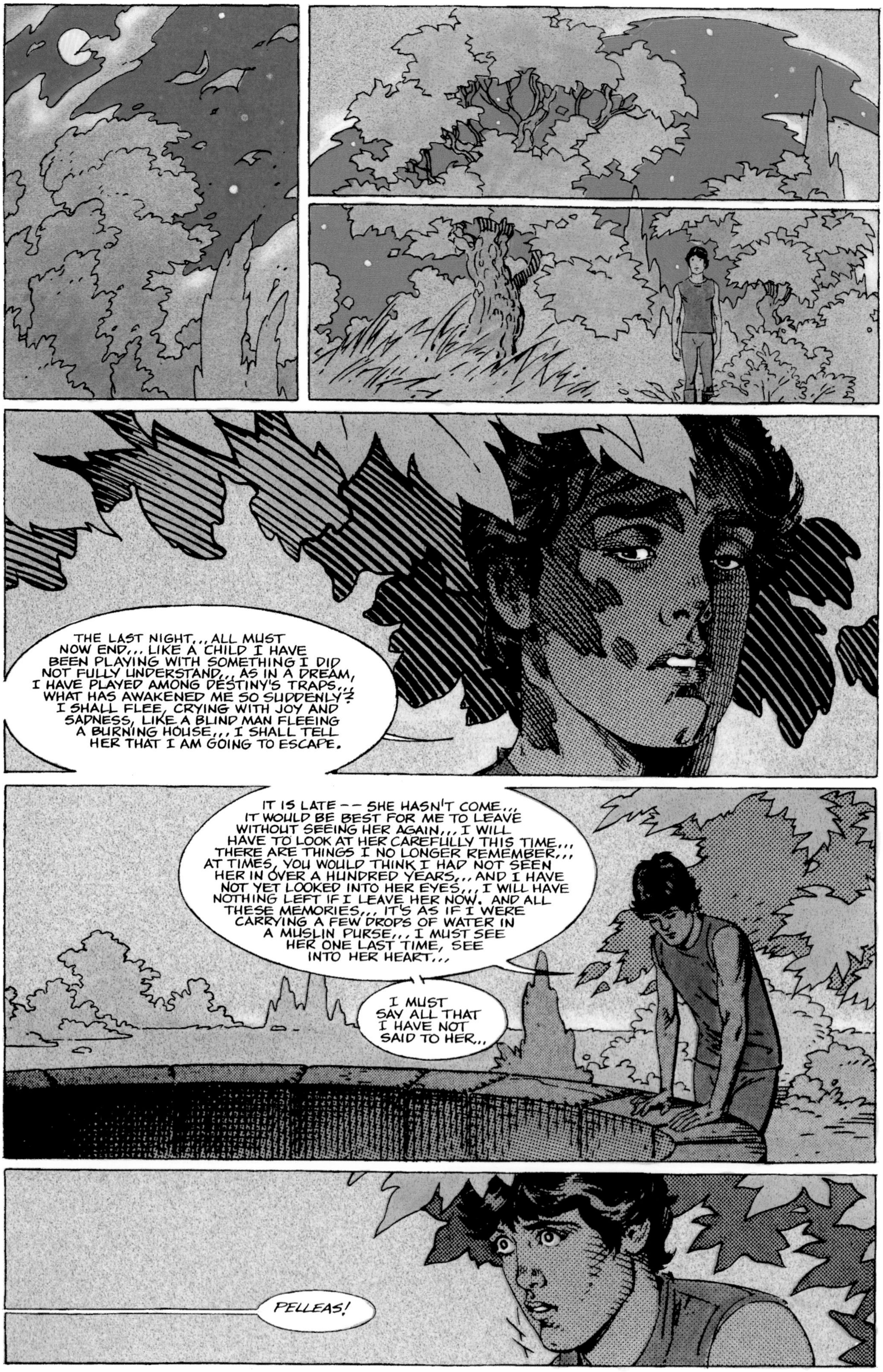

THE LAST NIGHT... ALL MUST NOW END... LIKE A CHILD I HAVE BEEN PLAYING WITH SOMETHING I DID NOT FULLY UNDERSTAND... AS IN A DREAM, I HAVE PLAYED AMONG DESTINY'S TRAPS... WHAT HAS AWAKENED ME SO SUDDENLY?! I SHALL FLEE, CRYING WITH JOY AND SADNESS, LIKE A BLIND MAN FLEEING A BURNING HOUSE... I SHALL TELL HER THAT I AM GOING TO ESCAPE.
IT IS LATE -- SHE HASN'T COME... IT WOULD BE BEST FOR ME TO LEAVE WITHOUT SEEING HER AGAIN... I WILL HAVE TO LOOK AT HER CAREFULLY THIS TIME... THERE ARE THINGS I NO LONGER REMEMBER... AT TIMES, YOU WOULD THINK I HAD NOT SEEN HER IN OVER A HUNDRED YEARS... AND I HAVE NOT YET LOOKED INTO HER EYES... I WILL HAVE NOTHING LEFT IF I LEAVE HER NOW. AND ALL THESE MEMORIES... IT'S AS IF I WERE CARRYING A FEW DROPS OF WATER IN A MUSLIN PURSE... I MUST SEE HER ONE LAST TIME, SEE INTO HER HEART...
I MUST SAY ALL THAT I HAVE NOT SAID TO HER...
PELLEAS!

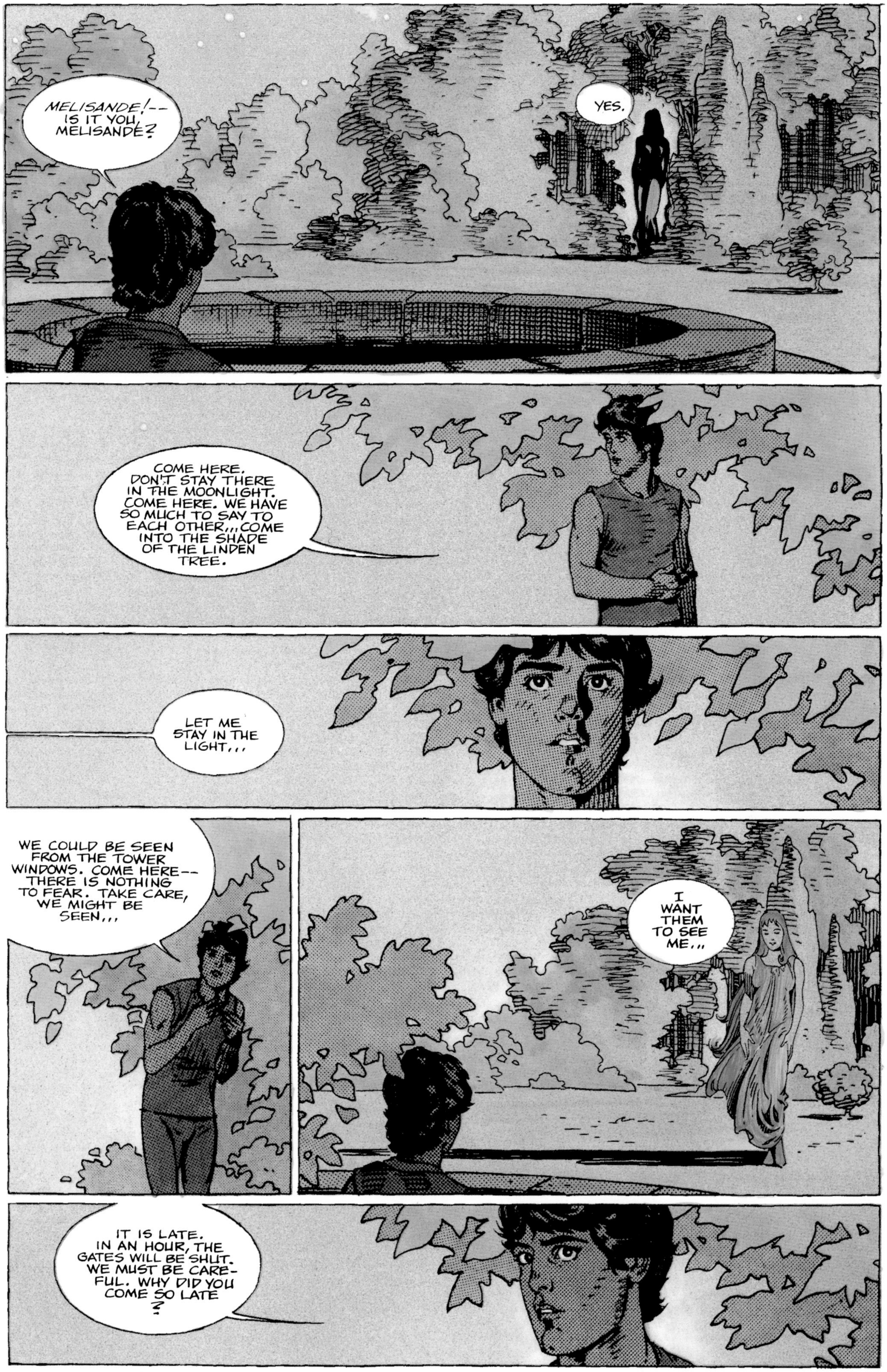
MELISANDE!-- IS IT YOU, MELISANDE?
YES.
COME HERE. DON'T STAY THERE IN THE MOONLIGHT. COME HERE. WE HAVE SO MUCH TO SAY TO EACH OTHER,,, COME INTO THE SHADE OF THE LINDEN TREE.
LET ME STAY IN THE LIGHT,,,
WE COULD BE SEEN FROM THE TOWER WINDOWS. COME HERE-- THERE IS NOTHING TO FEAR. TAKE CARE, WE MIGHT BE SEEN,,,
I WANT THEM TO SEE ME,,,
IT IS LATE. IN AN HOUR, THE GATES WILL BE SHUT. WE MUST BE CARE-FUL. WHY DID YOU COME SO LATE?

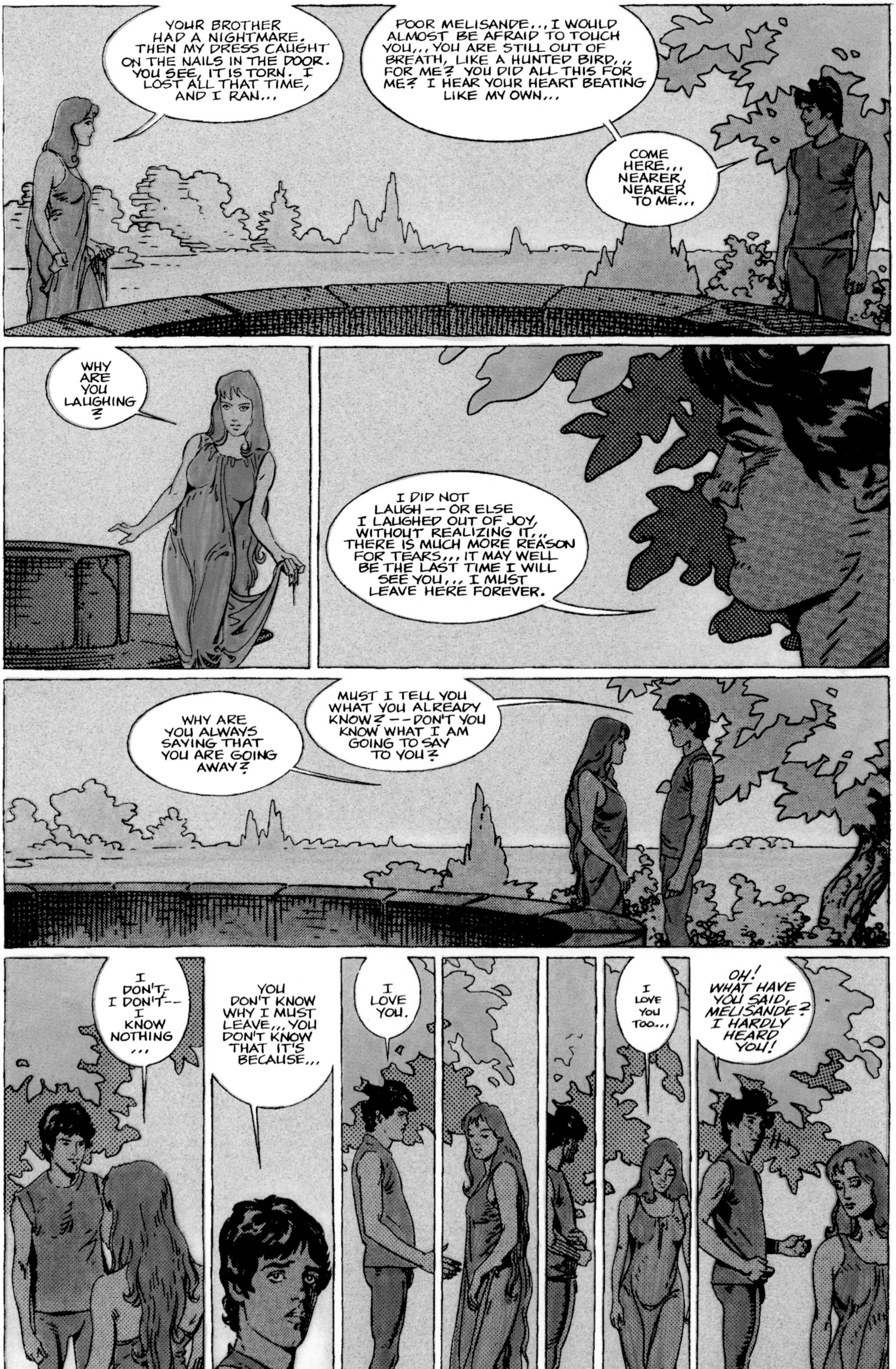
YOUR BROTHER HAD A NIGHTMARE. THEN MY DRESS CAUGHT ON THE NAILS IN THE DOOR. YOU SEE, IT IS TORN. I LOST ALL THAT TIME, AND I RAN...
POOR MELISANDE... I WOULD ALMOST BE AFRAID TO TOUCH YOU... YOU ARE STILL OUT OF BREATH, LIKE A HUNTED BIRD... FOR ME? YOU DID ALL THIS FOR ME? I HEAR YOUR HEART BEATING LIKE MY OWN...
COME HERE... NEARER, NEARER TO ME...
WHY ARE YOU LAUGHING?
I DID NOT LAUGH -- OR ELSE I LAUGHED OUT OF JOY, WITHOUT REALIZING IT... THERE IS MUCH MORE REASON FOR TEARS... IT MAY WELL BE THE LAST TIME I WILL SEE YOU... I MUST LEAVE HERE FOREVER.
WHY ARE YOU ALWAYS SAYING THAT YOU ARE GOING AWAY?
MUST I TELL YOU WHAT YOU ALREADY KNOW? -- DON'T YOU KNOW WHAT I AM GOING TO SAY TO YOU?
I DON'T- I DON'T-- I KNOW NOTHING ...
YOU DON'T KNOW WHY I MUST LEAVE... YOU DON'T KNOW THAT IT'S BECAUSE...
I LOVE YOU.
I LOVE YOU TOO...
OH! WHAT HAVE YOU SAID, MELISANDE? I HARDLY HEARD YOU!

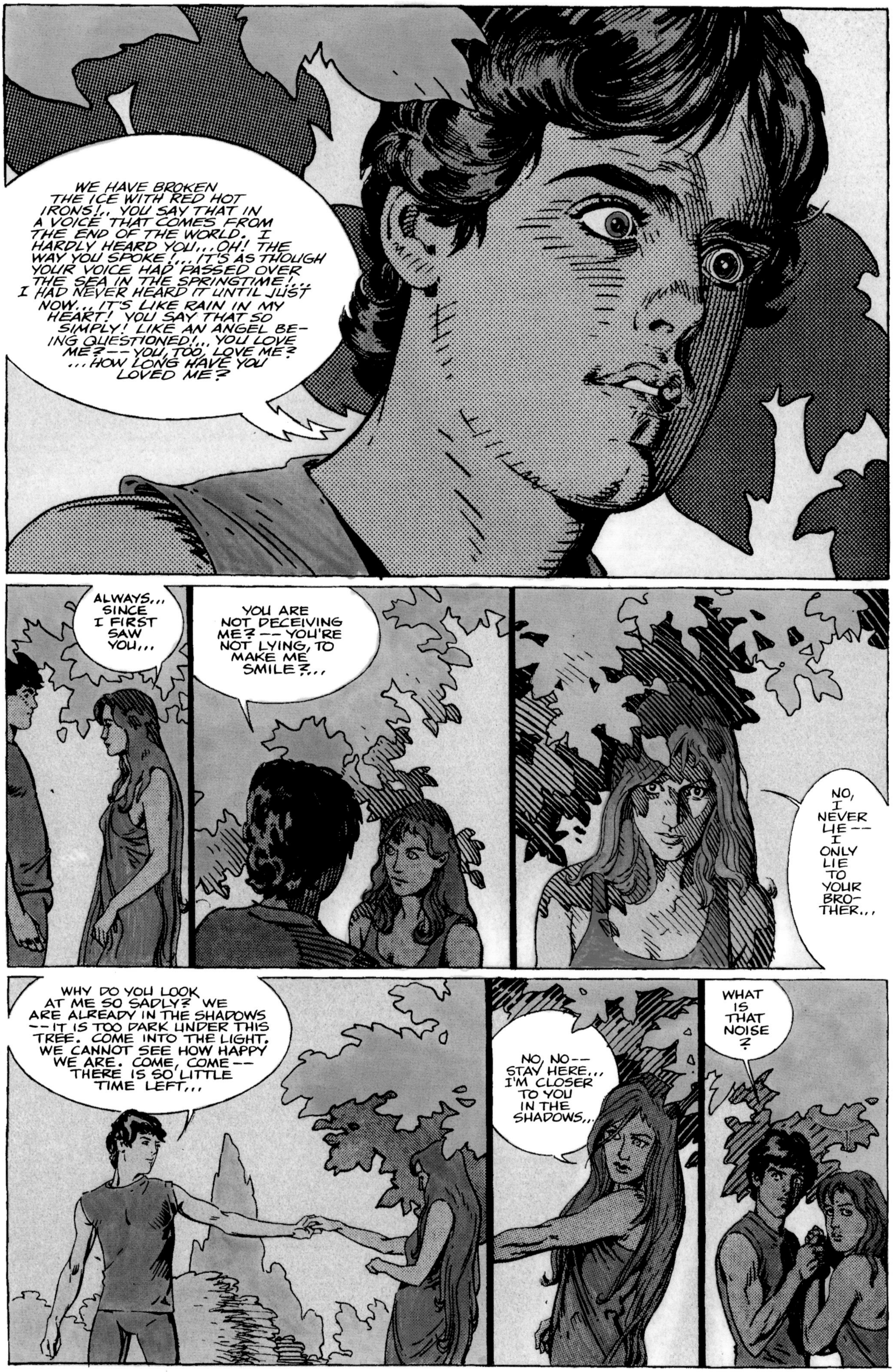
WE HAVE BROKEN THE ICE WITH RED HOT IRONS!.. YOU SAY THAT IN A VOICE THAT COMES FROM THE END OF THE WORLD. I HARDLY HEARD YOU...OH! THE WAY YOU SPOKE!...IT'S AS THOUGH YOUR VOICE HAD PASSED OVER THE SEA IN THE SPRINGTIME!... I HAD NEVER HEARD IT UNTIL JUST NOW... IT'S LIKE RAIN IN MY HEART! YOU SAY THAT SO SIMPLY! LIKE AN ANGEL BEING QUESTIONED!.. YOU LOVE ME?-- YOU, TOO, LOVE ME? ...HOW LONG HAVE YOU LOVED ME?
ALWAYS... SINCE I FIRST SAW YOU...
YOU ARE NOT DECEIVING ME? -- YOU'RE NOT LYING, TO MAKE ME SMILE?...
NO, I NEVER LIE -- I ONLY LIE TO YOUR BROTHER...
WHY DO YOU LOOK AT ME SO SADLY? WE ARE ALREADY IN THE SHADOWS -- IT IS TOO DARK UNDER THIS TREE. COME INTO THE LIGHT. WE CANNOT SEE HOW HAPPY WE ARE. COME, COME -- THERE IS SO LITTLE TIME LEFT...
NO, NO-- STAY HERE... I'M CLOSER TO YOU IN THE SHADOWS...
WHAT IS THAT NOISE?

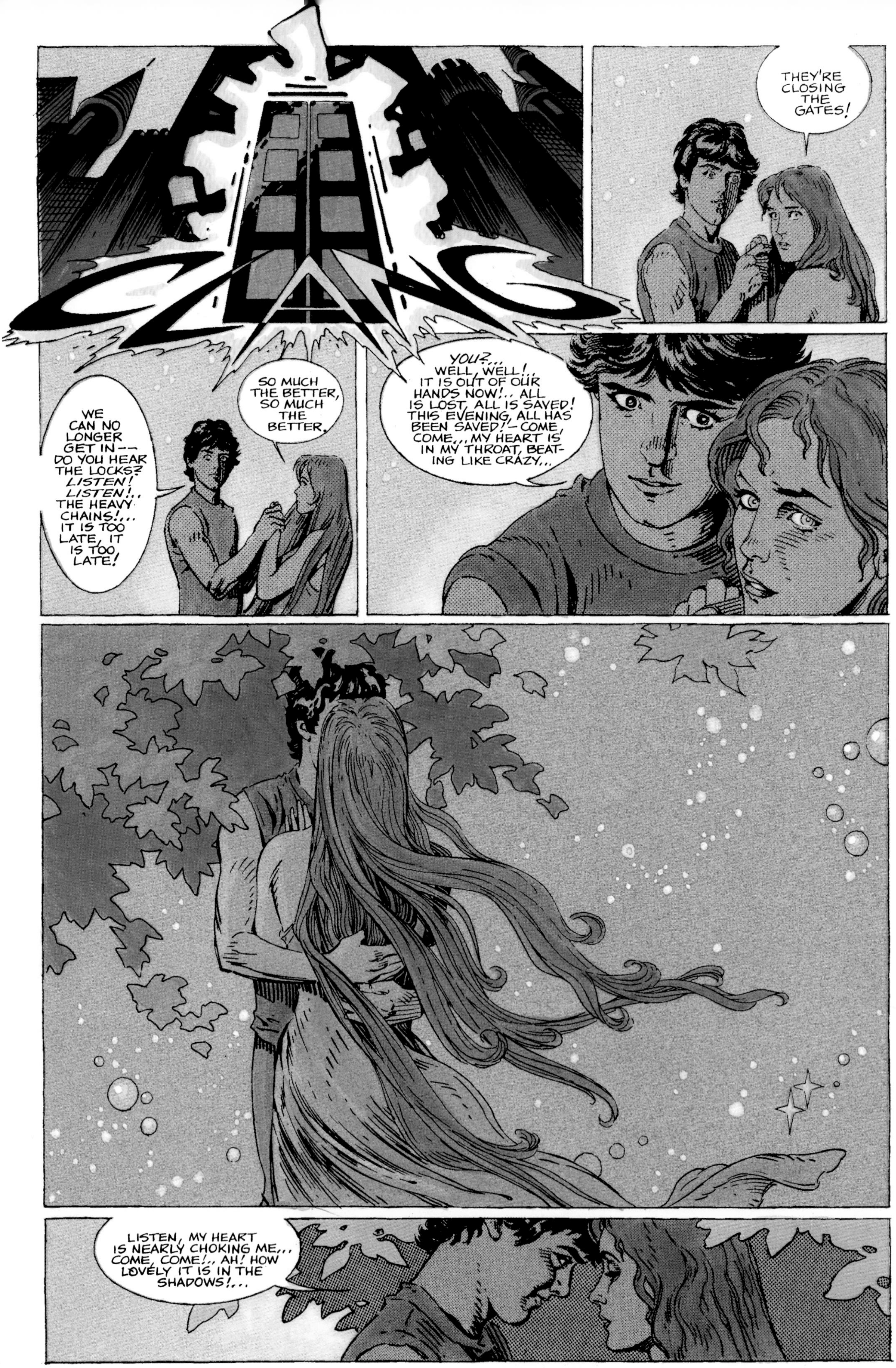
CLANG
THEY'RE CLOSING THE GATES!
WE CAN NO LONGER GET IN -- DO YOU HEAR THE LOCKS? LISTEN! LISTEN!.. THE HEAVY CHAINS!... IT IS TOO LATE, IT IS TOO LATE!
SO MUCH THE BETTER, SO MUCH THE BETTER.
YOU?... WELL, WELL!.. IT IS OUT OF OUR HANDS NOW!.. ALL IS LOST, ALL IS SAVED! THIS EVENING, ALL HAS BEEN SAVED! -- COME, COME... MY HEART IS IN MY THROAT, BEATING LIKE CRAZY...
LISTEN, MY HEART IS NEARLY CHOKING ME... COME, COME!.. AH! HOW LOVELY IT IS IN THE SHADOWS!...

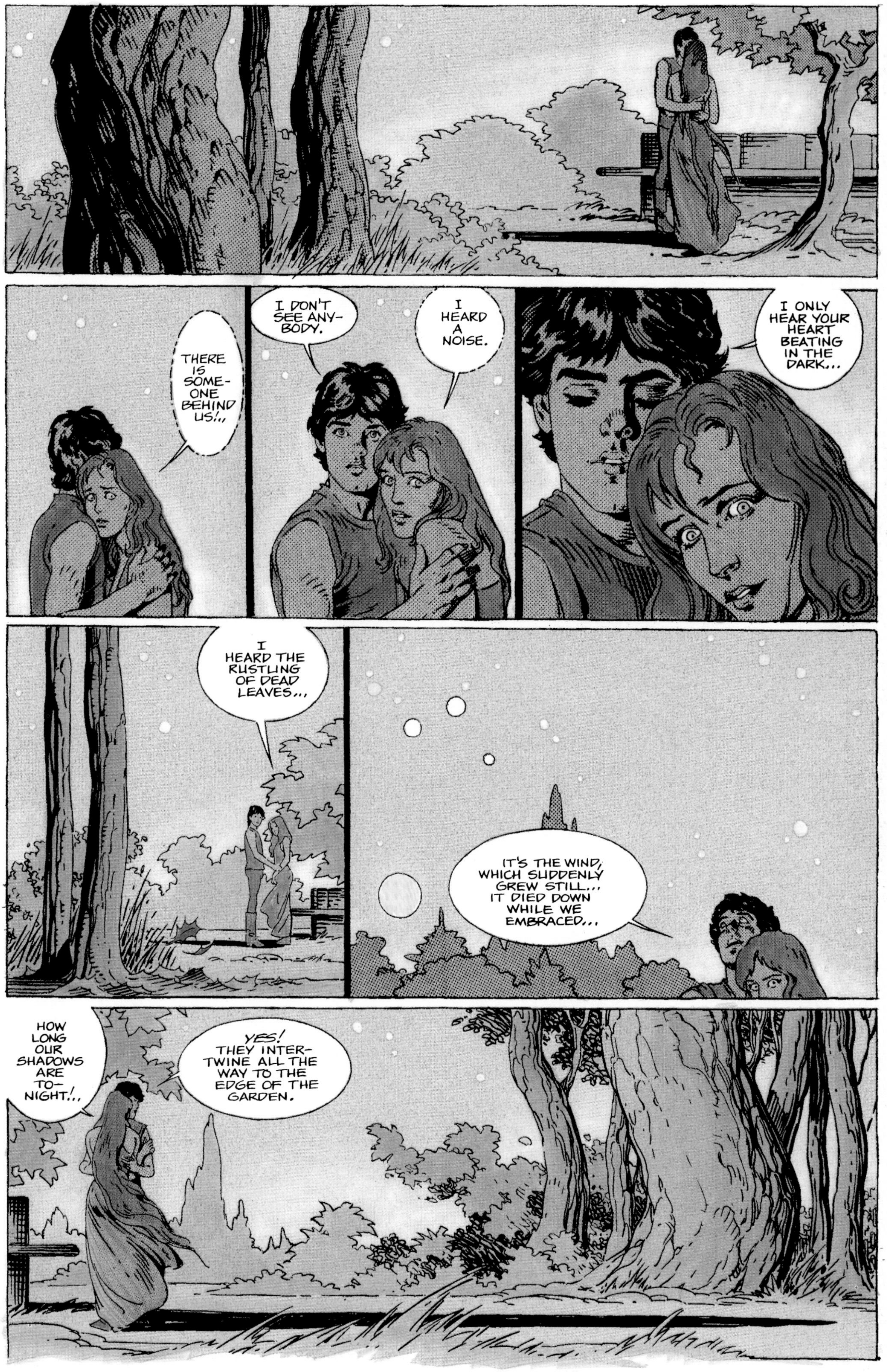
THERE IS SOME-ONE BEHIND US!..
I DON'T SEE ANY-BODY.
I HEARD A NOISE.
I ONLY HEAR YOUR HEART BEATING IN THE DARK...
I HEARD THE RUSTLING OF DEAD LEAVES...
IT'S THE WIND, WHICH SUDDENLY GREW STILL... IT DIED DOWN WHILE WE EMBRACED...
HOW LONG OUR SHADOWS ARE TO-NIGHT!..
YES! THEY INTER-TWINE ALL THE WAY TO THE EDGE OF THE GARDEN.

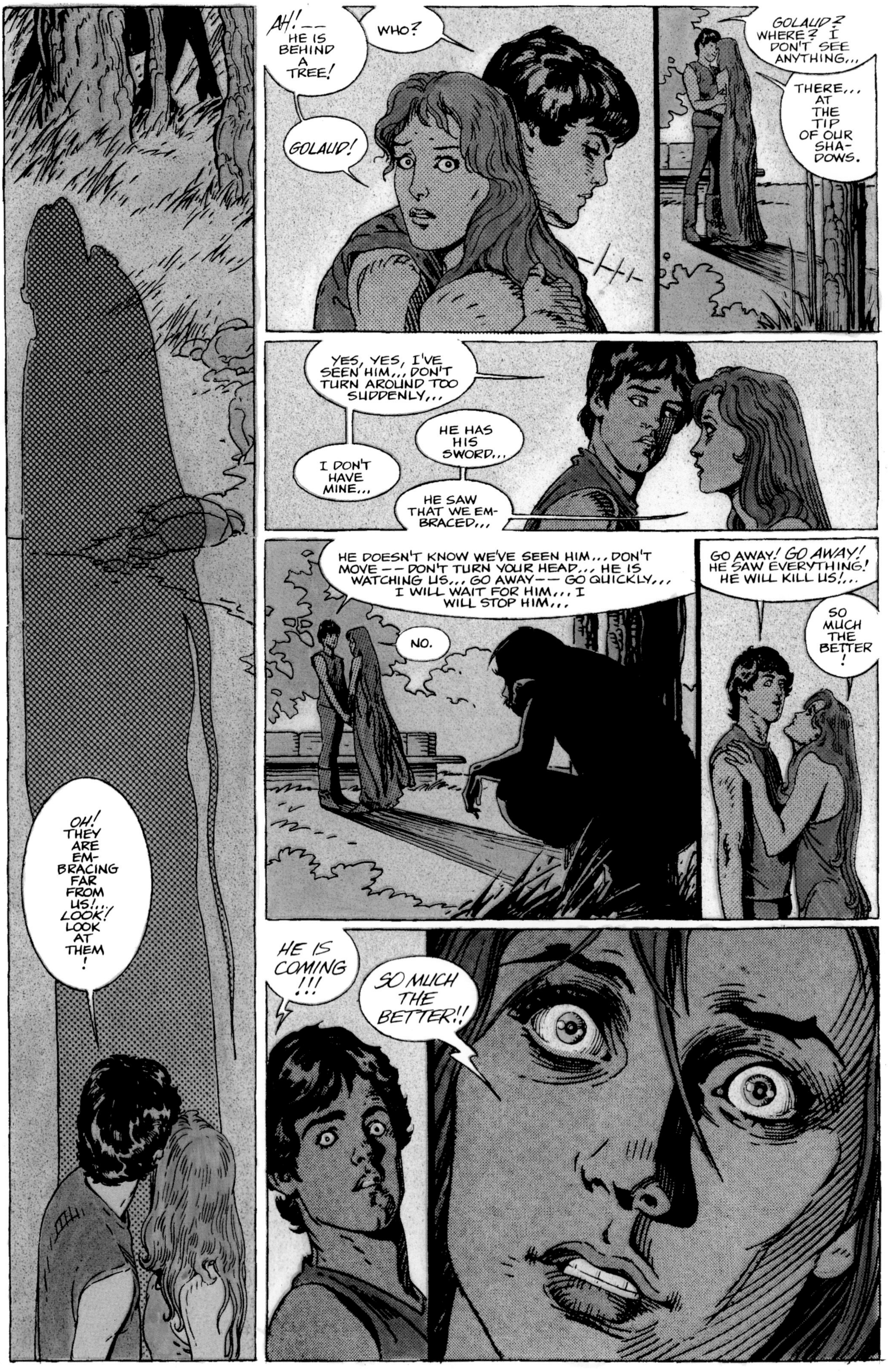
AH!-- HE IS BEHIND A TREE!
WHO?
GOLAUD!
GOLAUD? WHERE? I DON'T SEE ANYTHING...
THERE... AT THE TIP OF OUR SHA-DOWS.
YES, YES, I'VE SEEN HIM... DON'T TURN AROUND TOO SUDDENLY...
I DON'T HAVE MINE...
HE HAS HIS SWORD...
HE SAW THAT WE EM-BRACED...
HE DOESN'T KNOW WE'VE SEEN HIM... DON'T MOVE -- DON'T TURN YOUR HEAD... HE IS WATCHING US... GO AWAY-- GO QUICKLY... I WILL WAIT FOR HIM... I WILL STOP HIM...
NO.
OH! THEY ARE EM-BRACING FAR FROM US!... LOOK! LOOK AT THEM!
GO AWAY! GO AWAY! HE SAW EVERYTHING! HE WILL KILL US!...
SO MUCH THE BETTER!
HE IS COMING!!!
SO MUCH THE BETTER!!

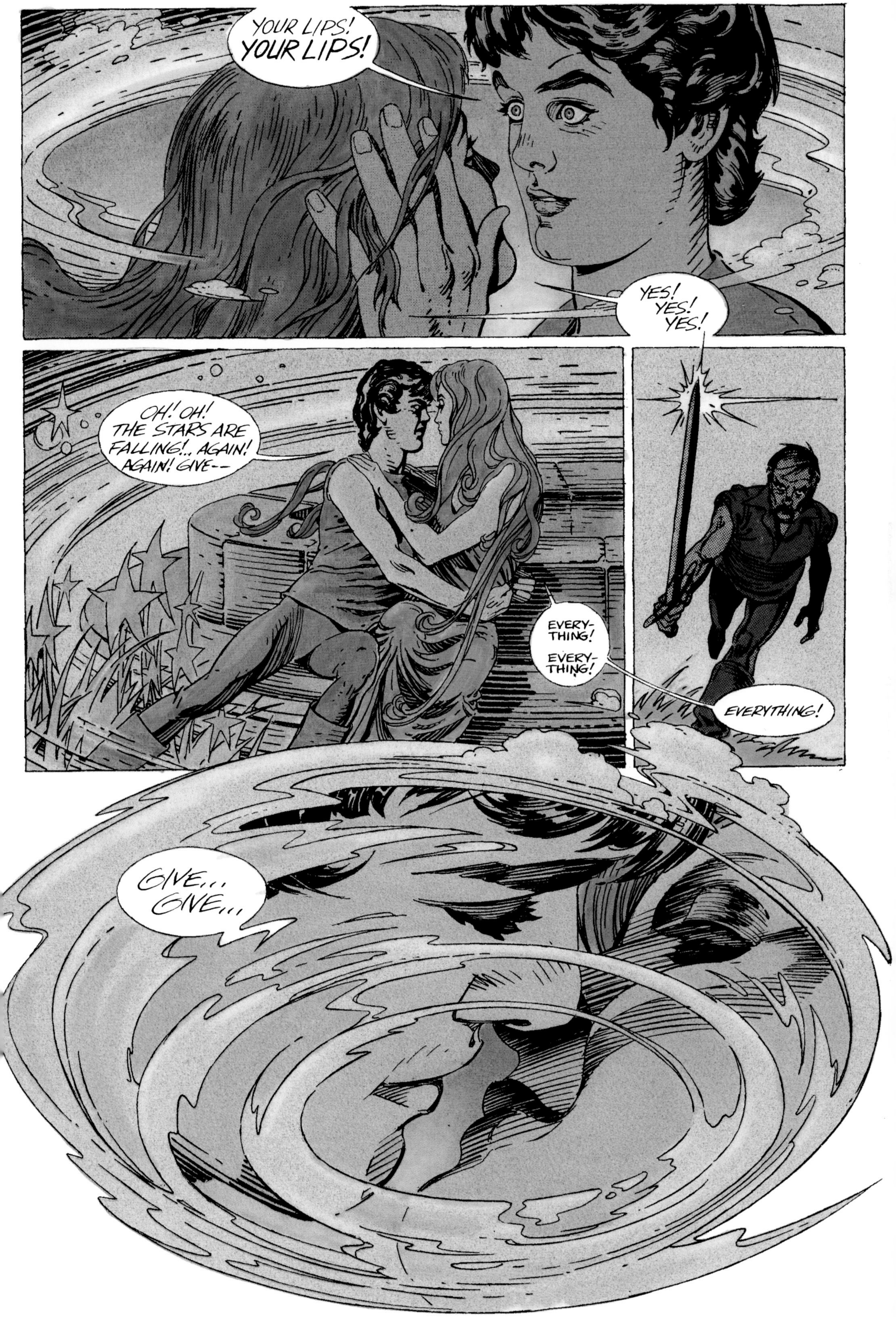
YOUR LIPS! YOUR LIPS!
YES! YES! YES!
OH! OH! THE STARS ARE FALLING!.. AGAIN! AGAIN! GIVE--
EVERY-THING! EVERY-THING!
EVERYTHING!
GIVE... GIVE...

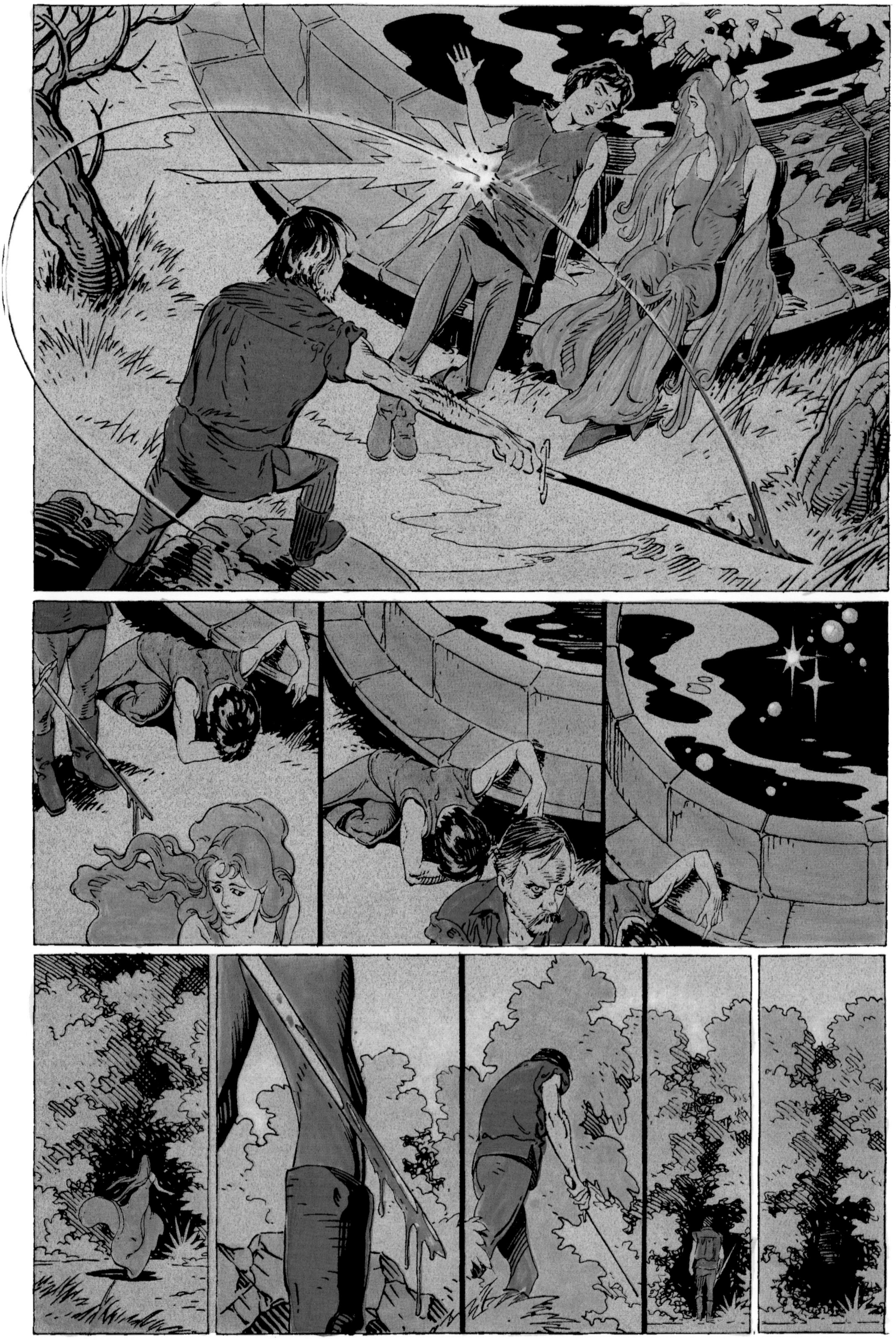

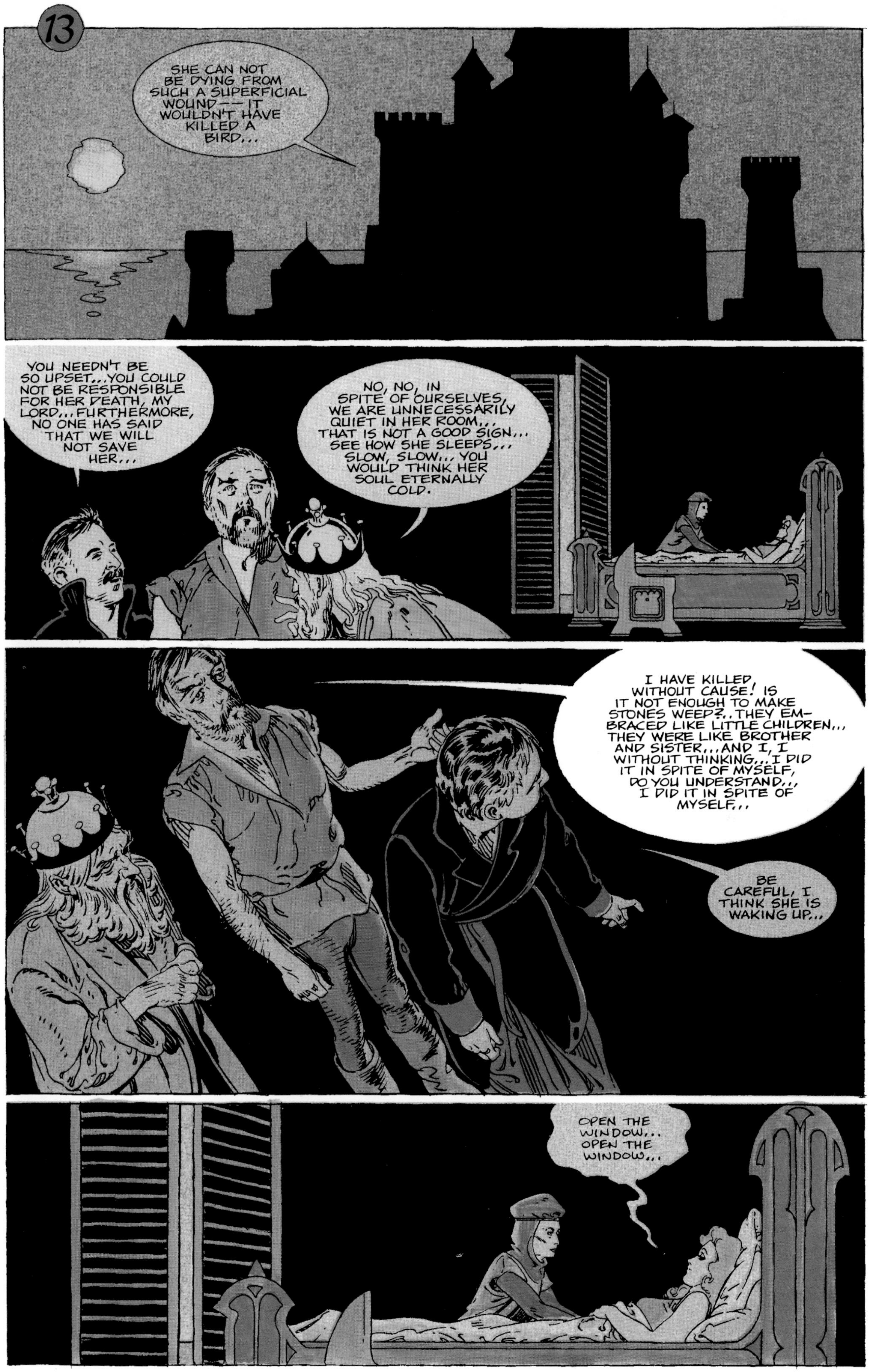
13
SHE CAN NOT BE DYING FROM SUCH A SUPERFICIAL WOUND-- IT WOULDN'T HAVE KILLED A BIRD...
YOU NEEDN'T BE SO UPSET... YOU COULD NOT BE RESPONSIBLE FOR HER DEATH, MY LORD... FURTHERMORE, NO ONE HAS SAID THAT WE WILL NOT SAVE HER...
NO, NO, IN SPITE OF OURSELVES, WE ARE UNNECESSARILY QUIET IN HER ROOM... THAT IS NOT A GOOD SIGN... SEE HOW SHE SLEEPS... SLOW, SLOW... YOU WOULD THINK HER SOUL ETERNALLY COLD.
I HAVE KILLED, WITHOUT CAUSE! IS IT NOT ENOUGH TO MAKE STONES WEEP?.. THEY EMBRACED LIKE LITTLE CHILDREN... THEY WERE LIKE BROTHER AND SISTER... AND I, I WITHOUT THINKING... I DID IT IN SPITE OF MYSELF, DO YOU UNDERSTAND... I DID IT IN SPITE OF MYSELF...
BE CAREFUL, I THINK SHE IS WAKING UP...
OPEN THE WINDOW... OPEN THE WINDOW...

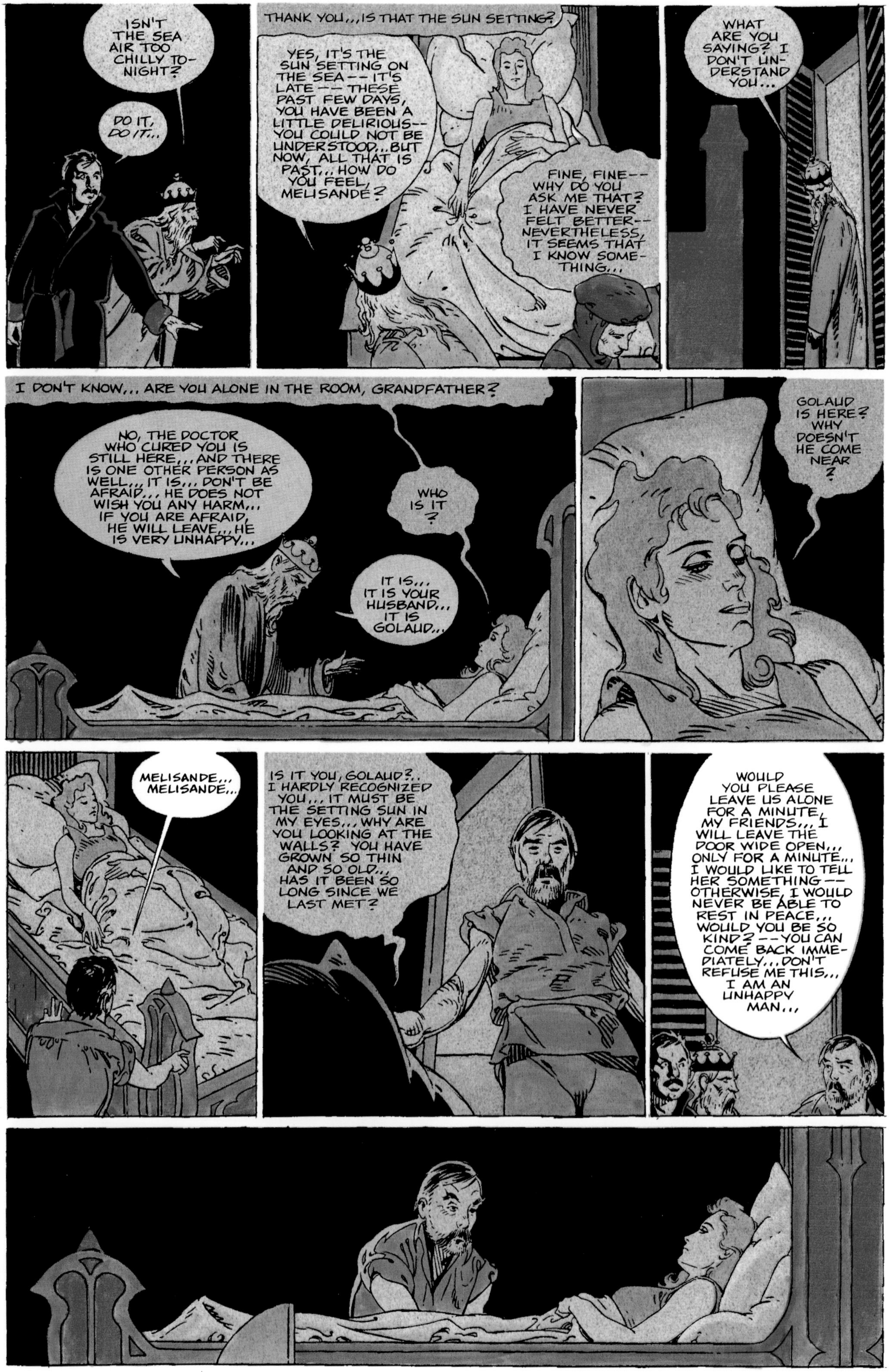
ISN'T THE SEA AIR TOO CHILLY TO-NIGHT?
DO IT, DO IT...
THANK YOU,,, IS THAT THE SUN SETTING?
YES, IT'S THE SUN SETTING ON THE SEA -- IT'S LATE -- THESE PAST FEW DAYS, YOU HAVE BEEN A LITTLE DELIRIOUS-- YOU COULD NOT BE UNDERSTOOD...BUT NOW, ALL THAT IS PAST... HOW DO YOU FEEL, MELISANDE?
FINE, FINE-- WHY DO YOU ASK ME THAT? I HAVE NEVER FELT BETTER-- NEVERTHELESS, IT SEEMS THAT I KNOW SOME-THING...
WHAT ARE YOU SAYING? I DON'T UN-DERSTAND YOU...
I DON'T KNOW,.. ARE YOU ALONE IN THE ROOM, GRANDFATHER?
NO, THE DOCTOR WHO CURED YOU IS STILL HERE,,, AND THERE IS ONE OTHER PERSON AS WELL,,, IT IS,,, DON'T BE AFRAID,,, HE DOES NOT WISH YOU ANY HARM,,, IF YOU ARE AFRAID, HE WILL LEAVE,,, HE IS VERY UNHAPPY,,,
WHO IS IT?
IT IS,,, IT IS YOUR HUSBAND,,, IT IS GOLAUD,,,
GOLAUD IS HERE? WHY DOESN'T HE COME NEAR?
MELISANDE,,, MELISANDE,,,
IS IT YOU, GOLAUD?.. I HARDLY RECOGNIZED YOU,,, IT MUST BE THE SETTING SUN IN MY EYES,,, WHY ARE YOU LOOKING AT THE WALLS? YOU HAVE GROWN SO THIN AND SO OLD,,, HAS IT BEEN SO LONG SINCE WE LAST MET?
WOULD YOU PLEASE LEAVE US ALONE FOR A MINUTE, MY FRIENDS,,, I WILL LEAVE THE DOOR WIDE OPEN,,, ONLY FOR A MINUTE,,, I WOULD LIKE TO TELL HER SOMETHING -- OTHERWISE, I WOULD NEVER BE ABLE TO REST IN PEACE,,, WOULD YOU BE SO KIND? --YOU CAN COME BACK IMME-DIATELY,,, DON'T REFUSE ME THIS,,, I AM AN UNHAPPY MAN,,,

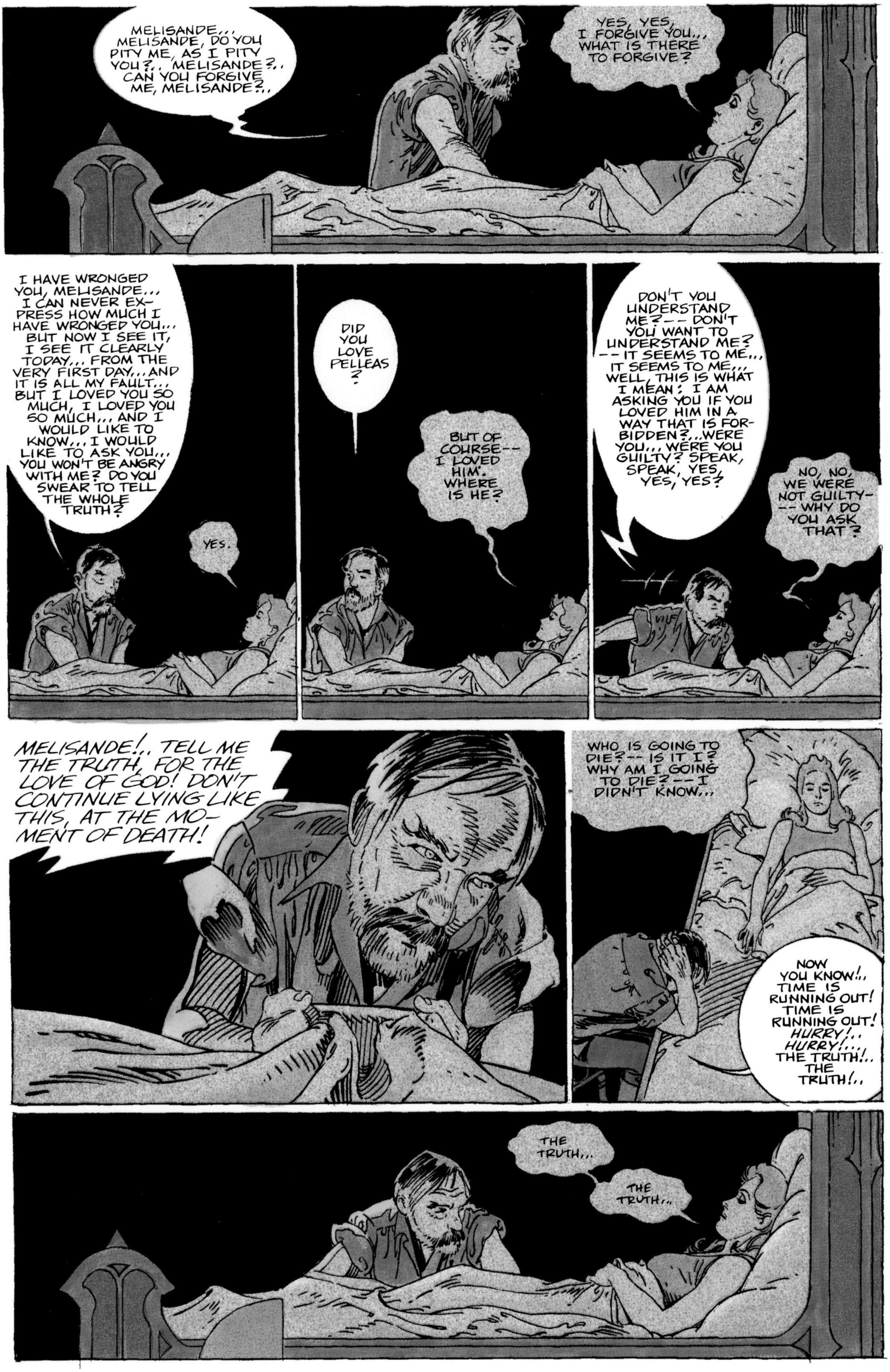
MELISANDE... MELISANDE, DO YOU PITY ME, AS I PITY YOU?.. MELISANDE?.. CAN YOU FORGIVE ME, MELISANDE?..
YES, YES, I FORGIVE YOU... WHAT IS THERE TO FORGIVE?
I HAVE WRONGED YOU, MELISANDE... I CAN NEVER EX-PRESS HOW MUCH I HAVE WRONGED YOU... BUT NOW I SEE IT, I SEE IT CLEARLY TODAY... FROM THE VERY FIRST DAY... AND IT IS ALL MY FAULT... BUT I LOVED YOU SO MUCH, I LOVED YOU SO MUCH... AND I WOULD LIKE TO KNOW... I WOULD LIKE TO ASK YOU... YOU WON'T BE ANGRY WITH ME? DO YOU SWEAR TO TELL THE WHOLE TRUTH?
YES.
DID YOU LOVE PELLEAS?
BUT OF COURSE-- I LOVED HIM. WHERE IS HE?
DON'T YOU UNDERSTAND ME?-- DON'T YOU WANT TO UNDERSTAND ME? -- IT SEEMS TO ME... IT SEEMS TO ME... WELL, THIS IS WHAT I MEAN: I AM ASKING YOU IF YOU LOVED HIM IN A WAY THAT IS FOR-BIDDEN?... WERE YOU... WERE YOU GUILTY? SPEAK, SPEAK, YES, YES, YES?
NO, NO, WE WERE NOT GUILTY- -- WHY DO YOU ASK THAT?
MELISANDE!.. TELL ME THE TRUTH, FOR THE LOVE OF GOD! DON'T CONTINUE LYING LIKE THIS, AT THE MO-MENT OF DEATH!
WHO IS GOING TO DIE?-- IS IT I? WHY AM I GOING TO DIE?-- I DIDN'T KNOW...
NOW YOU KNOW!.. TIME IS RUNNING OUT! TIME IS RUNNING OUT! HURRY!.. HURRY!... THE TRUTH!.. THE TRUTH!..
THE TRUTH...
THE TRUTH...

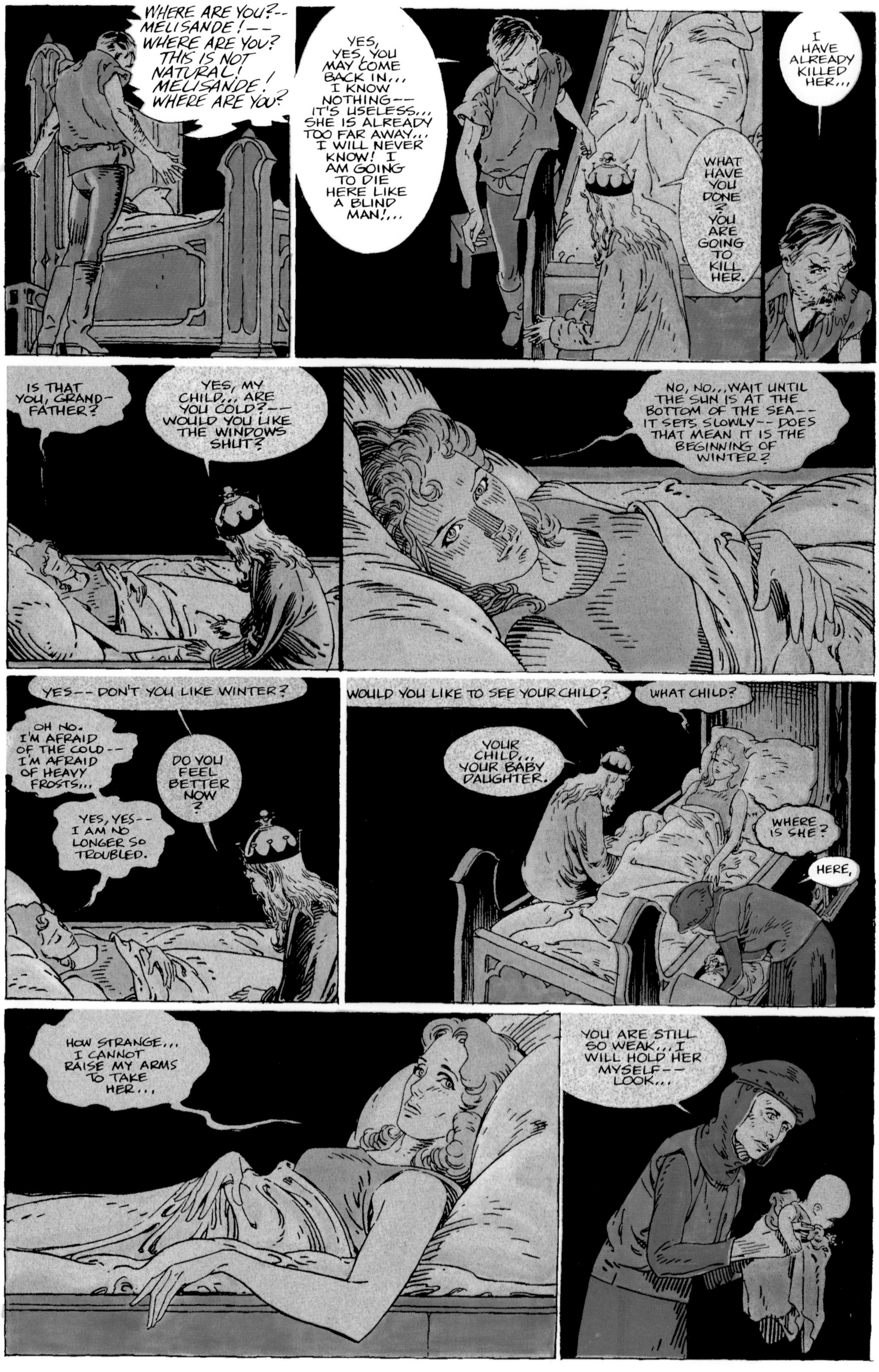
WHERE ARE YOU?-- MELISANDE!-- WHERE ARE YOU? THIS IS NOT NATURAL! MELISANDE! WHERE ARE YOU?
YES, YES, YOU MAY COME BACK IN... I KNOW NOTHING-- IT'S USELESS... SHE IS ALREADY TOO FAR AWAY... I WILL NEVER KNOW! I AM GOING TO DIE HERE LIKE A BLIND MAN!...
WHAT HAVE YOU DONE? YOU ARE GOING TO KILL HER.
I HAVE ALREADY KILLED HER...
IS THAT YOU, GRAND-FATHER?
YES, MY CHILD... ARE YOU COLD?-- WOULD YOU LIKE THE WINDOWS SHUT?
NO, NO... WAIT UNTIL THE SUN IS AT THE BOTTOM OF THE SEA-- IT SETS SLOWLY-- DOES THAT MEAN IT IS THE BEGINNING OF WINTER?
YES-- DON'T YOU LIKE WINTER?
OH NO. I'M AFRAID OF THE COLD-- I'M AFRAID OF HEAVY FROSTS...
DO YOU FEEL BETTER NOW?
YES, YES-- I AM NO LONGER SO TROUBLED.
WOULD YOU LIKE TO SEE YOUR CHILD?
WHAT CHILD?
YOUR CHILD... YOUR BABY DAUGHTER.
WHERE IS SHE?
HERE.
HOW STRANGE... I CANNOT RAISE MY ARMS TO TAKE HER...
YOU ARE STILL SO WEAK... I WILL HOLD HER MYSELF-- LOOK...

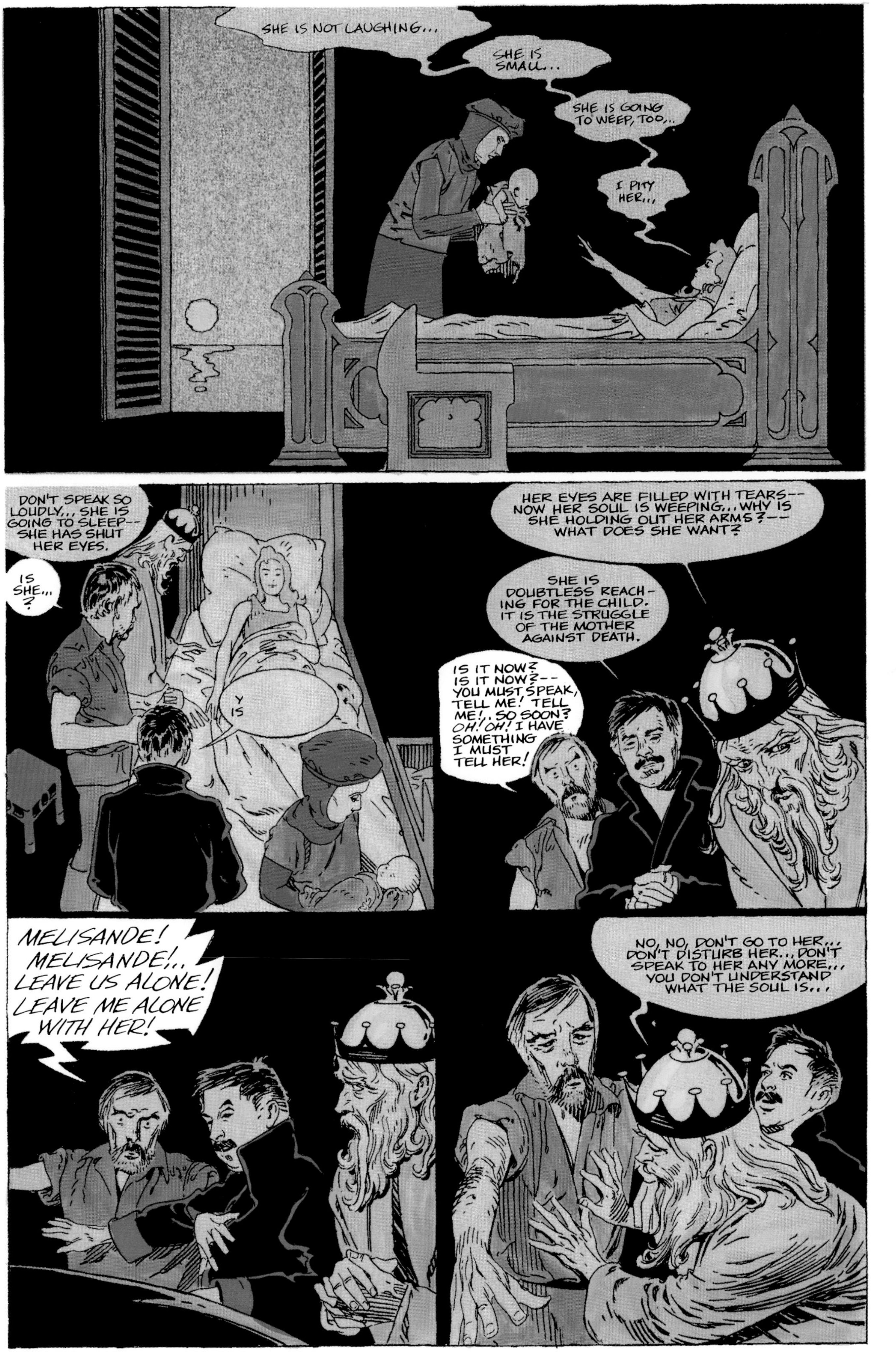
SHE IS NOT LAUGHING...
SHE IS SMALL...
SHE IS GOING TO WEEP, TOO,...
I PITY HER,..
DON'T SPEAK SO LOUDLY,.. SHE IS GOING TO SLEEP-- SHE HAS SHUT HER EYES.
IS SHE...?
HER EYES ARE FILLED WITH TEARS-- NOW HER SOUL IS WEEPING... WHY IS SHE HOLDING OUT HER ARMS?-- WHAT DOES SHE WANT?
SHE IS DOUBTLESS REACHING FOR THE CHILD. IT IS THE STRUGGLE OF THE MOTHER AGAINST DEATH.
IS IT NOW? IS IT NOW?-- YOU MUST SPEAK, TELL ME! TELL ME!.. SO SOON? OH! OH! I HAVE SOMETHING I MUST TELL HER!
MELISANDE! MELISANDE!.. LEAVE US ALONE! LEAVE ME ALONE WITH HER!
NO, NO, DON'T GO TO HER... DON'T DISTURB HER... DON'T SPEAK TO HER ANY MORE... YOU DON'T UNDERSTAND WHAT THE SOUL IS...

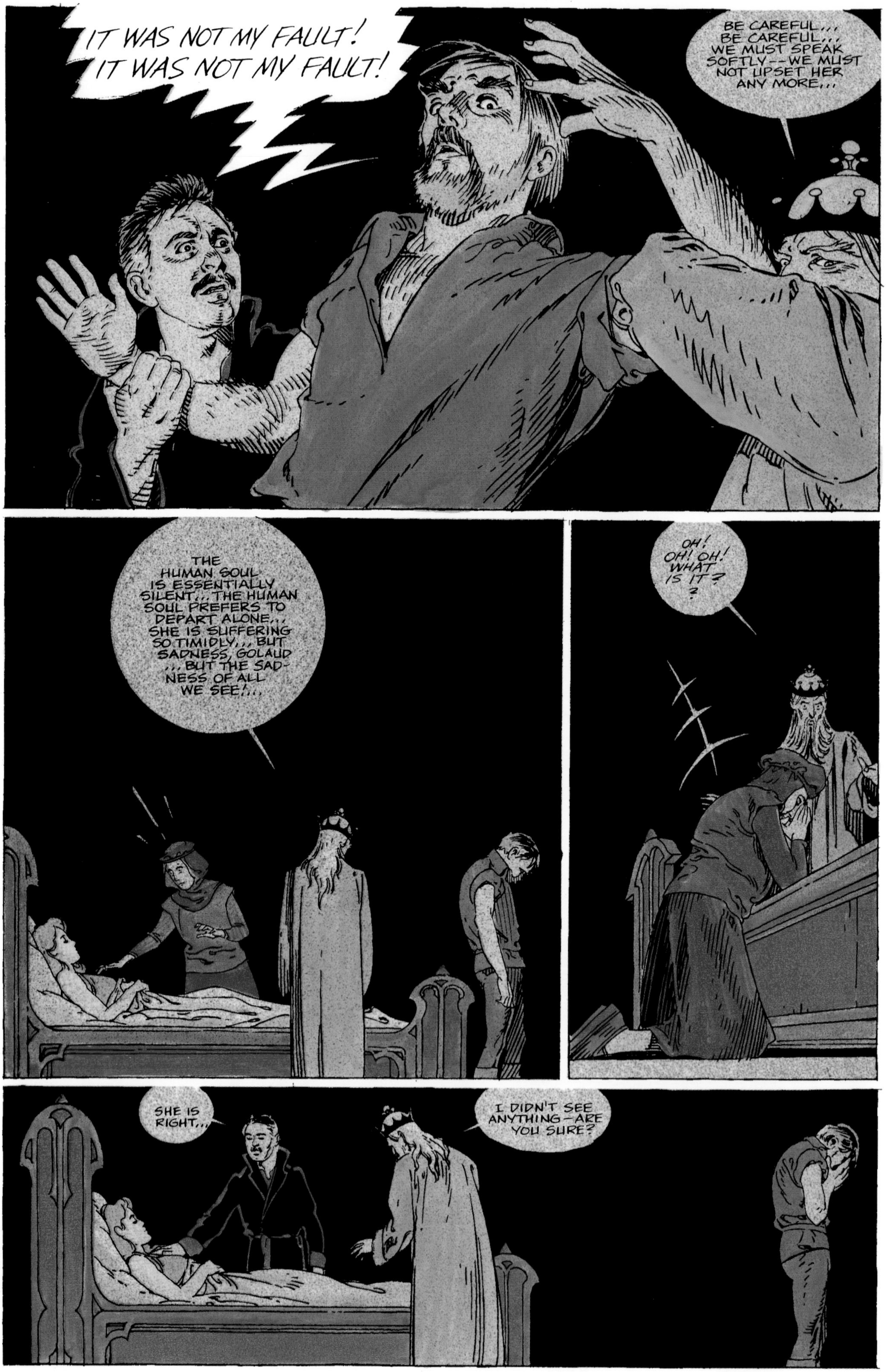
IT WAS NOT MY FAULT! IT WAS NOT MY FAULT!
BE CAREFUL... BE CAREFUL... WE MUST SPEAK SOFTLY--WE MUST NOT UPSET HER ANY MORE...
THE HUMAN SOUL IS ESSENTIALLY SILENT... THE HUMAN SOUL PREFERS TO DEPART ALONE... SHE IS SUFFERING SO TIMIDLY... BUT SADNESS, GOLAUD ... BUT THE SADNESS OF ALL WE SEE!...
OH! OH! OH! WHAT IS IT? ?
SHE IS RIGHT...
I DIDN'T SEE ANYTHING--ARE YOU SURE?

YES.

YES.

I HEARD NOTHING... SO QUICKLY, SO SUDDENLY... SHE HAS GONE WITHOUT SAYING ANYTHING...

DON'T STAY HERE, GOLAUD... SHE NEEDS SILENCE NOW... COME, COME... IT IS HORRIBLY AWFUL, BUT IT IS NOT YOUR FAULT... SHE WAS SUCH A CALM, TIMID, AND SILENT CREATURE... SHE WAS A POOR MYSTERIOUS BEING, LIKE ALL OF US... THERE SHE IS, AS THOUGH SHE WERE HER CHILD'S OLDER SISTER...

-- COME -- THE CHILD SHOULD NOT STAY HERE IN THIS ROOM... SHE MUST LIVE, NOW, IN HER PLACE...

IT'S THE POOR LITTLE THING'S TURN...

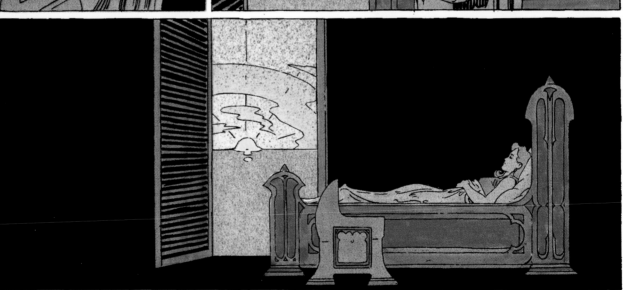

FIN

63

Ein Heldentraum

INTRODUCTION

H ugo Wolf (1860-1903) was one of the most prolific and successful com-
posers of German Lied (art song). The text of his song Ein Heldentraum is bleak and despairing. The following adaptation of his song into
graphic story form illustrates how a separate visual thread can play against a
text to produce a wholely new interpretation.

P. Craig Russell

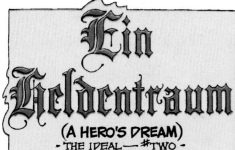

Ein Heldentraum

(A HERO'S DREAM)

• THE IDEAL — #TWO •

AFTER HUGO WOLF'S SETTING OF GOETHE'S POEM~

DER NEUE AMADIS

SCRIPT Patrick Mason • ART P. Craig Russell

LETTERING - BILL PEARSON

IN MEMORIUM - W. WOOD

= OPUS 20 =

TO THOSE OUTSIDE, THAT HOUSE MUST HAVE SEEMED A PRISON WHERE I, AS A SICK AND BEDRIDDEN CHILD, WAS HELD IN THE OPPRESSIVE PALLOR WHICH CLUNG SO FEARFULLY TO ITS WALLS.

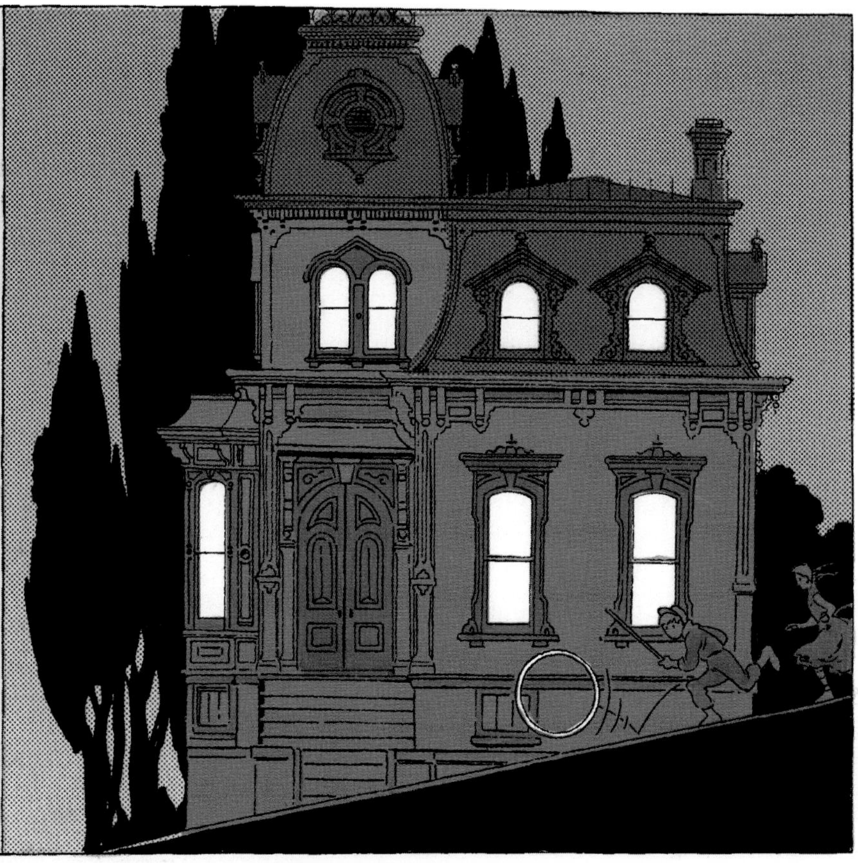

I, HOWEVER, REALLY DID NOT KNOW WHILE GROWING UP THERE THAT THE SOUNDS I HEARD WERE NOT PERHAPS BEETHOVEN'S TRIUMPHANT AND TERRIBLE SPRING MARCHING BY —

OR THAT THE LIGHT WHICH FILTERED THROUGH TO ME WAS NOT THE SAME WHICH GUIDED MILLET'S PEASANTS HOME.

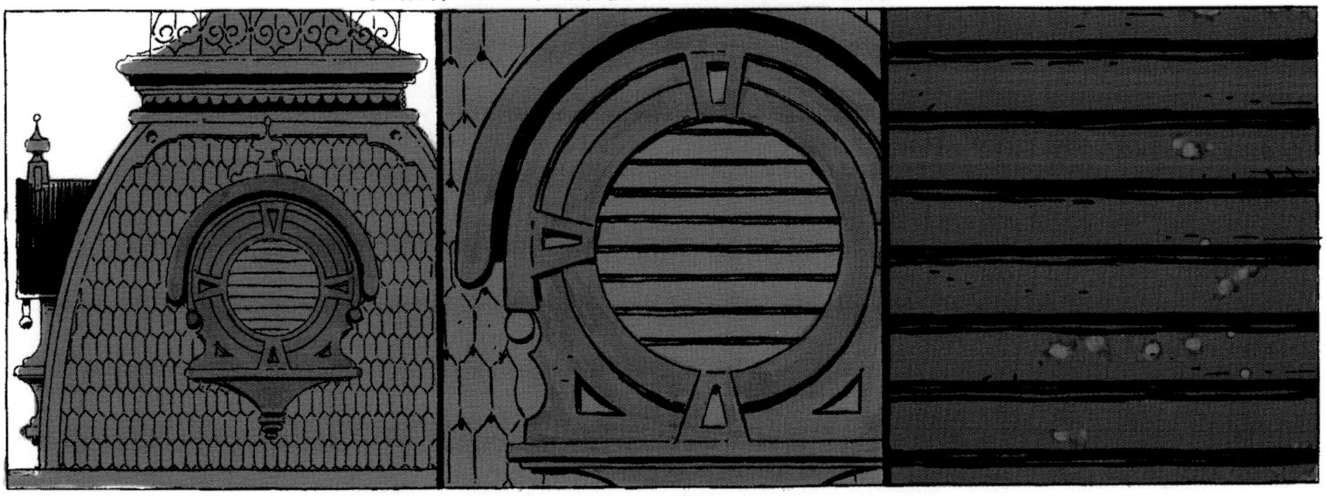

THE FULL GLARE OF NOON, THE DEEP LAUGHTER OF VICTORIOUS YOUNG LOVERS NEVER REACHED ME... OR, IF IT DID...

...I DIDN'T NOTICE. FOR SURROUNDING ME WERE DOORS, WINDOWS, TURRETED GATES TO A BRIGHT, ENCHANTING WORLD WHICH WAS ALWAYS NEW – AND ALWAYS MINE.

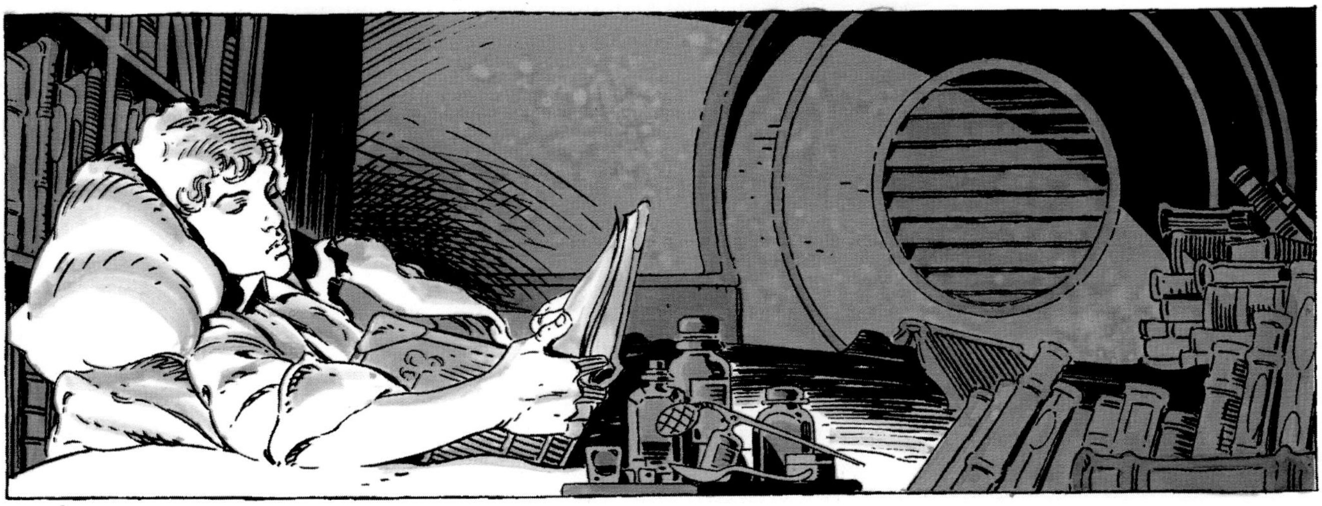

A WORLD REVEALING ITS BROADENING VISTAS TO MY HORIZON-HUNGRY EYES.

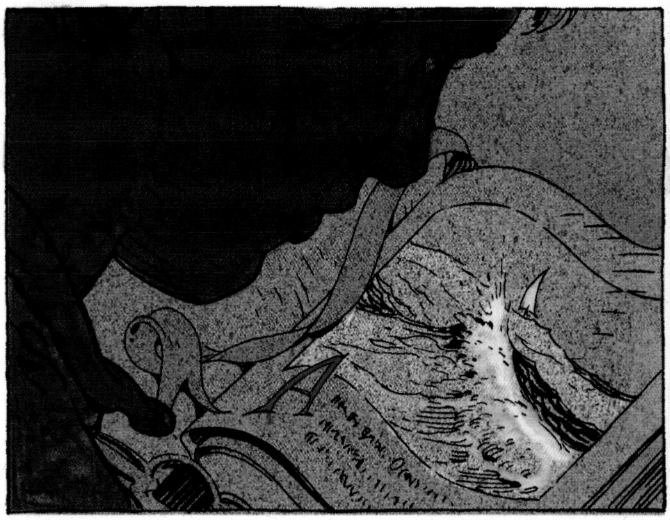

I WAS FREE THERE...

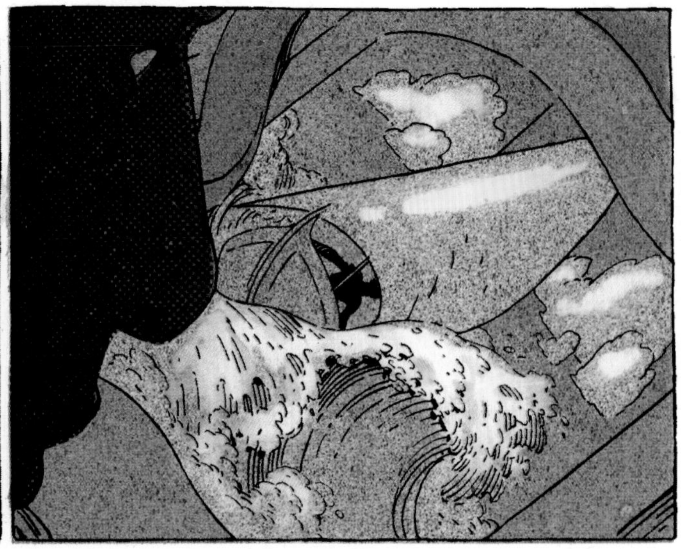

FREE TO FEEL THE SHARP, STINGING SALT WIND OF DISTANT SEAS LASHING MY FACE.

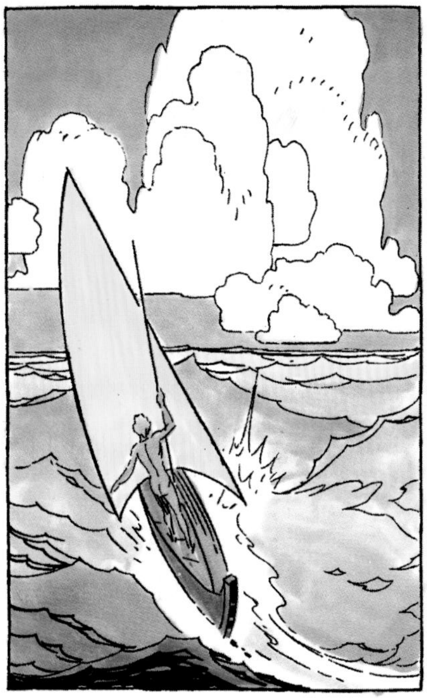

EVERY NEED, EMERGENT AND PRIMAL, WAS MET BY THE VERY ENVIRONMENT WHICH HAD CREATED THE NECESSITY.

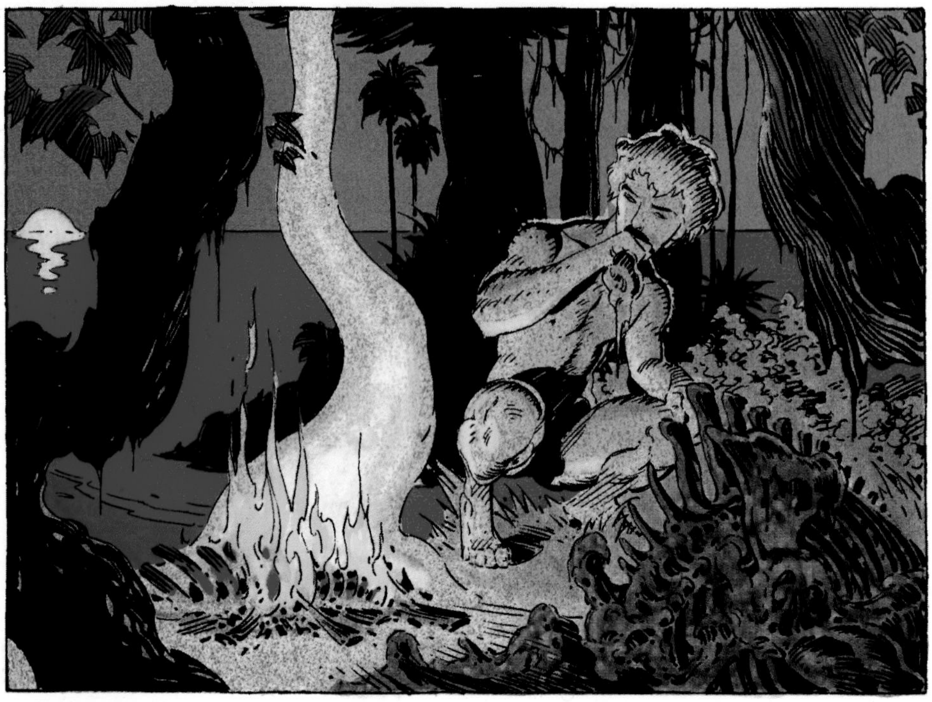

LIFE WAS SWORD AND BLOOD AND UNSOUGHT-FOR ADVENTURE AT EVERY TURN, WHERE WEAK MEN FOLLOWED THE STRONG VISION OF A STRONGER DREAMER.

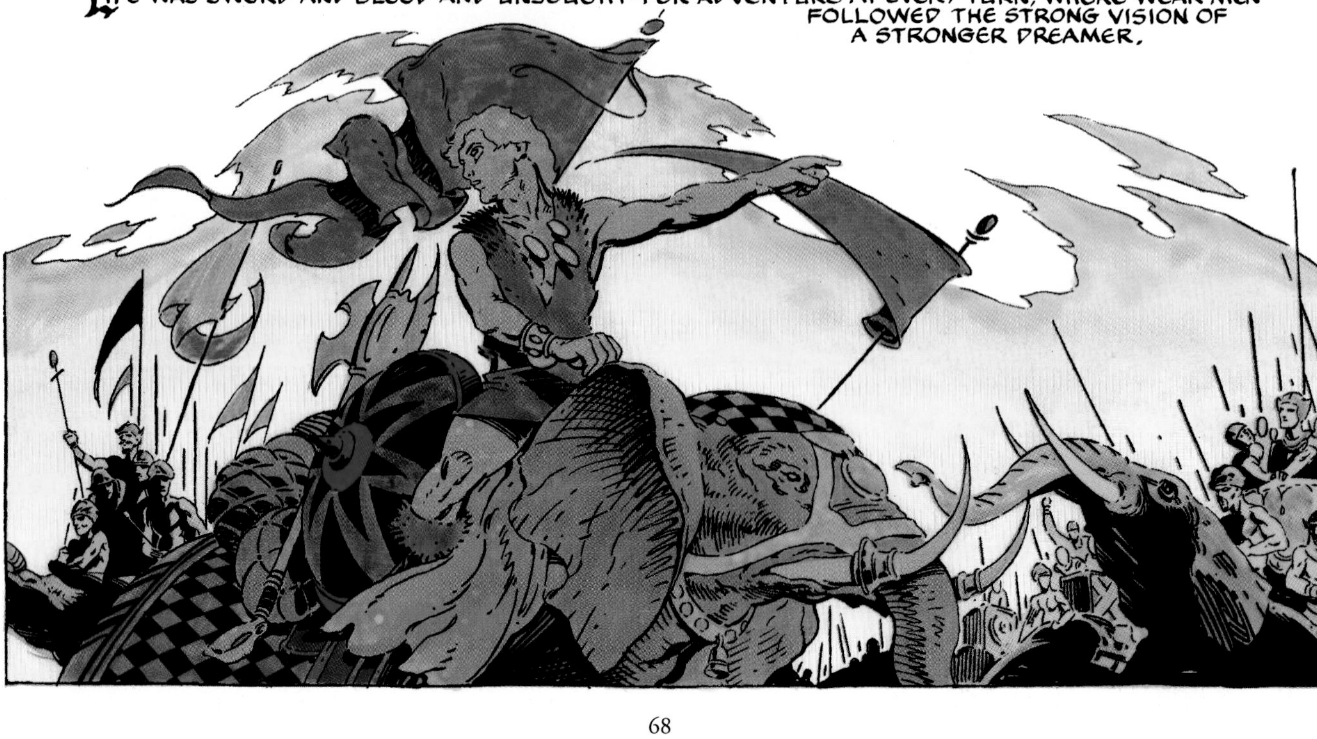

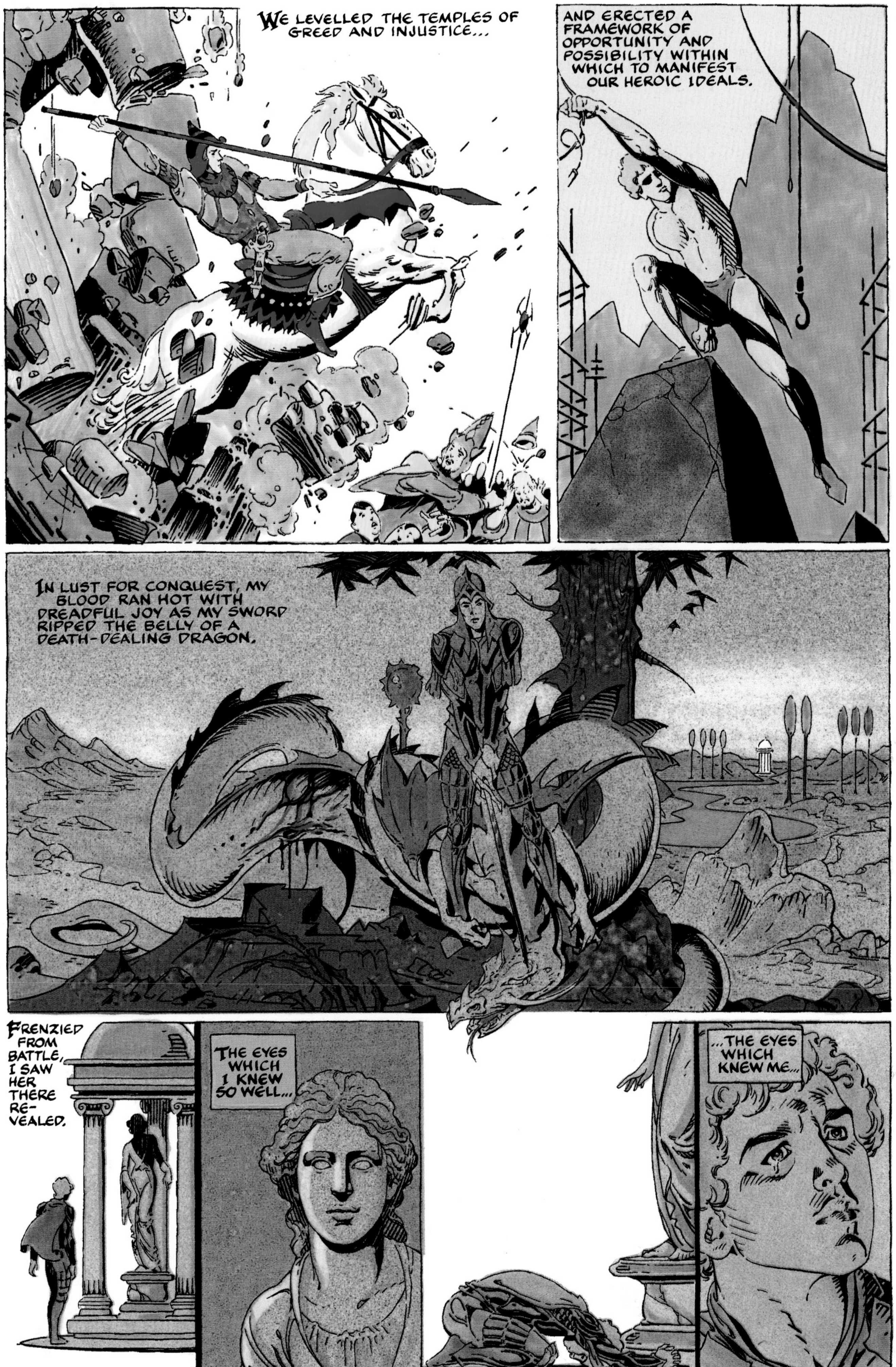

WE LEVELLED THE TEMPLES OF GREED AND INJUSTICE...
AND ERECTED A FRAMEWORK OF OPPORTUNITY AND POSSIBILITY WITHIN WHICH TO MANIFEST OUR HEROIC IDEALS.
IN LUST FOR CONQUEST, MY BLOOD RAN HOT WITH DREADFUL JOY AS MY SWORD RIPPED THE BELLY OF A DEATH-DEALING DRAGON.
FRENZIED FROM BATTLE, I SAW HER THERE RE-VEALED.
THE EYES WHICH I KNEW SO WELL...
...THE EYES WHICH KNEW ME...

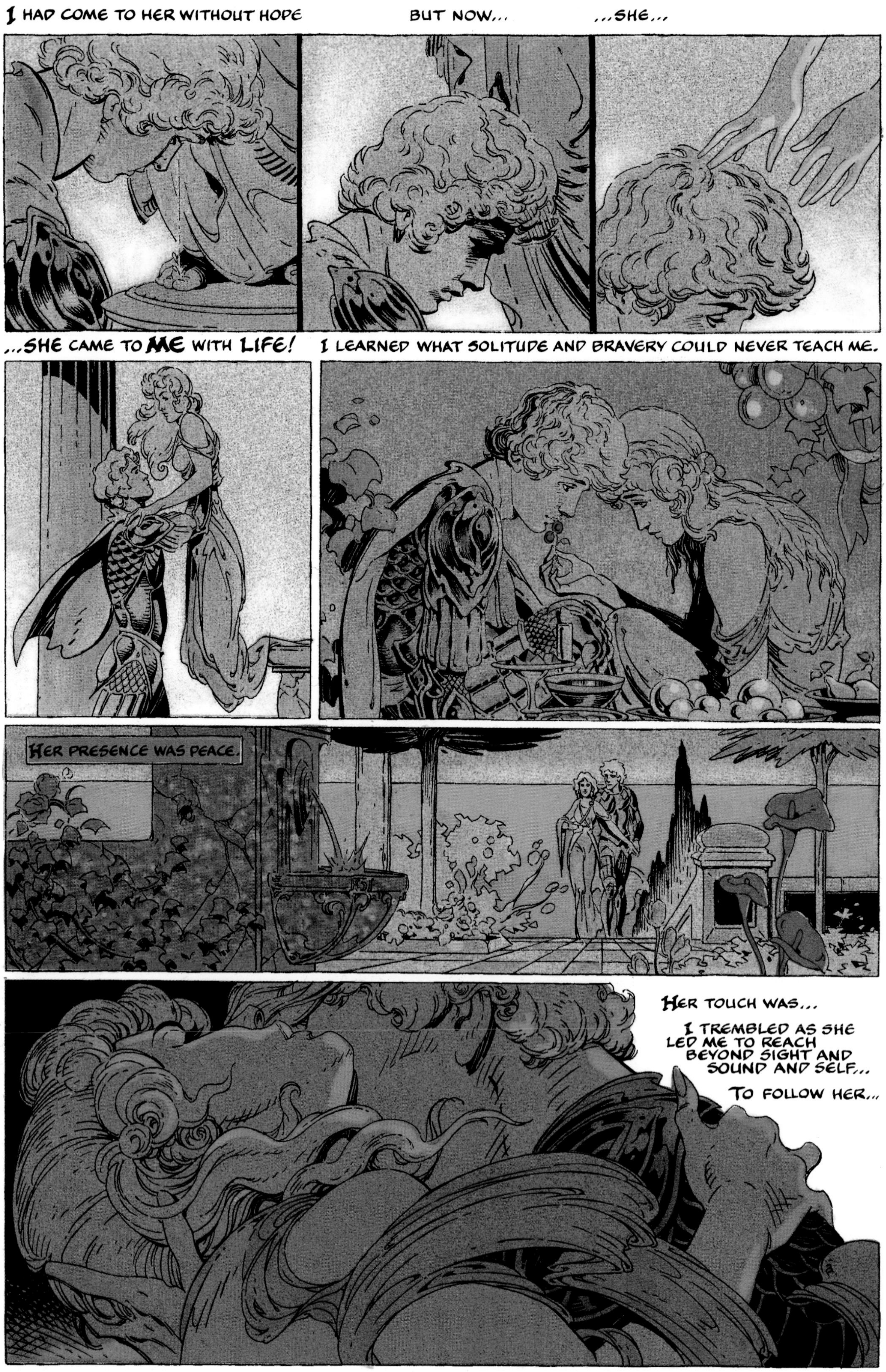
I HAD COME TO HER WITHOUT HOPE
BUT NOW...
...SHE...
...SHE CAME TO ME WITH LIFE!
I LEARNED WHAT SOLITUDE AND BRAVERY COULD NEVER TEACH ME.
HER PRESENCE WAS PEACE.
HER TOUCH WAS...
I TREMBLED AS SHE LED ME TO REACH BEYOND SIGHT AND SOUND AND SELF...
TO FOLLOW HER...

TO JOIN HER. YES!
ALL OF LIFE HAD CONSPIRED
TO BRING ME TO THIS...

UNAFRAID AND
FINALLY WHOLE
AND HEALED.
I KNEW IT!
I KNEW
IT!

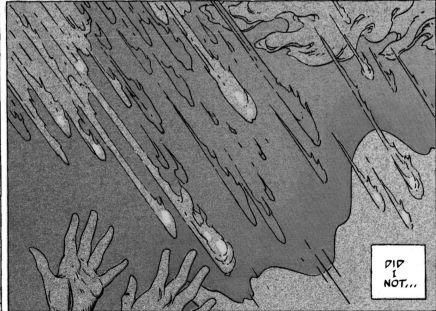

DID
I
NOT...

71

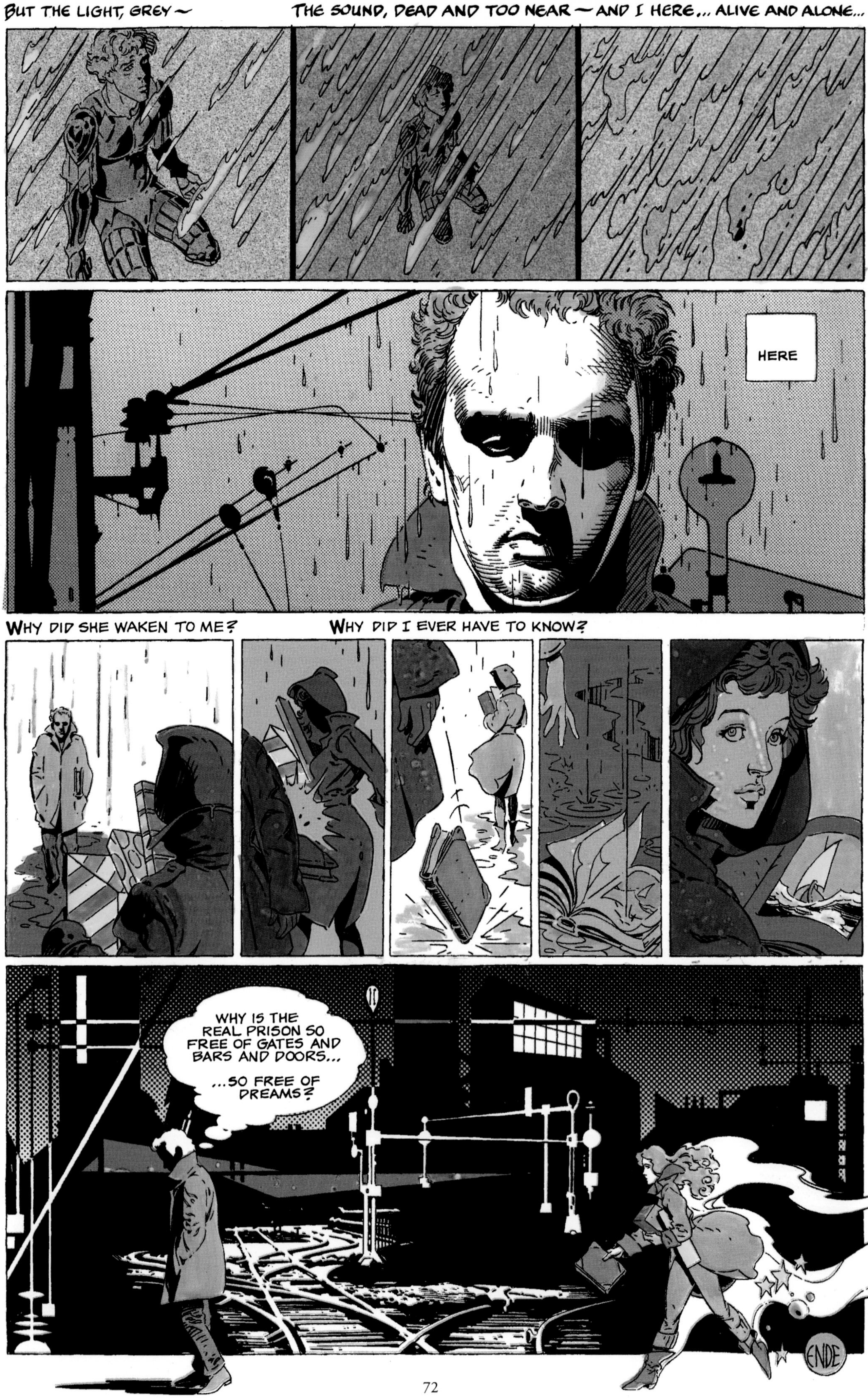

BUT THE LIGHT, GREY~
THE SOUND, DEAD AND TOO NEAR ~ AND I HERE... ALIVE AND ALONE...
HERE
WHY DID SHE WAKEN TO ME?
WHY DID I EVER HAVE TO KNOW?
WHY IS THE REAL PRISON SO FREE OF GATES AND BARS AND DOORS...
...SO FREE OF DREAMS?
ENDE

THE GODFATHER'S CODE

INTRODUCTION

Francis Robinson, in notes written for James Levine's recording of the opera wrote:

"There is no way to render that title and all its implications into English. 'Rustic Chivalry', the literal translation? Forget it. The Godfather's Code comes nearest."

Mascagni, like his fellow and contemporary composer Leoncavallo (whose *Pagliacci* can be seen in volume two of this series as *The Clowns*), provided in *Cavalleria Rusticana* an early example of *verismo* (realism), a late 19th century art movement set on sweeping out the gods and goddesses of grand opera in favor of the denizens of the real world.

The catalyst for composition was the announcement of an open competition. Public performance was the prize. The 26 year old composer responded with an adaptation of a play of the same name and in so doing produced a work that took the world by storm. Like a later era's Orson Welles with his Citizen Kane, Mascagni's Cavalleria Rusticana was also a first effort he was never able to top, such a blazing success that ever after, each new work, no matter how successful in its own right, was found wanting. In later years the composer lamented 'I was crowned king too soon'.

Astute readers (and filmgoers) may notice that the opera directed by Francis Ford Coppola in The Godfather 3 as the great concluding set piece (and by far the highlight of the film) was Cavalleria Rusticana.

The Godfather's Code, indeed.

P. Craig Russell

PROLOGUE • TURIDDU'S SERENADE

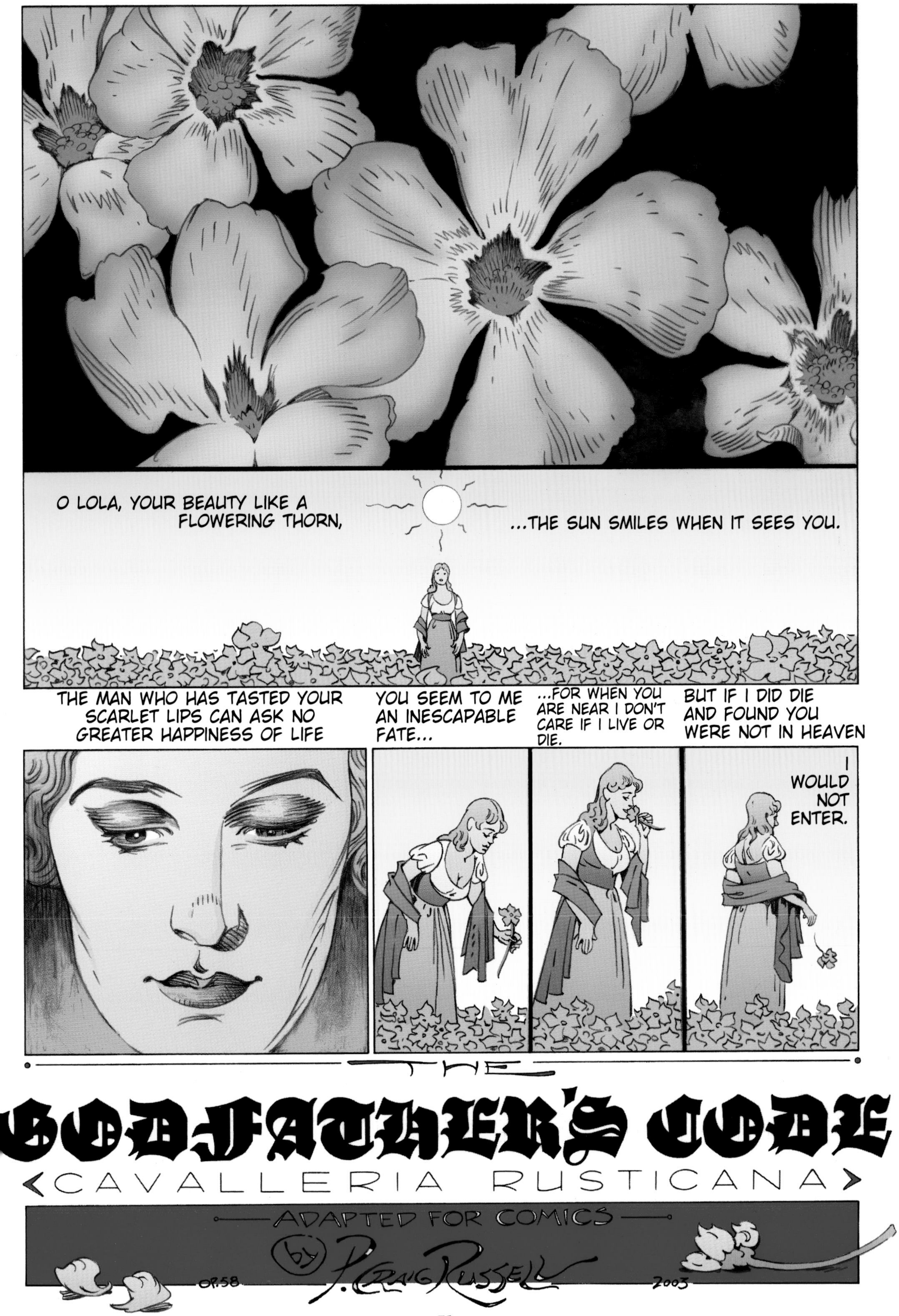
O LOLA, YOUR BEAUTY LIKE A FLOWERING THORN,
...THE SUN SMILES WHEN IT SEES YOU.
THE MAN WHO HAS TASTED YOUR SCARLET LIPS CAN ASK NO GREATER HAPPINESS OF LIFE
YOU SEEM TO ME AN INESCAPABLE FATE...
...FOR WHEN YOU ARE NEAR I DON'T CARE IF I LIVE OR DIE.
BUT IF I DID DIE AND FOUND YOU WERE NOT IN HEAVEN
I WOULD NOT ENTER.
THE
GODFATHER'S CODE
<CAVALLERIA RUSTICANA>
ADAPTED FOR COMICS
by P. CRAIG RUSSELL
OP. 58
2003

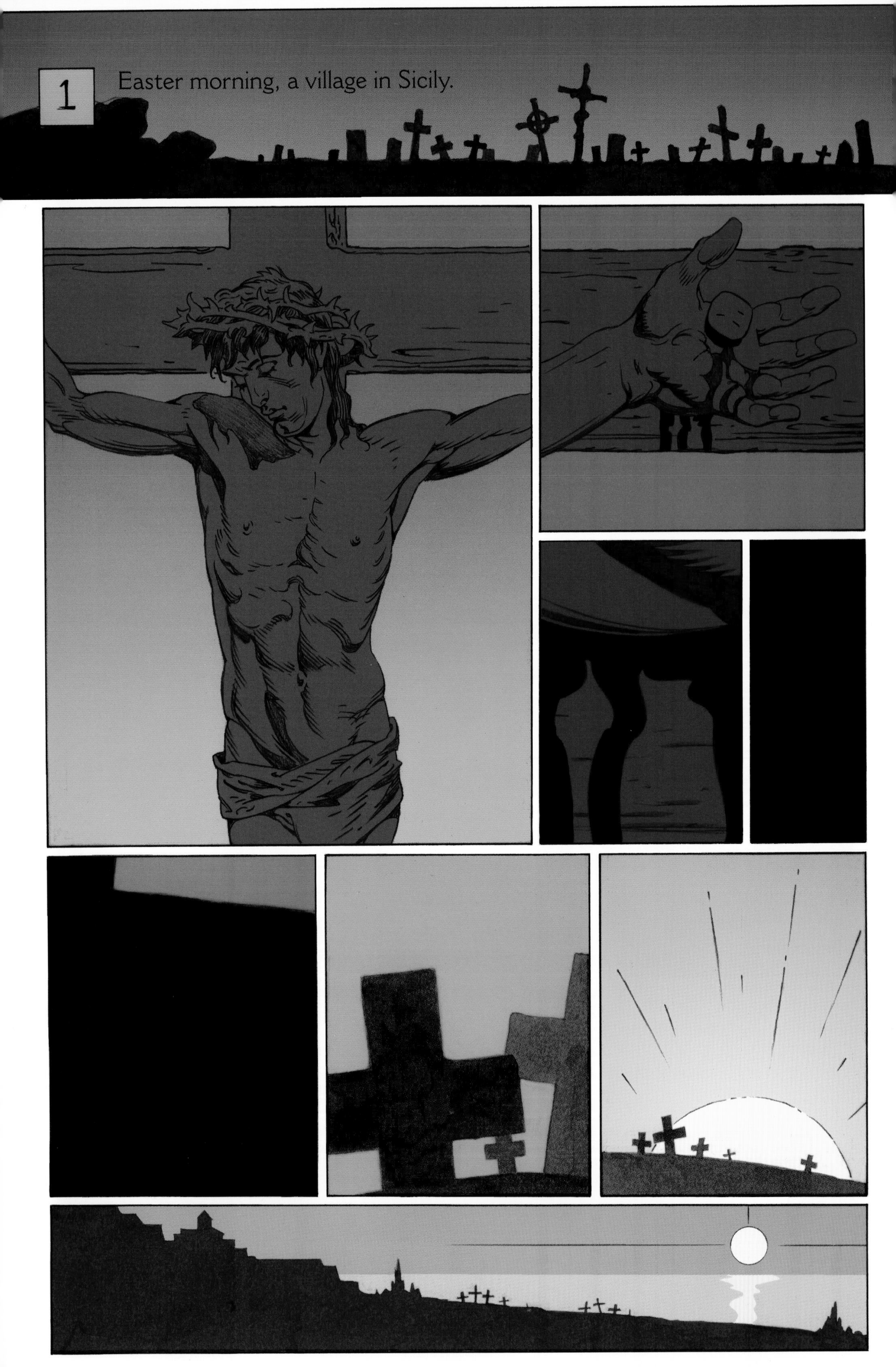
1
Easter morning, a village in Sicily.

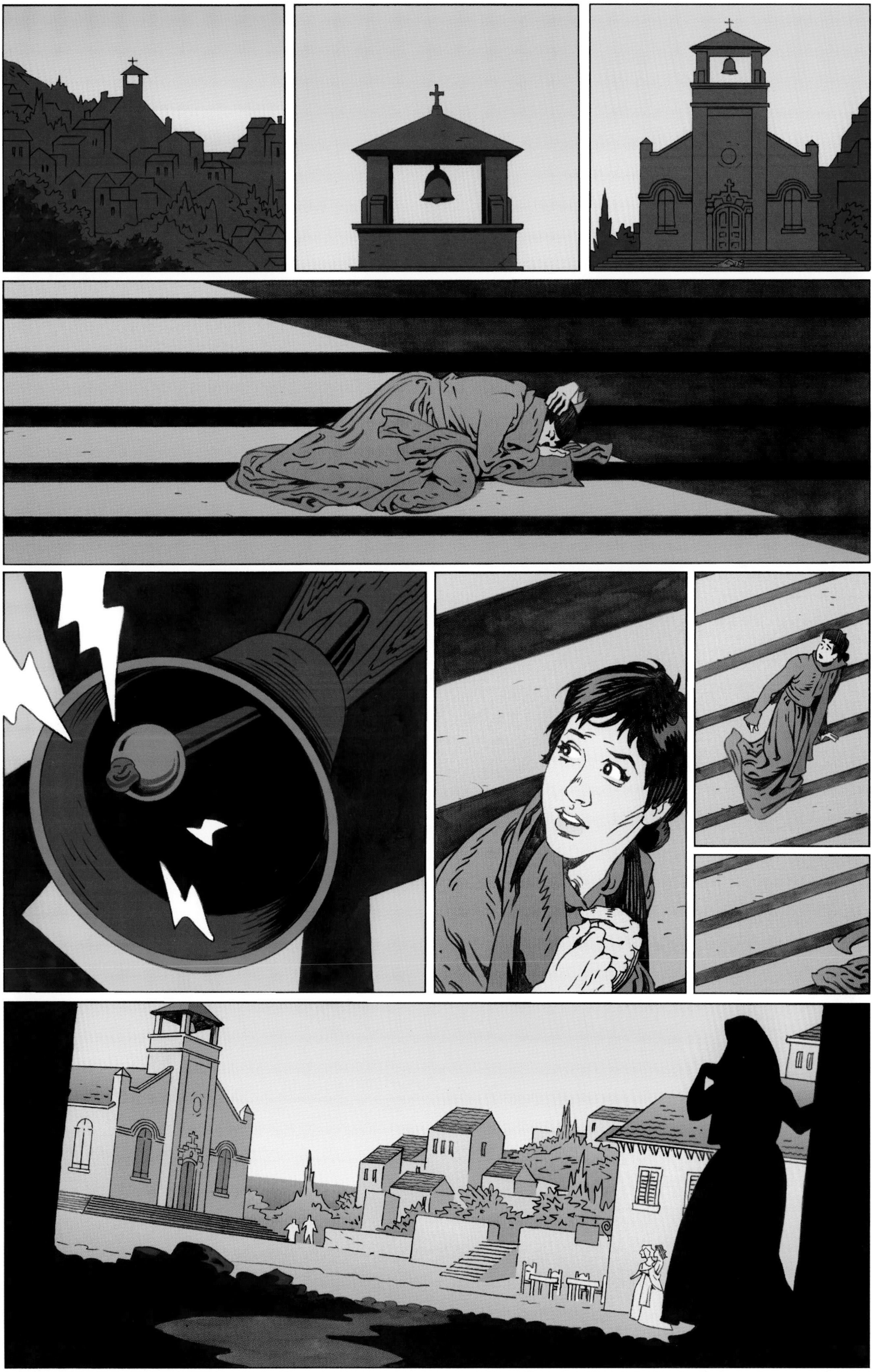

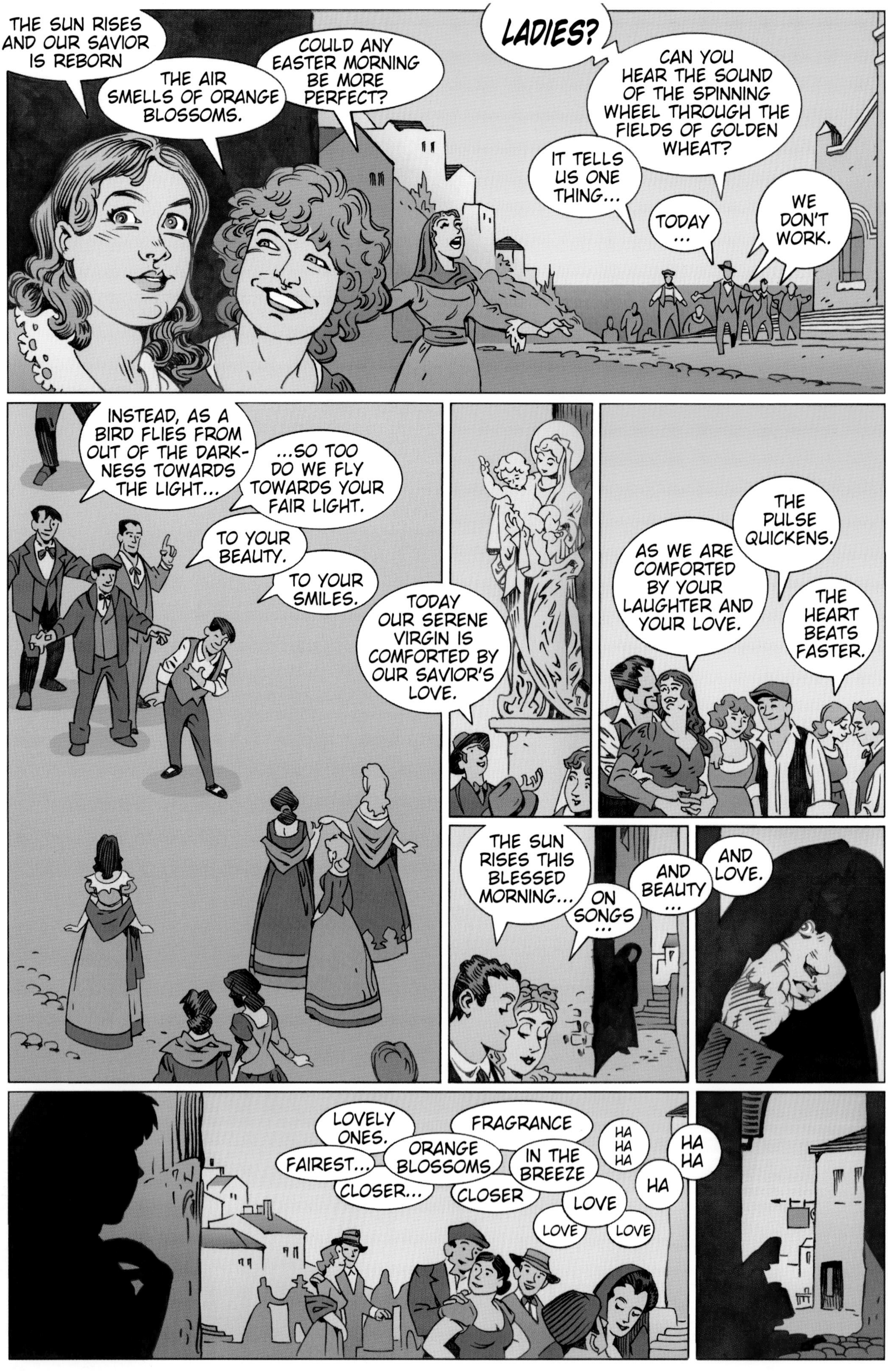
THE SUN RISES AND OUR SAVIOR IS REBORN
THE AIR SMELLS OF ORANGE BLOSSOMS.
COULD ANY EASTER MORNING BE MORE PERFECT?
LADIES?
CAN YOU HEAR THE SOUND OF THE SPINNING WHEEL THROUGH THE FIELDS OF GOLDEN WHEAT?
IT TELLS US ONE THING...
TODAY ...
WE DON'T WORK.
INSTEAD, AS A BIRD FLIES FROM OUT OF THE DARK-NESS TOWARDS THE LIGHT...
...SO TOO DO WE FLY TOWARDS YOUR FAIR LIGHT.
TO YOUR BEAUTY.
TO YOUR SMILES.
TODAY OUR SERENE VIRGIN IS COMFORTED BY OUR SAVIOR'S LOVE.
AS WE ARE COMFORTED BY YOUR LAUGHTER AND YOUR LOVE.
THE PULSE QUICKENS.
THE HEART BEATS FASTER.
THE SUN RISES THIS BLESSED MORNING...
ON SONGS ...
AND BEAUTY ...
AND LOVE.
LOVELY ONES.
FRAGRANCE
FAIREST...
ORANGE BLOSSOMS
IN THE BREEZE
CLOSER...
CLOSER
HA HA HA
HA HA
HA
LOVE
LOVE
LOVE

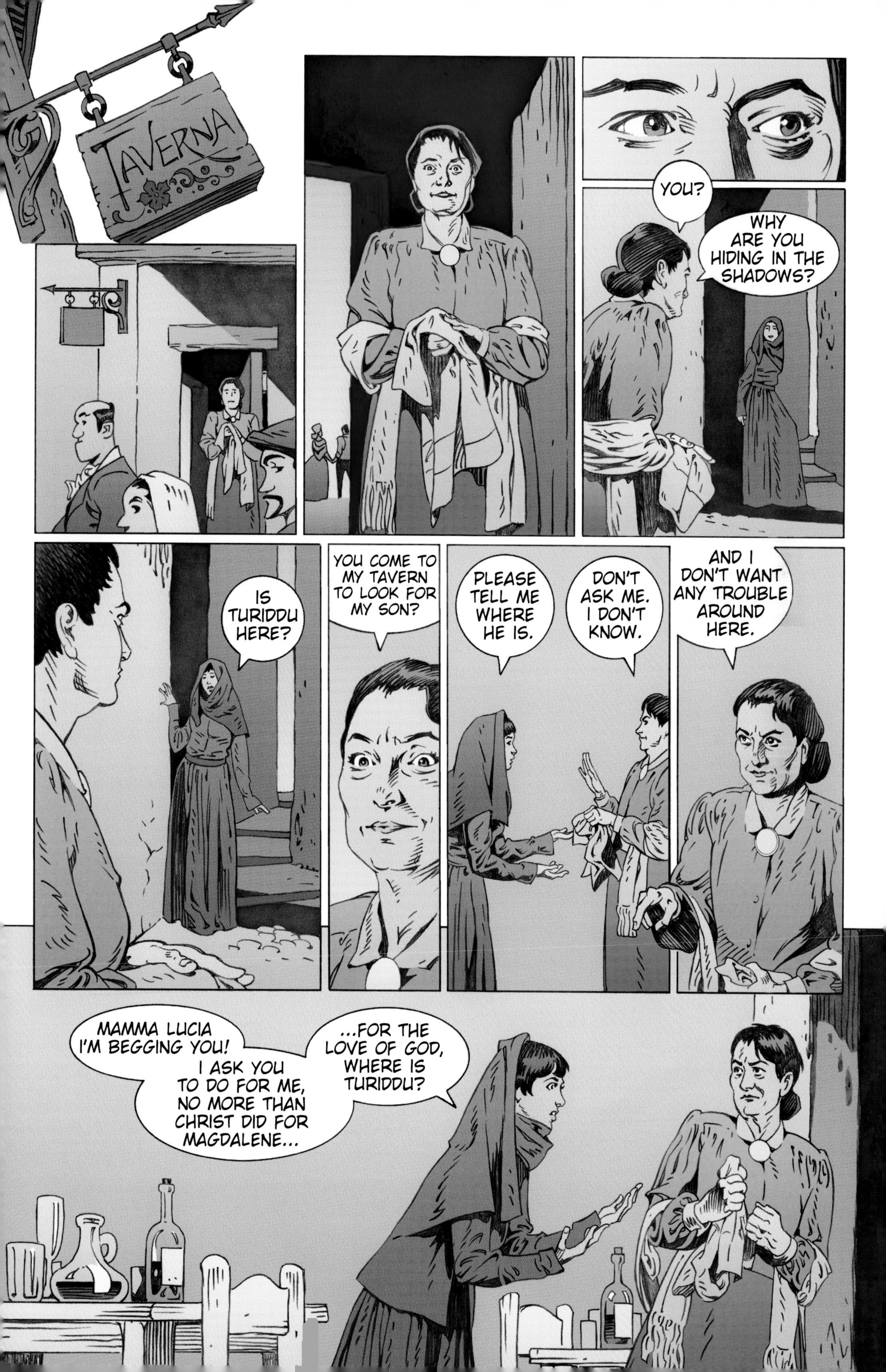
TAVERNA
YOU?
WHY ARE YOU HIDING IN THE SHADOWS?
IS TURIDDU HERE?
YOU COME TO MY TAVERN TO LOOK FOR MY SON?
PLEASE TELL ME WHERE HE IS.
DON'T ASK ME. I DON'T KNOW.
AND I DON'T WANT ANY TROUBLE AROUND HERE.
MAMMA LUCIA I'M BEGGING YOU!
I ASK YOU TO DO FOR ME, NO MORE THAN CHRIST DID FOR MAGDALENE...
...FOR THE LOVE OF GOD, WHERE IS TURIDDU?

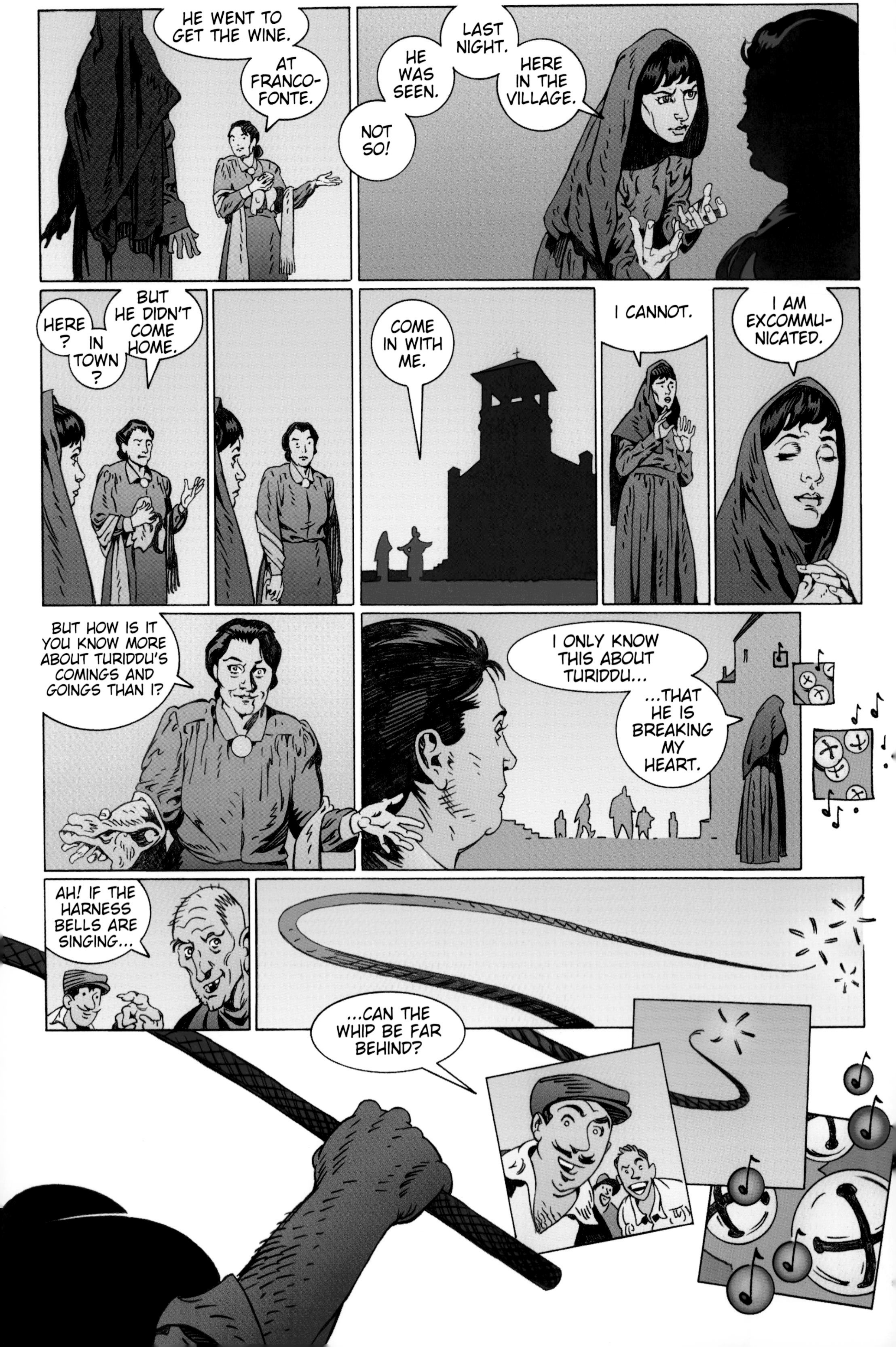
HE WENT TO GET THE WINE.
AT FRANCO-FONTE.
NOT SO!
HE WAS SEEN.
LAST NIGHT.
HERE IN THE VILLAGE.
HERE?
IN TOWN?
BUT HE DIDN'T COME HOME.
COME IN WITH ME.
I CANNOT.
I AM EXCOMMU-NICATED.
BUT HOW IS IT YOU KNOW MORE ABOUT TURIDDU'S COMINGS AND GOINGS THAN I?
I ONLY KNOW THIS ABOUT TURIDDU...
...THAT HE IS BREAKING MY HEART.
AH! IF THE HARNESS BELLS ARE SINGING...
...CAN THE WHIP BE FAR BEHIND?

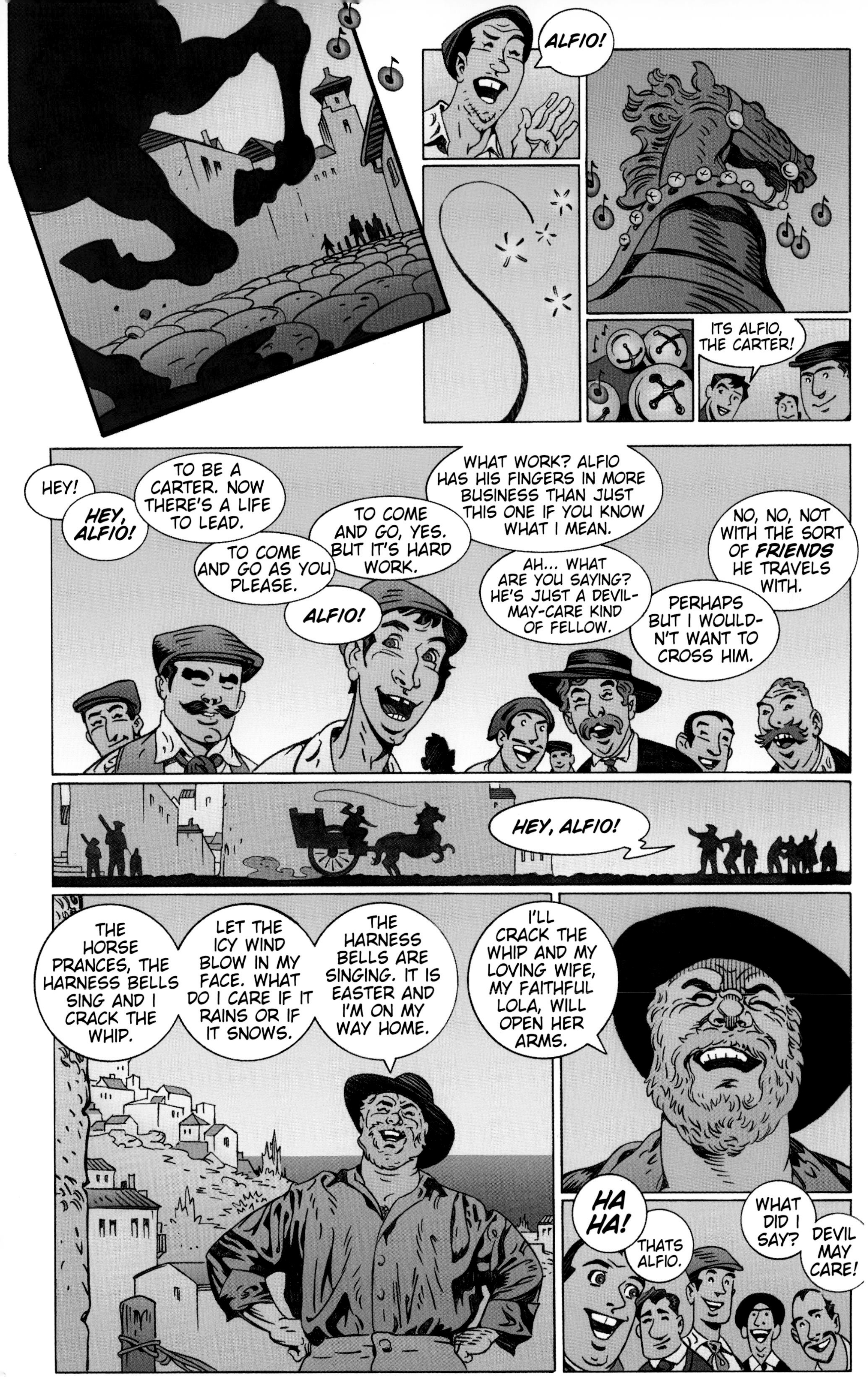
ALFIO!
ITS ALFIO, THE CARTER!
HEY!
HEY, ALFIO!
TO BE A CARTER. NOW THERE'S A LIFE TO LEAD.
TO COME AND GO AS YOU PLEASE.
TO COME AND GO, YES. BUT IT'S HARD WORK.
ALFIO!
WHAT WORK? ALFIO HAS HIS FINGERS IN MORE BUSINESS THAN JUST THIS ONE IF YOU KNOW WHAT I MEAN.
AH... WHAT ARE YOU SAYING? HE'S JUST A DEVIL-MAY-CARE KIND OF FELLOW.
NO, NO, NOT WITH THE SORT OF FRIENDS HE TRAVELS WITH.
PERHAPS BUT I WOULDN'T WANT TO CROSS HIM.
HEY, ALFIO!
THE HORSE PRANCES, THE HARNESS BELLS SING AND I CRACK THE WHIP.
LET THE ICY WIND BLOW IN MY FACE. WHAT DO I CARE IF IT RAINS OR IF IT SNOWS.
THE HARNESS BELLS ARE SINGING. IT IS EASTER AND I'M ON MY WAY HOME.
I'LL CRACK THE WHIP AND MY LOVING WIFE, MY FAITHFUL LOLA, WILL OPEN HER ARMS.
HA HA!
THATS ALFIO.
WHAT DID I SAY?
DEVIL MAY CARE!

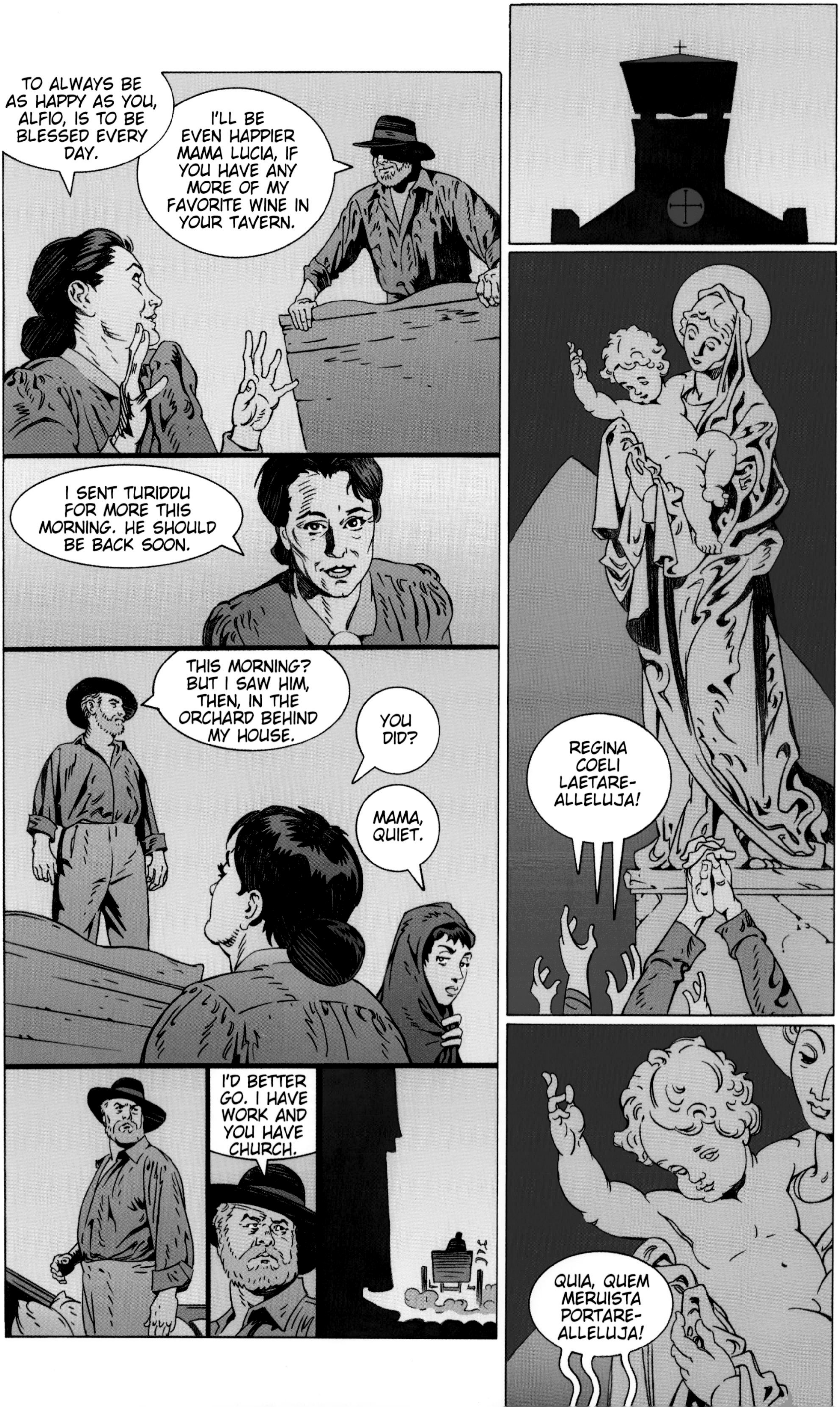
TO ALWAYS BE AS HAPPY AS YOU, ALFIO, IS TO BE BLESSED EVERY DAY.
I'LL BE EVEN HAPPIER MAMA LUCIA, IF YOU HAVE ANY MORE OF MY FAVORITE WINE IN YOUR TAVERN.
I SENT TURIDDU FOR MORE THIS MORNING. HE SHOULD BE BACK SOON.
THIS MORNING? BUT I SAW HIM, THEN, IN THE ORCHARD BEHIND MY HOUSE.
YOU DID?
MAMA, QUIET.
I'D BETTER GO. I HAVE WORK AND YOU HAVE CHURCH.
REGINA COELI LAETARE-ALLELUJA!
QUIA, QUEM MERUISTA PORTARE-ALLELUJA!

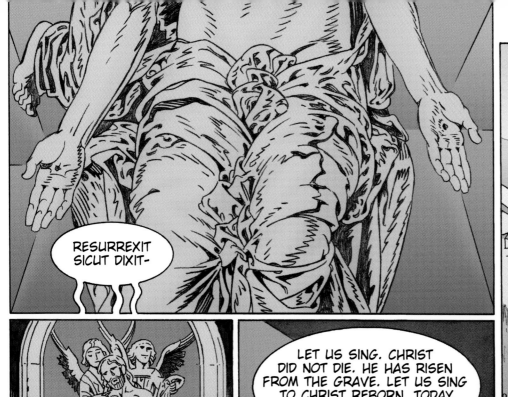

RESURREXIT SICUT DIXIT-

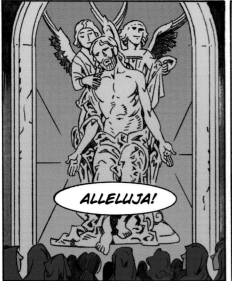

ALLELUJA!

LET US SING. CHRIST DID NOT DIE. HE HAS RISEN FROM THE GRAVE. LET US SING TO CHRIST REBORN. TODAY, HE ASCENDS TO THE GLORY OF HEAVEN.

SAN-TUZZA...

WHAT WAS THAT ABOUT?

WHY DID YOU TELL ME TO BE QUIET?

LET US SING, CHRIST DID NOT DIE.

LET US SING TO CHRIST REBORN

...TODAY HE ASCENDS TO THE GLORY OF HEAVEN.

ALLELUJA

ALLELUJA

ALLELUJA

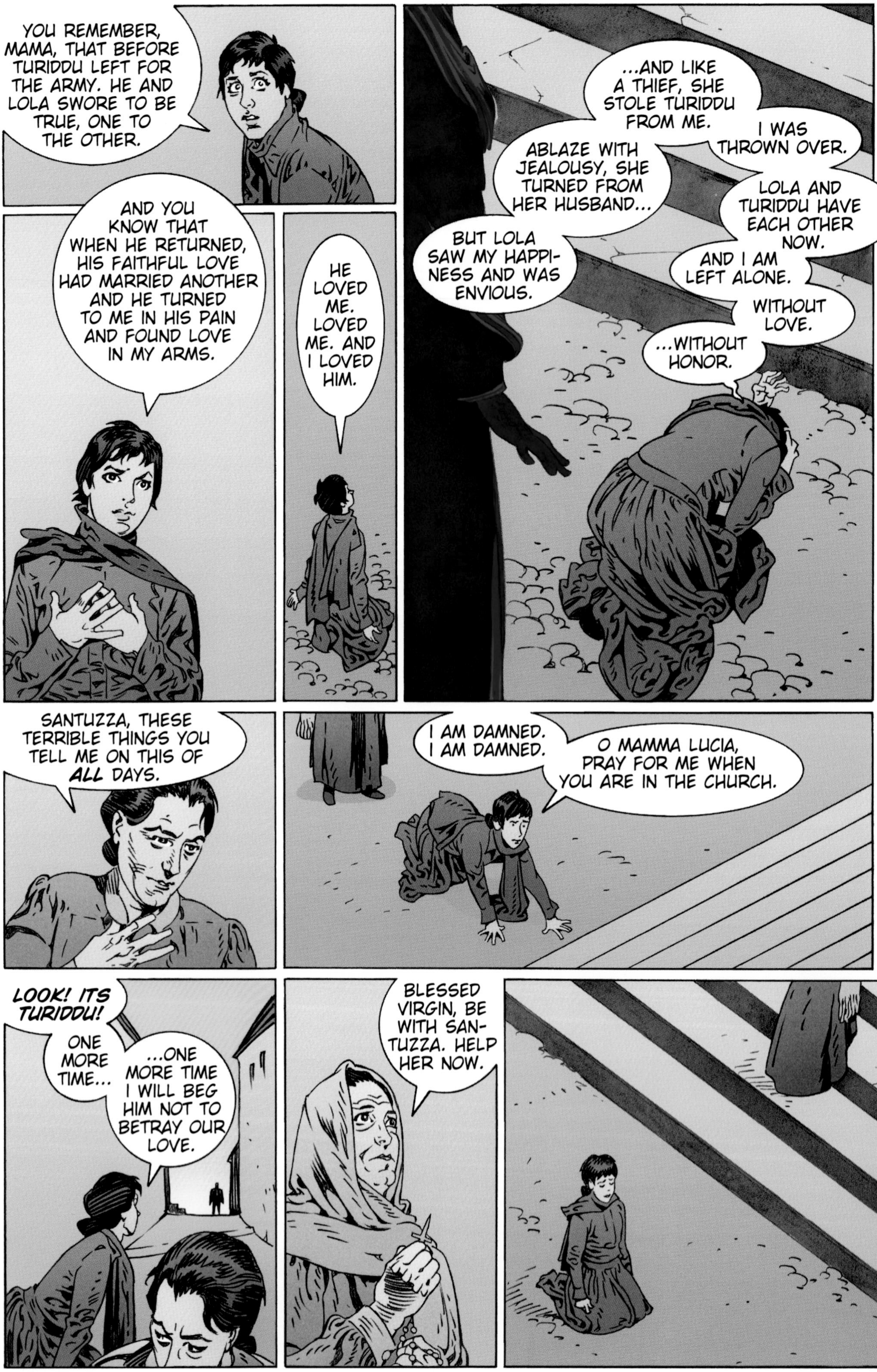
YOU REMEMBER, MAMA, THAT BEFORE TURIDDU LEFT FOR THE ARMY. HE AND LOLA SWORE TO BE TRUE, ONE TO THE OTHER.
AND YOU KNOW THAT WHEN HE RETURNED, HIS FAITHFUL LOVE HAD MARRIED ANOTHER AND HE TURNED TO ME IN HIS PAIN AND FOUND LOVE IN MY ARMS.
HE LOVED ME. LOVED ME. AND I LOVED HIM.
BUT LOLA SAW MY HAPPI-NESS AND WAS ENVIOUS.
ABLAZE WITH JEALOUSY, SHE TURNED FROM HER HUSBAND...
...AND LIKE A THIEF, SHE STOLE TURIDDU FROM ME.
I WAS THROWN OVER.
LOLA AND TURIDDU HAVE EACH OTHER NOW.
AND I AM LEFT ALONE.
WITHOUT LOVE.
...WITHOUT HONOR.
SANTUZZA, THESE TERRIBLE THINGS YOU TELL ME ON THIS OF ALL DAYS.
I AM DAMNED. I AM DAMNED.
O MAMMA LUCIA, PRAY FOR ME WHEN YOU ARE IN THE CHURCH.
LOOK! ITS TURIDDU!
ONE MORE TIME...
...ONE MORE TIME I WILL BEG HIM NOT TO BETRAY OUR LOVE.
BLESSED VIRGIN, BE WITH SAN-TUZZA. HELP HER NOW.

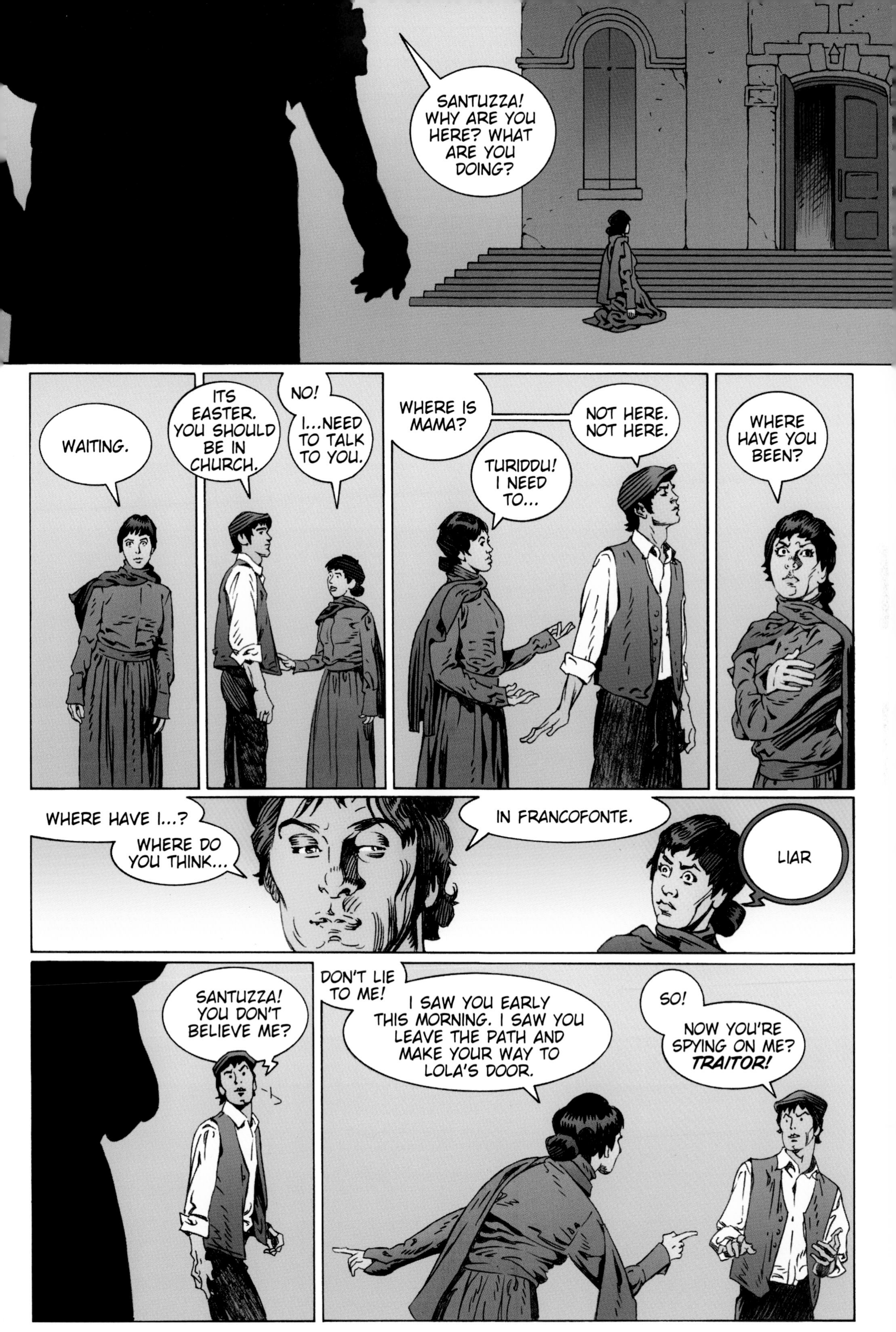
SANTUZZA! WHY ARE YOU HERE? WHAT ARE YOU DOING?
WAITING.
ITS EASTER. YOU SHOULD BE IN CHURCH.
NO!
I...NEED TO TALK TO YOU.
WHERE IS MAMA?
NOT HERE. NOT HERE.
TURIDDU! I NEED TO...
WHERE HAVE YOU BEEN?
WHERE HAVE I...?
WHERE DO YOU THINK...
IN FRANCOFONTE.
LIAR
SANTUZZA! YOU DON'T BELIEVE ME?
DON'T LIE TO ME!
I SAW YOU EARLY THIS MORNING. I SAW YOU LEAVE THE PATH AND MAKE YOUR WAY TO LOLA'S DOOR.
SO!
NOW YOU'RE SPYING ON ME? TRAITOR!

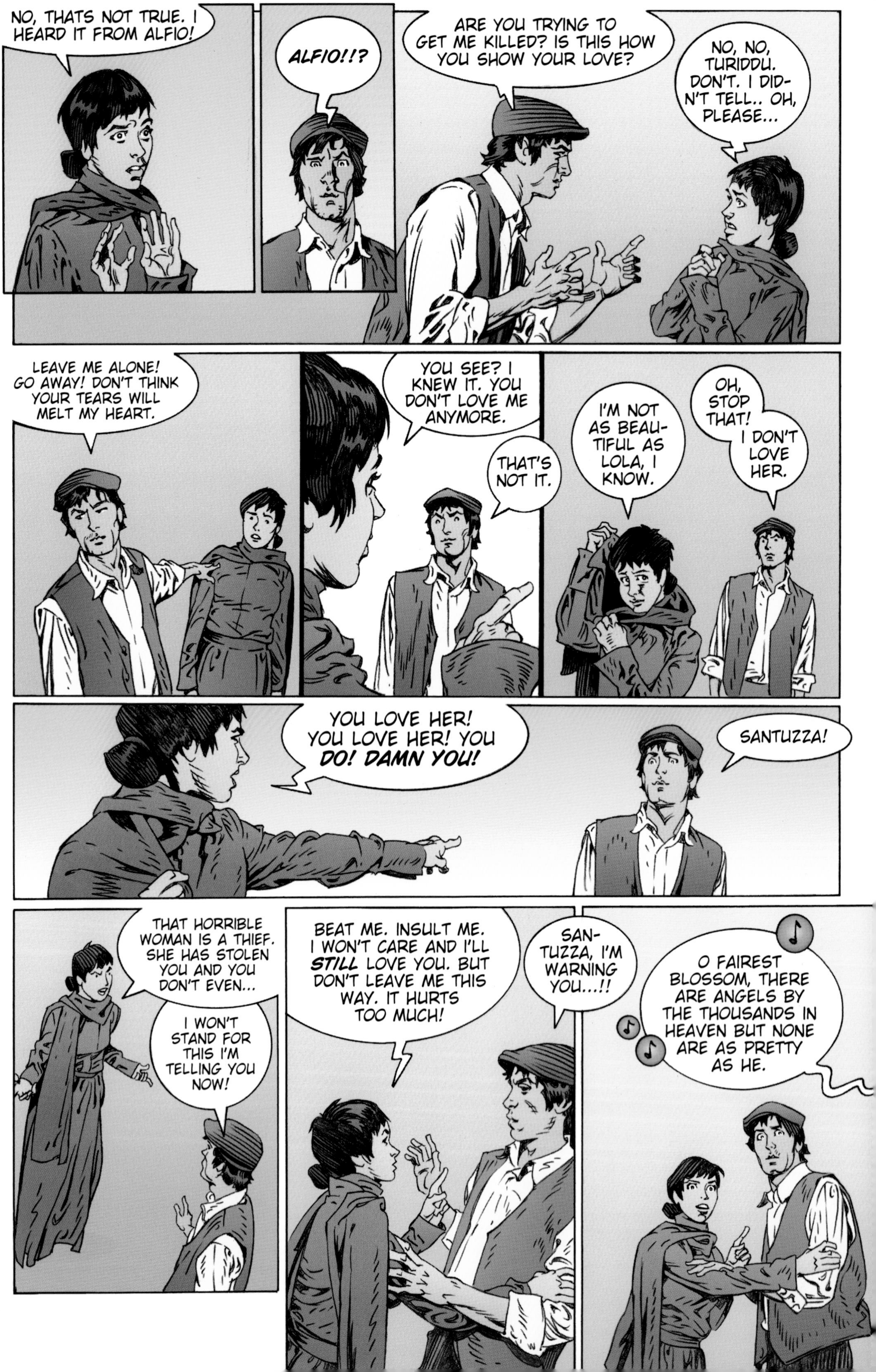
NO, THATS NOT TRUE. I HEARD IT FROM ALFIO!
ALFIO!!?
ARE YOU TRYING TO GET ME KILLED? IS THIS HOW YOU SHOW YOUR LOVE?
NO, NO, TURIDDU. DON'T. I DIDN'T TELL.. OH, PLEASE...
LEAVE ME ALONE! GO AWAY! DON'T THINK YOUR TEARS WILL MELT MY HEART.
YOU SEE? I KNEW IT. YOU DON'T LOVE ME ANYMORE.
THAT'S NOT IT.
I'M NOT AS BEAUTIFUL AS LOLA, I KNOW.
OH, STOP THAT! I DON'T LOVE HER.
YOU LOVE HER! YOU LOVE HER! YOU DO! DAMN YOU!
SANTUZZA!
THAT HORRIBLE WOMAN IS A THIEF. SHE HAS STOLEN YOU AND YOU DON'T EVEN...
I WON'T STAND FOR THIS I'M TELLING YOU NOW!
BEAT ME. INSULT ME. I WON'T CARE AND I'LL STILL LOVE YOU. BUT DON'T LEAVE ME THIS WAY. IT HURTS TOO MUCH!
SANTUZZA, I'M WARNING YOU...!!
O FAIREST BLOSSOM, THERE ARE ANGELS BY THE THOUSANDS IN HEAVEN BUT NONE ARE AS PRETTY AS HE.

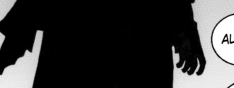 OH, TURIDDU!

HELLO, SANTUZZA

HAVE YOU SEEN ALFIO? HAS HE BEEN BY YET?

 ALFIO?

I HAVEN'T SEEN HIM. BUT I JUST GOT HERE.

 PERHAPS HE'S STILL AT THE BLACKSMITHS BUT I CAN'T WAIT ALL DAY.

 ARE YOU ATTENDING CHURCH IN THE STREET?

 NO... BUT...UM... SANTUZZA WAS JUST TELLING ME...

 I WAS TELLING HIM THAT THIS IS EASTER SUNDAY AND THERE IS NOTHING THAT GOD DOES NOT SEE.

 AND YOU, SANTUZZA, WHY AREN'T YOU IN CHURCH?

 NOT I.

ONLY THOSE WITHOUT SIN MAY ATTEND.

 YOU SHOULD MAKE THE ATTEMPT.

I PRAISE GOD EVERYDAY AND BOW MY HEAD BEFORE HIM.

 OH, WELL SAID, LOLA! COMING FROM YOU!

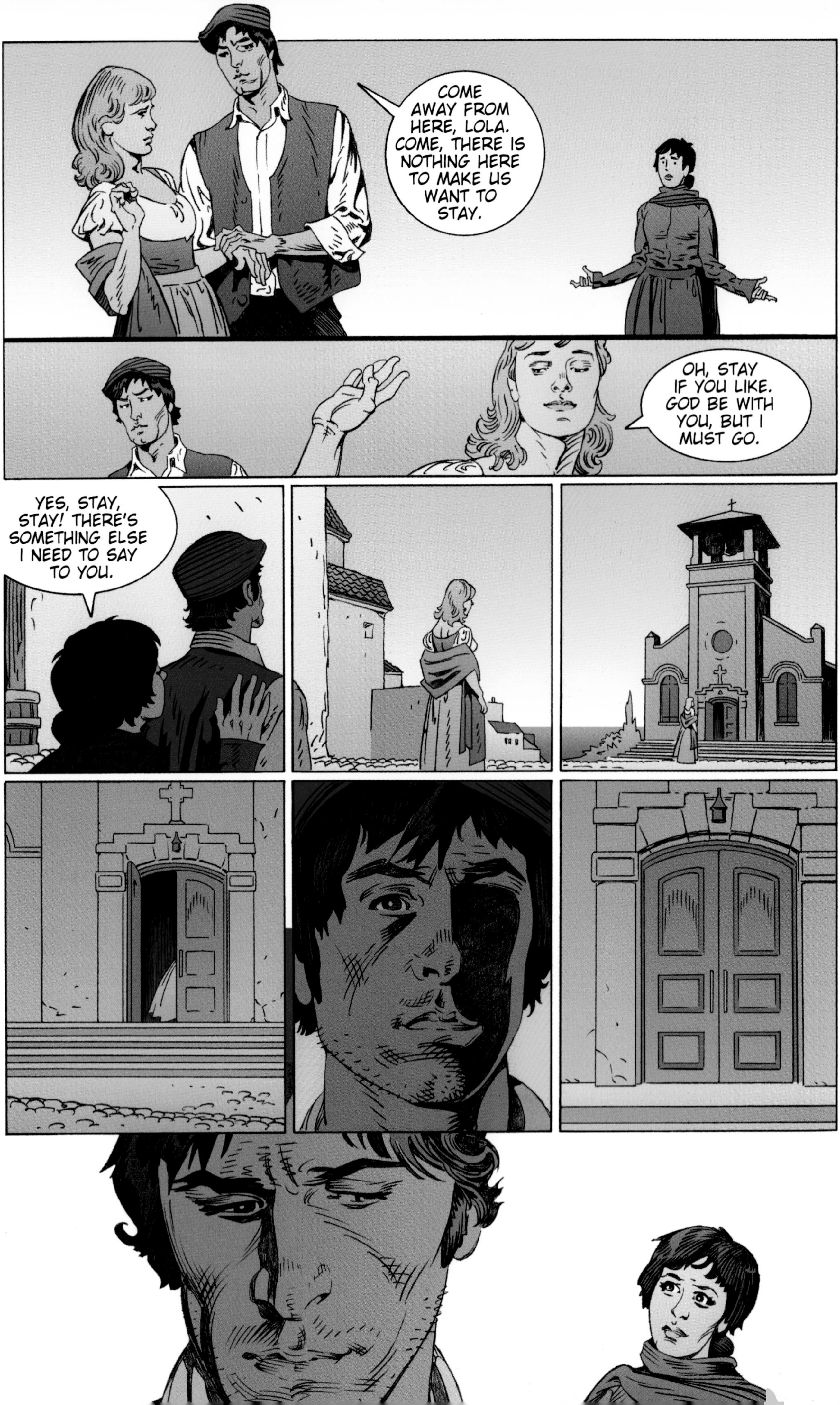
COME AWAY FROM HERE, LOLA. COME, THERE IS NOTHING HERE TO MAKE US WANT TO STAY.
OH, STAY IF YOU LIKE. GOD BE WITH YOU, BUT I MUST GO.
YES, STAY, STAY! THERE'S SOMETHING ELSE I NEED TO SAY TO YOU.

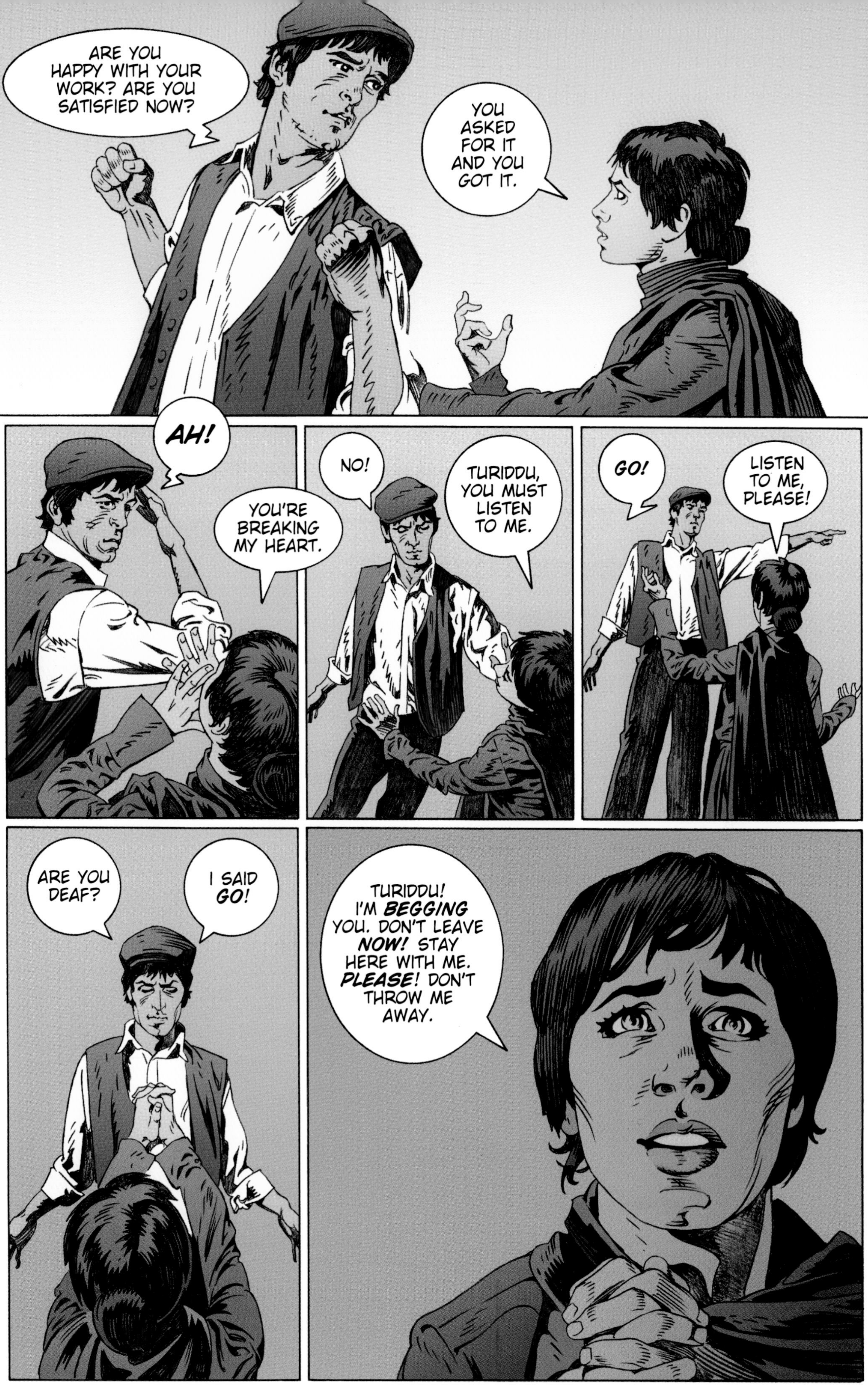

ARE YOU HAPPY WITH YOUR WORK? ARE YOU SATISFIED NOW?
YOU ASKED FOR IT AND YOU GOT IT.
AH!
YOU'RE BREAKING MY HEART.
NO!
TURIDDU, YOU MUST LISTEN TO ME.
GO!
LISTEN TO ME, PLEASE!
ARE YOU DEAF?
I SAID GO!
TURIDDU! I'M BEGGING YOU. DON'T LEAVE NOW! STAY HERE WITH ME. PLEASE! DON'T THROW ME AWAY.

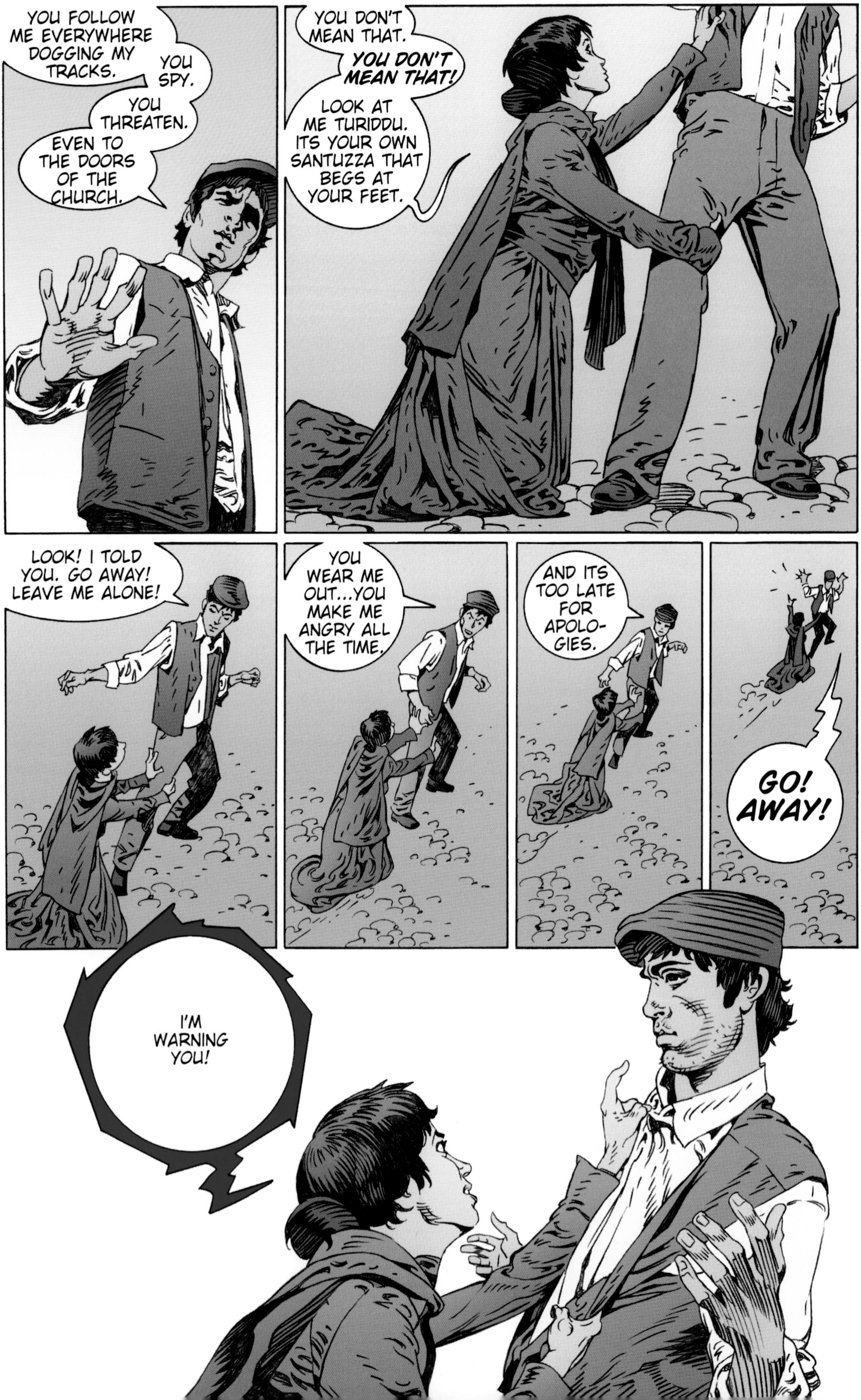

YOU FOLLOW ME EVERYWHERE DOGGING MY TRACKS.
YOU SPY.
YOU THREATEN.
EVEN TO THE DOORS OF THE CHURCH.
YOU DON'T MEAN THAT.
YOU DON'T MEAN THAT!
LOOK AT ME TURIDDU. ITS YOUR OWN SANTUZZA THAT BEGS AT YOUR FEET.
LOOK! I TOLD YOU. GO AWAY! LEAVE ME ALONE!
YOU WEAR ME OUT...YOU MAKE ME ANGRY ALL THE TIME.
AND ITS TOO LATE FOR APOLO-GIES.
GO! AWAY!
I'M WARNING YOU!

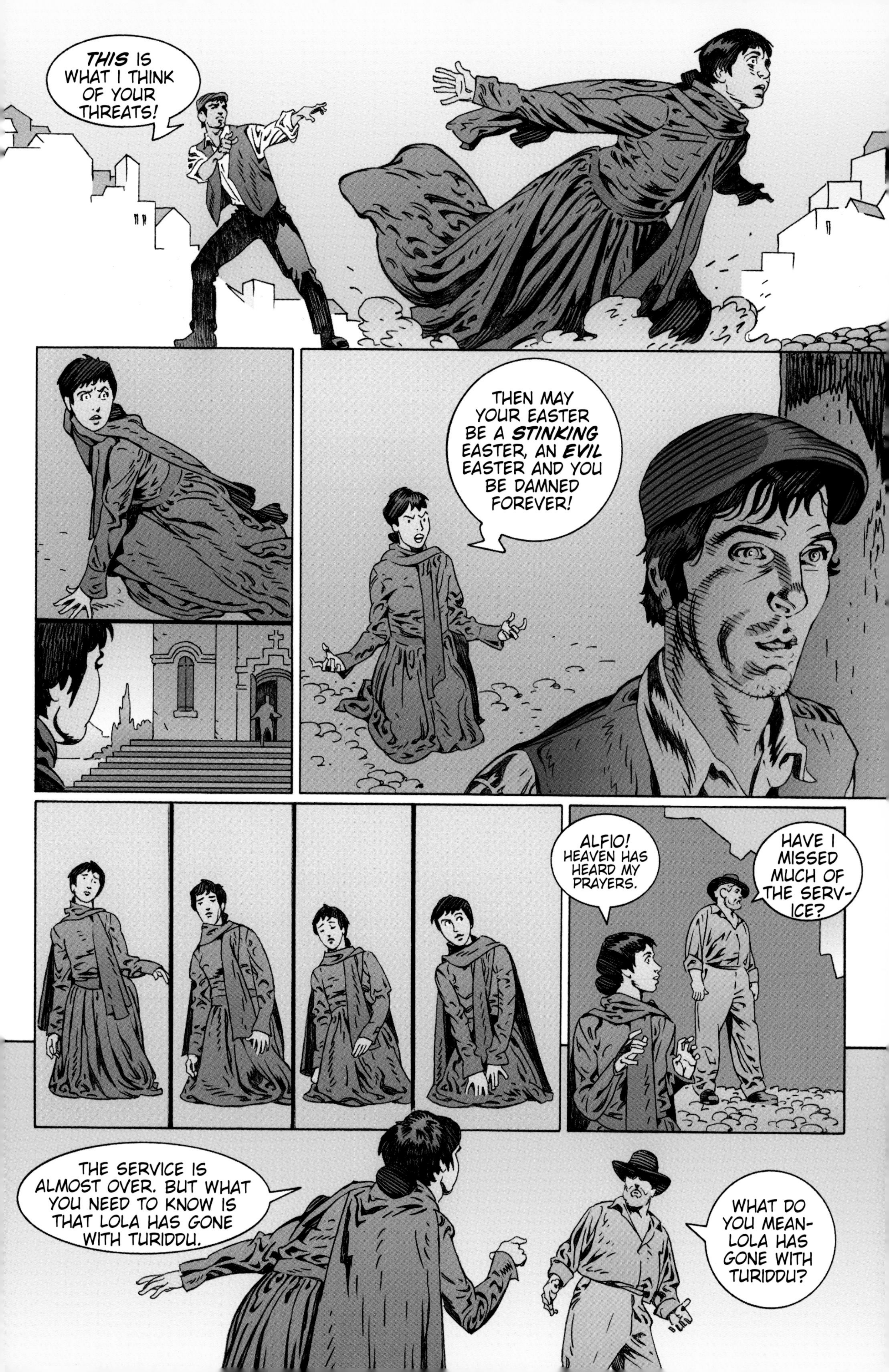
THIS IS WHAT I THINK OF YOUR THREATS!
THEN MAY YOUR EASTER BE A STINKING EASTER, AN EVIL EASTER AND YOU BE DAMNED FOREVER!
ALFIO! HEAVEN HAS HEARD MY PRAYERS.
HAVE I MISSED MUCH OF THE SERV-ICE?
THE SERVICE IS ALMOST OVER. BUT WHAT YOU NEED TO KNOW IS THAT LOLA HAS GONE WITH TURIDDU.
WHAT DO YOU MEAN-LOLA HAS GONE WITH TURIDDU?

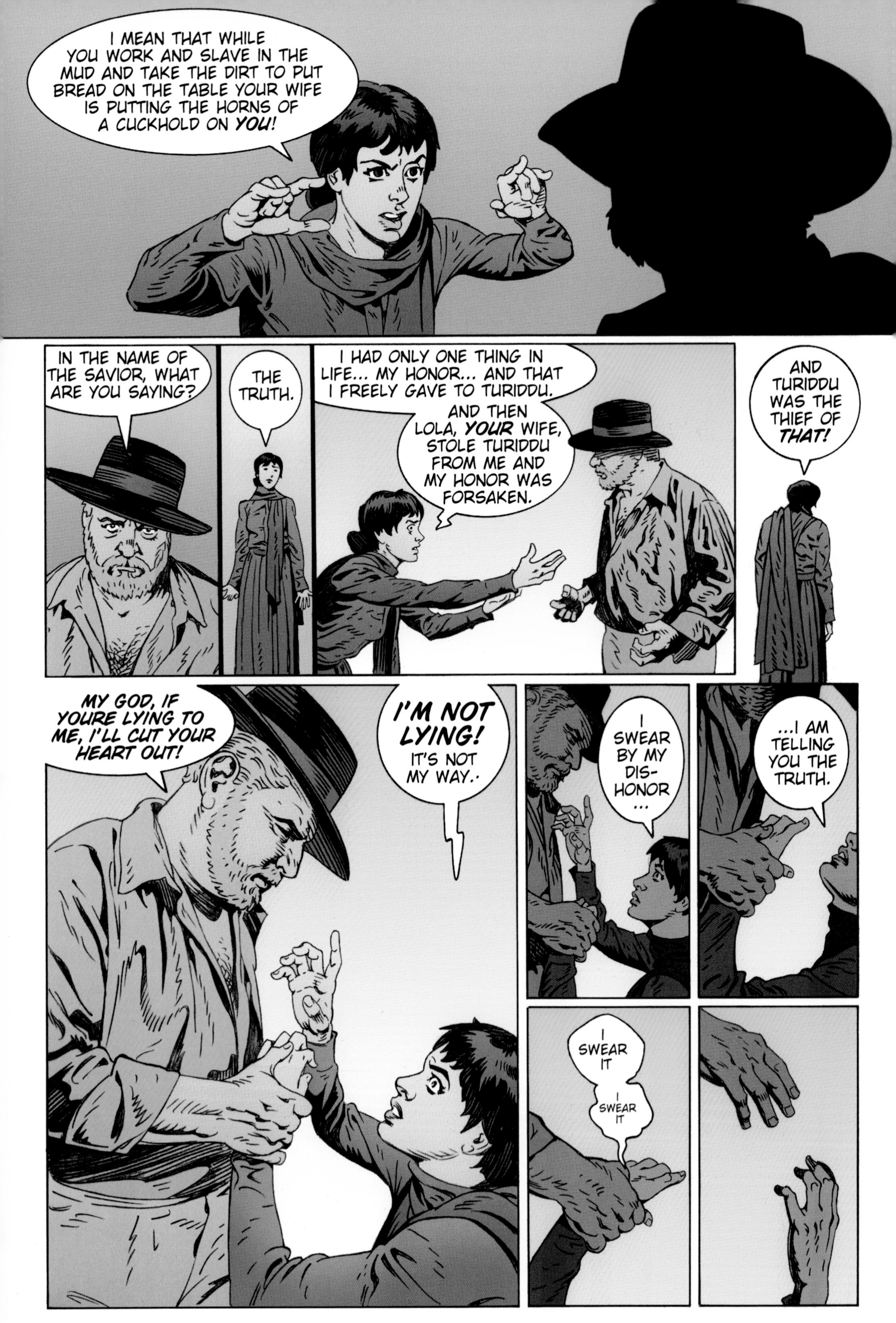
I MEAN THAT WHILE YOU WORK AND SLAVE IN THE MUD AND TAKE THE DIRT TO PUT BREAD ON THE TABLE YOUR WIFE IS PUTTING THE HORNS OF A CUCKHOLD ON YOU!
IN THE NAME OF THE SAVIOR, WHAT ARE YOU SAYING?
THE TRUTH.
I HAD ONLY ONE THING IN LIFE... MY HONOR... AND THAT I FREELY GAVE TO TURIDDU.
AND THEN LOLA, YOUR WIFE, STOLE TURIDDU FROM ME AND MY HONOR WAS FORSAKEN.
AND TURIDDU WAS THE THIEF OF THAT!
MY GOD, IF YOURE LYING TO ME, I'LL CUT YOUR HEART OUT!
I'M NOT LYING! IT'S NOT MY WAY..
I SWEAR BY MY DIS- HONOR ...
...I AM TELLING YOU THE TRUTH.
I SWEAR IT
I SWEAR IT

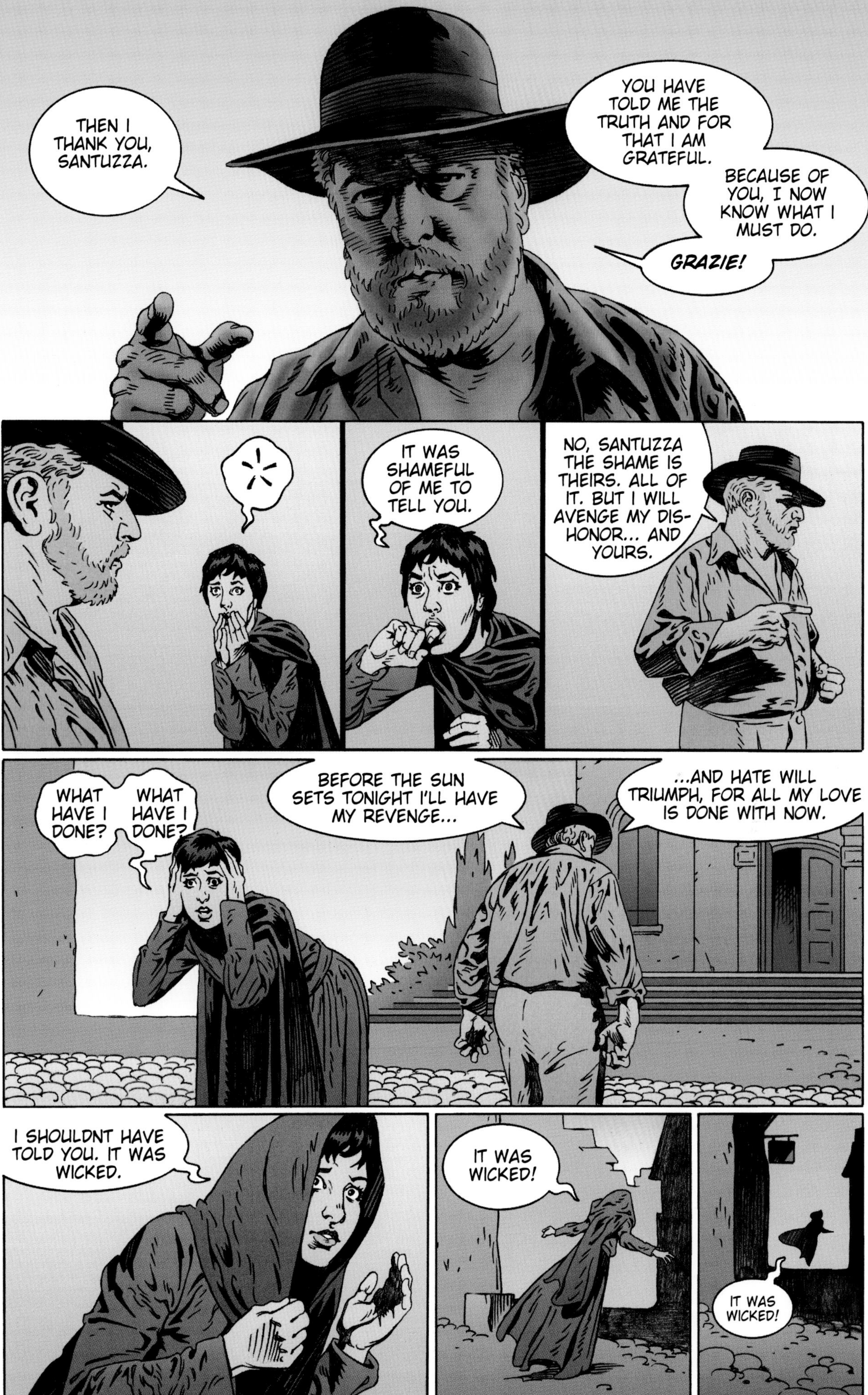
THEN I THANK YOU, SANTUZZA.
YOU HAVE TOLD ME THE TRUTH AND FOR THAT I AM GRATEFUL.
BECAUSE OF YOU, I NOW KNOW WHAT I MUST DO.
GRAZIE!
!
IT WAS SHAMEFUL OF ME TO TELL YOU.
NO, SANTUZZA THE SHAME IS THEIRS. ALL OF IT. BUT I WILL AVENGE MY DISHONOR... AND YOURS.
WHAT HAVE I DONE?
WHAT HAVE I DONE?
BEFORE THE SUN SETS TONIGHT I'LL HAVE MY REVENGE...
...AND HATE WILL TRIUMPH, FOR ALL MY LOVE IS DONE WITH NOW.
I SHOULDNT HAVE TOLD YOU. IT WAS WICKED.
IT WAS WICKED!
IT WAS WICKED!

INTERMEZZO

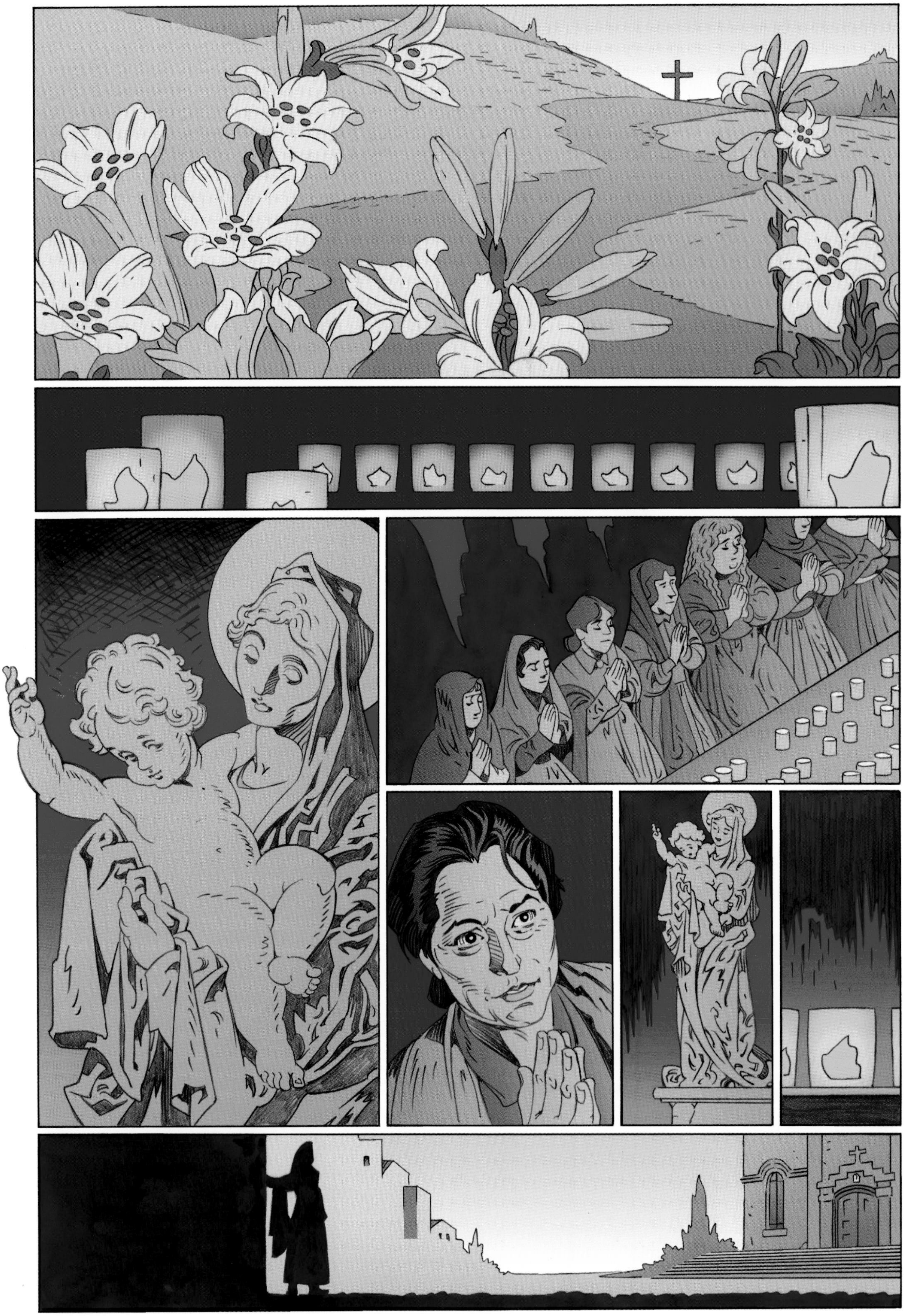

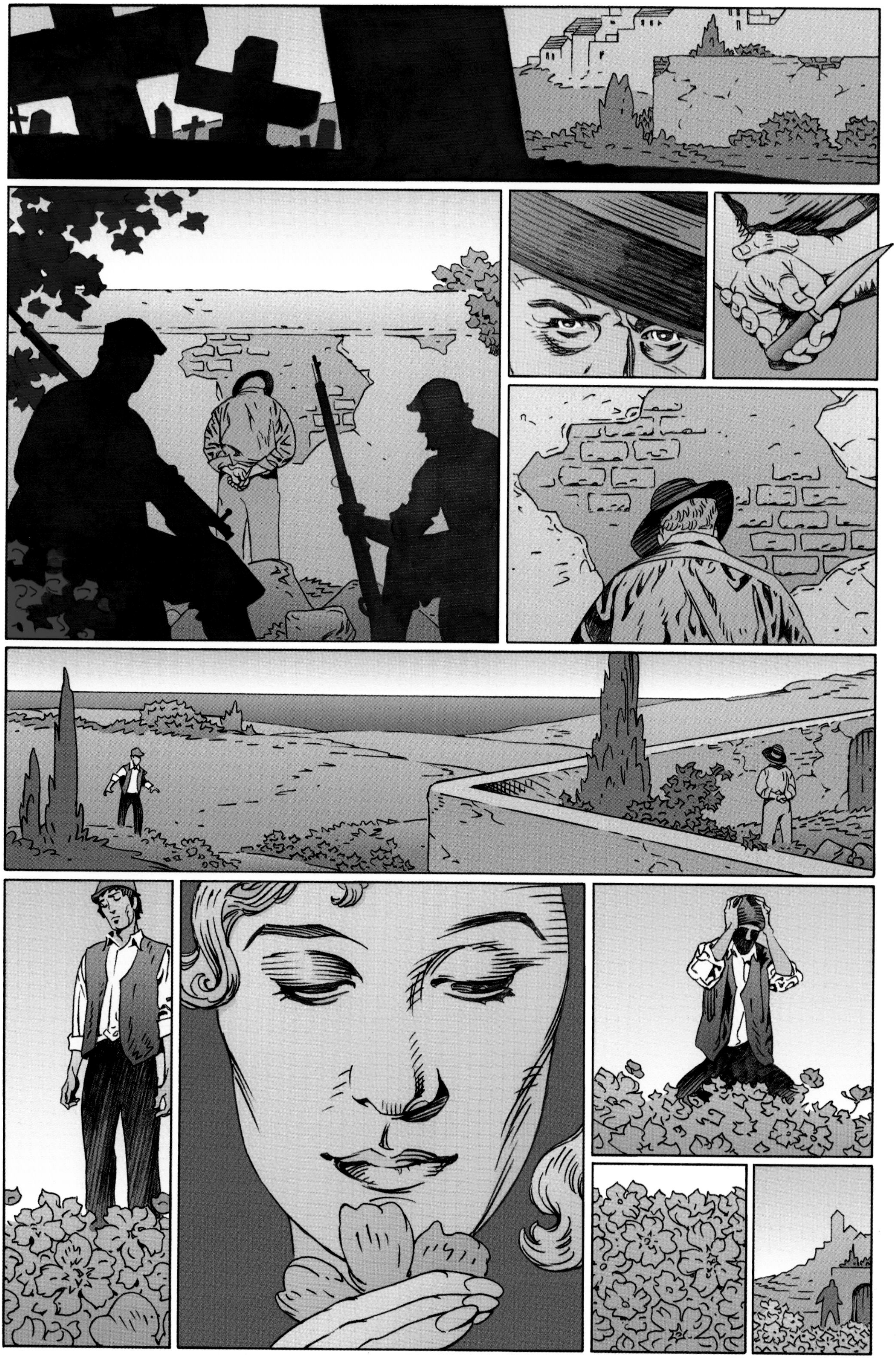

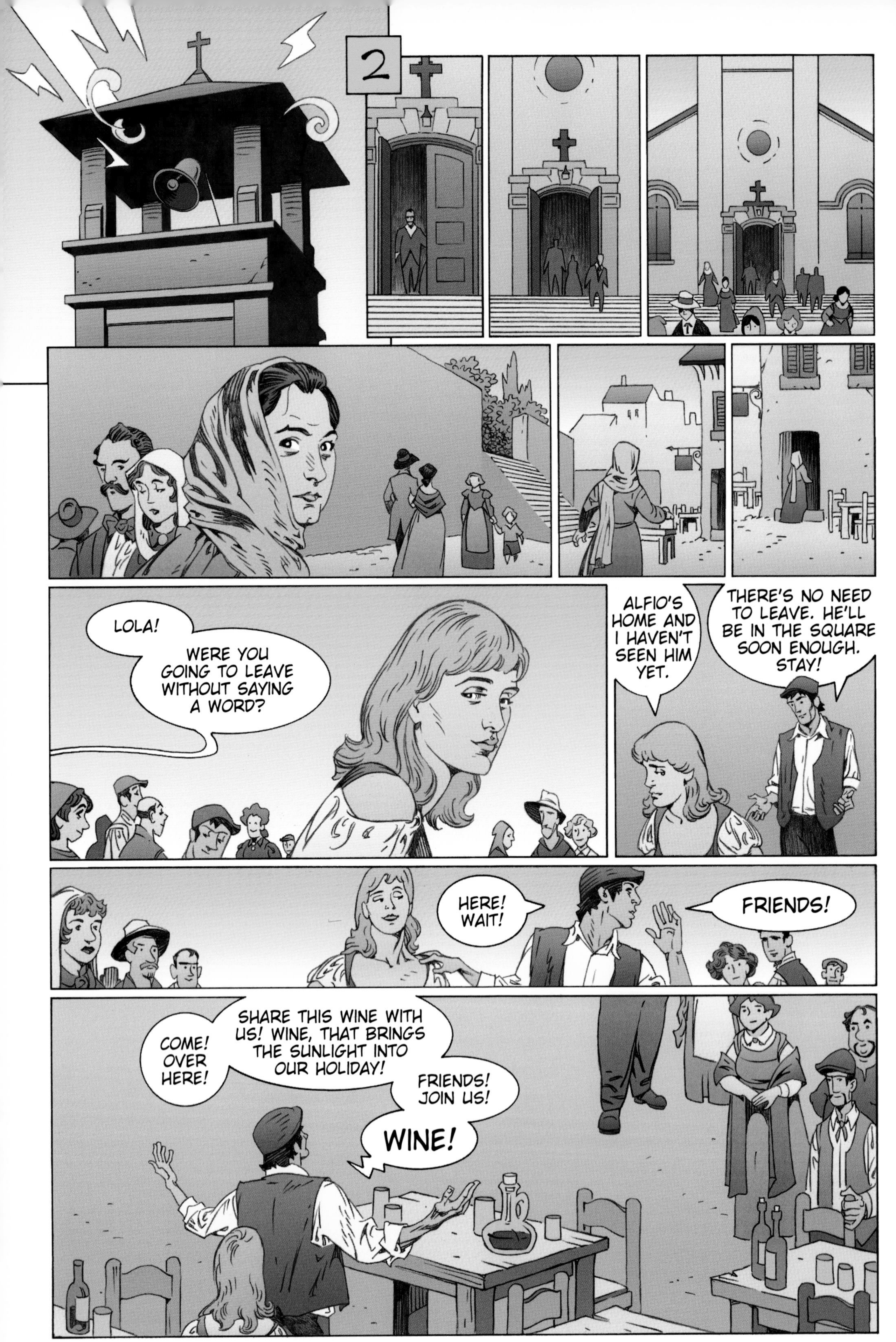
2
LOLA!
WERE YOU GOING TO LEAVE WITHOUT SAYING A WORD?
ALFIO'S HOME AND I HAVEN'T SEEN HIM YET.
THERE'S NO NEED TO LEAVE. HE'LL BE IN THE SQUARE SOON ENOUGH. STAY!
HERE! WAIT!
FRIENDS!
COME! OVER HERE!
SHARE THIS WINE WITH US! WINE, THAT BRINGS THE SUNLIGHT INTO OUR HOLIDAY!
FRIENDS! JOIN US!
WINE!

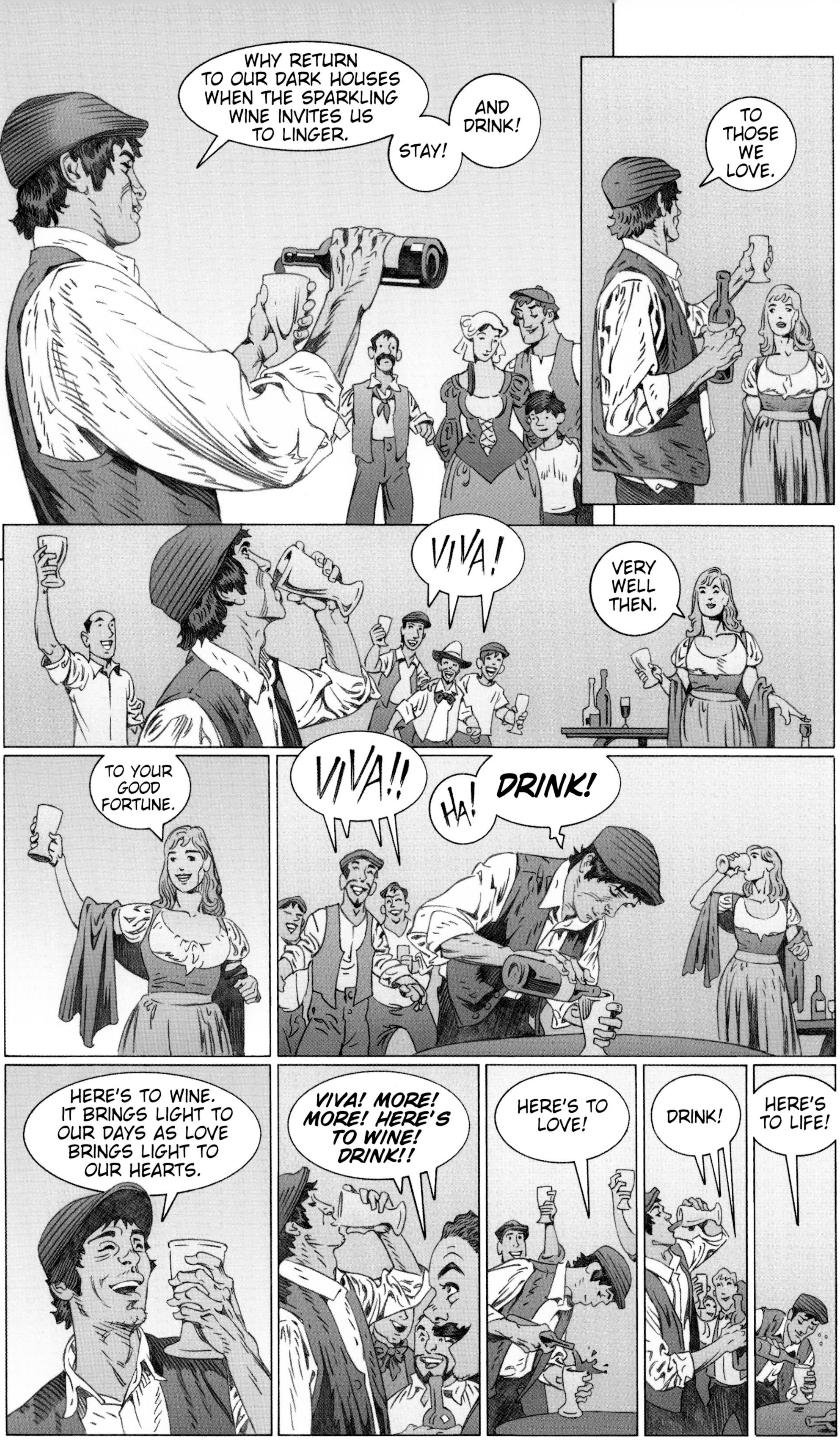
WHY RETURN TO OUR DARK HOUSES WHEN THE SPARKLING WINE INVITES US TO LINGER.
STAY!
AND DRINK!
TO THOSE WE LOVE.
VIVA!
VERY WELL THEN.
TO YOUR GOOD FORTUNE.
VIVA!!
HA!
DRINK!
HERE'S TO WINE. IT BRINGS LIGHT TO OUR DAYS AS LOVE BRINGS LIGHT TO OUR HEARTS.
VIVA! MORE! MORE! HERE'S TO WINE! DRINK!!
HERE'S TO LOVE!
DRINK!
HERE'S TO LIFE!

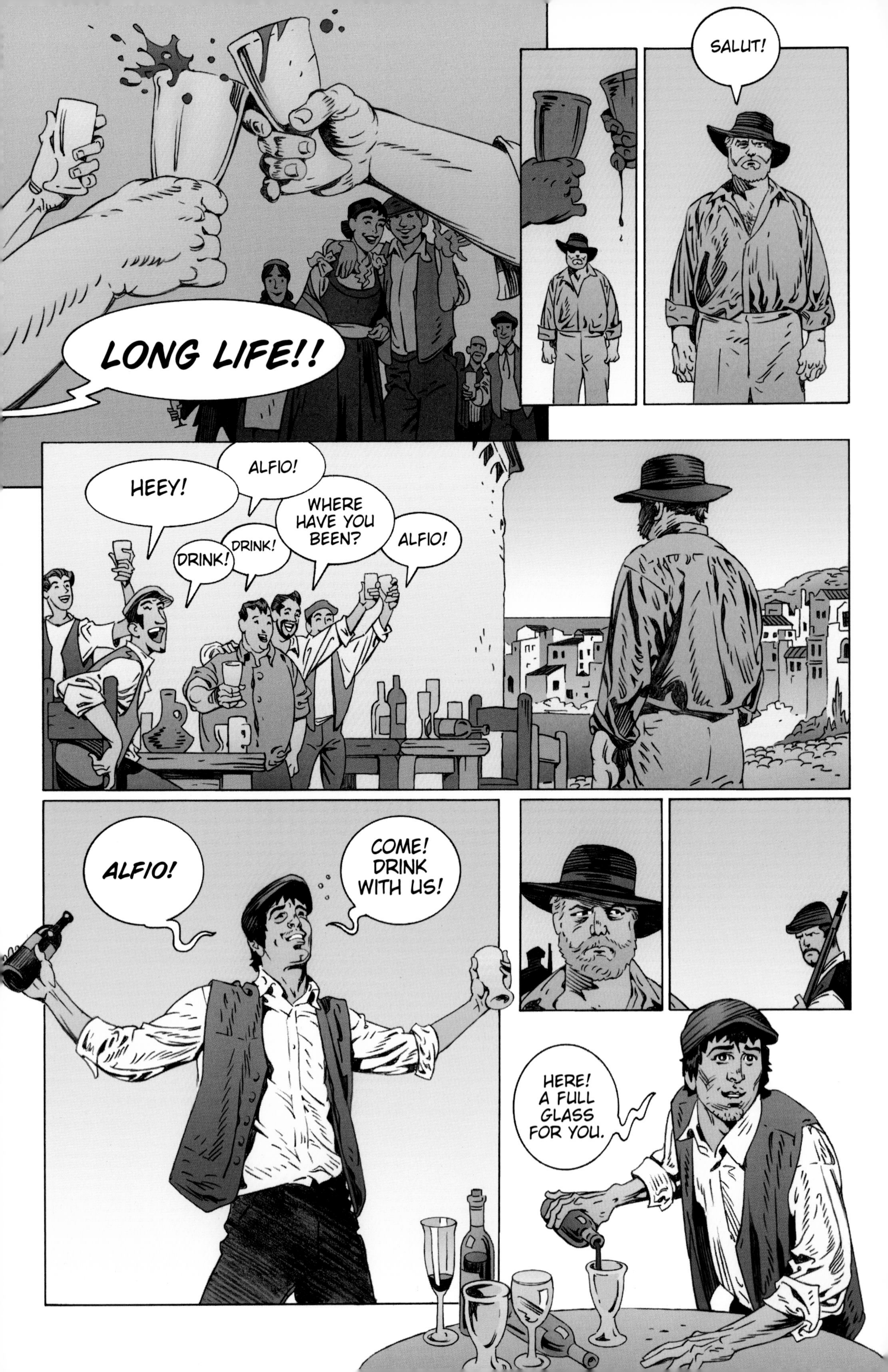
LONG LIFE!!
SALUT!
HEEY!
ALFIO!
DRINK!
DRINK!
WHERE HAVE YOU BEEN?
ALFIO!
ALFIO!
COME! DRINK WITH US!
HERE! A FULL GLASS FOR YOU.

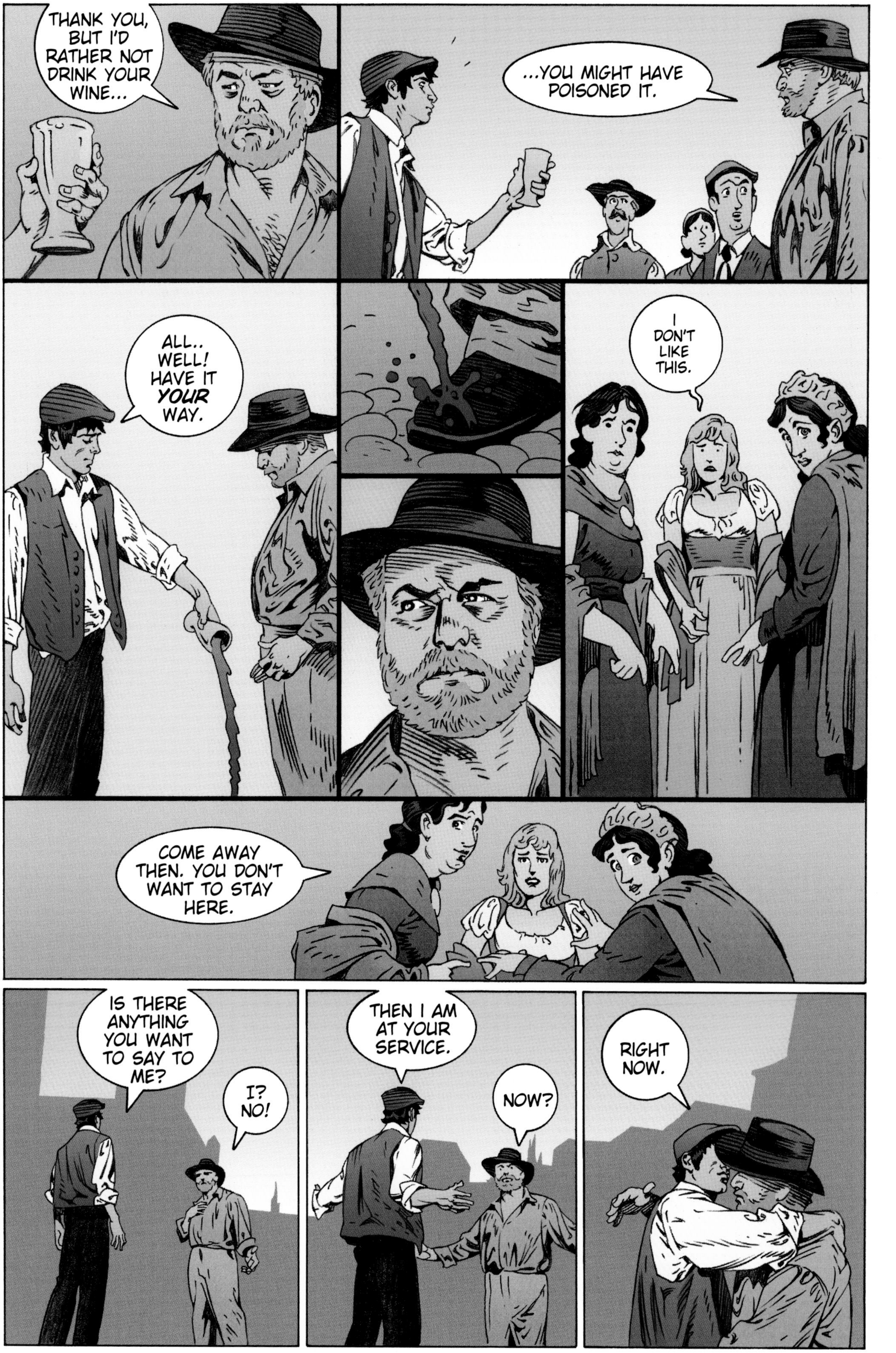
THANK YOU, BUT I'D RATHER NOT DRINK YOUR WINE...
...YOU MIGHT HAVE POISONED IT.
ALL.. WELL! HAVE IT YOUR WAY.
I DON'T LIKE THIS.
COME AWAY THEN. YOU DON'T WANT TO STAY HERE.
IS THERE ANYTHING YOU WANT TO SAY TO ME?
I? NO!
THEN I AM AT YOUR SERVICE.
NOW?
RIGHT NOW.

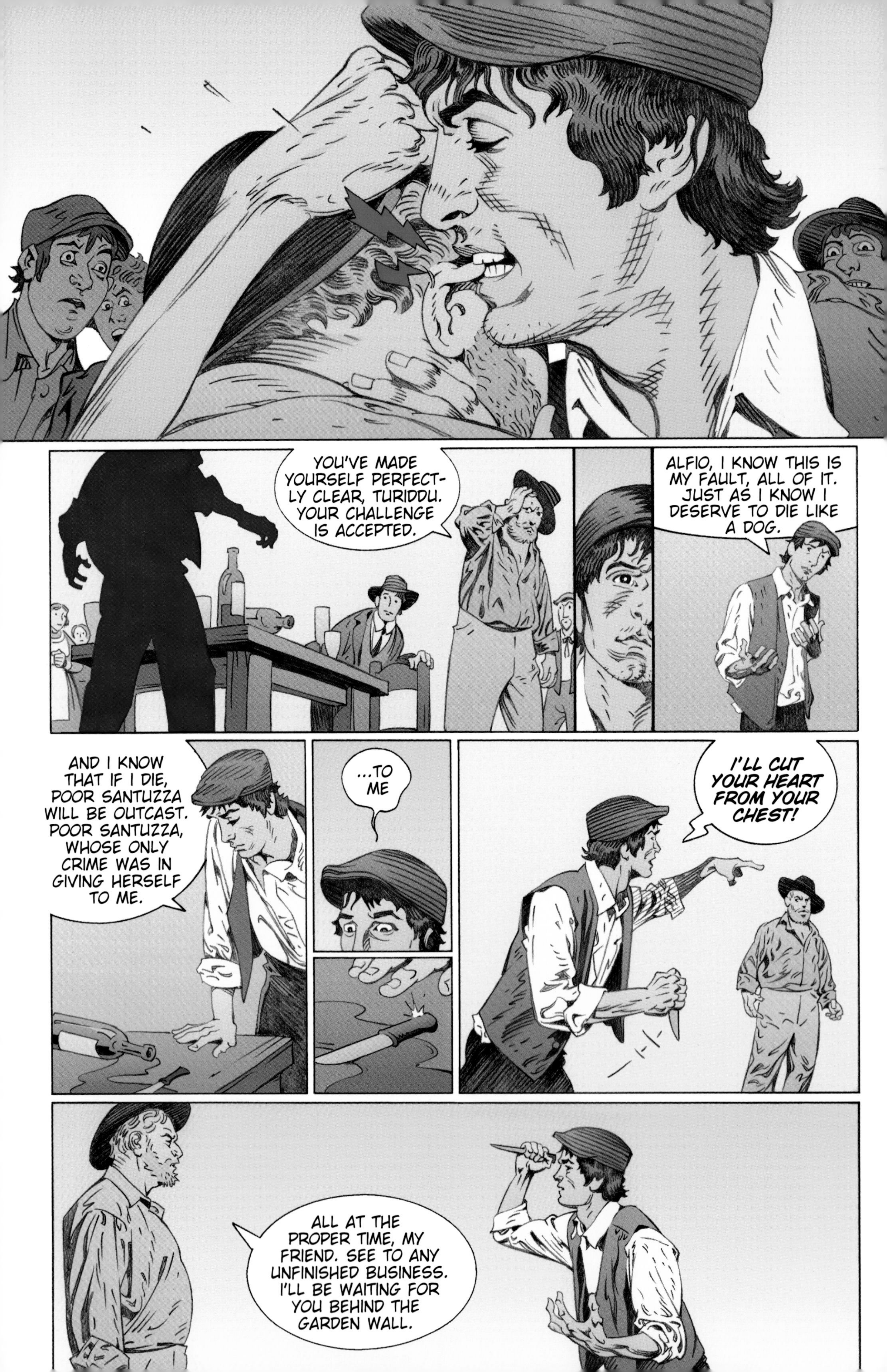

YOU'VE MADE YOURSELF PERFECTLY CLEAR, TURIDDU. YOUR CHALLENGE IS ACCEPTED.
ALFIO, I KNOW THIS IS MY FAULT, ALL OF IT. JUST AS I KNOW I DESERVE TO DIE LIKE A DOG.
AND I KNOW THAT IF I DIE, POOR SANTUZZA WILL BE OUTCAST. POOR SANTUZZA, WHOSE ONLY CRIME WAS IN GIVING HERSELF TO ME.
...TO ME
I'LL CUT YOUR HEART FROM YOUR CHEST!
ALL AT THE PROPER TIME, MY FRIEND. SEE TO ANY UNFINISHED BUSINESS. I'LL BE WAITING FOR YOU BEHIND THE GARDEN WALL.

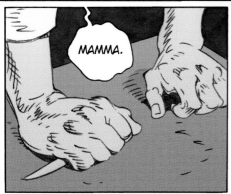

MAMMA.

MAMMA!

TURIDDU...

WHAT IS IT?

MAMMA.. I... I'VE HAD TOO MUCH WINE, I THINK, IT'S VERY STRONG AND I'M A LITTLE DRUNK. I'M GOING TO WALK IT OFF.

AND ALSO... ALSO... ARE YOU LISTENING, MAMMA?

BUT FIRST, GIVE ME YOUR BLESSING LIKE YOU DID WHEN I LEFT HOME TO BE A SOLDIER.

IF ANYTHING SHOULD HAPPEN TO ME YOU MUST TAKE CARE OF SANTUZZA. I'VE PROMISED TO MARRY HER AND SHE HAS NO ONE ELSE.

DO YOU UNDERSTAND ME, MAMMA?

HAPPEN TO YOU?! WHAT ARE YOU SAYING?

OH... NOTHING ITS JUST THE WINE SPEAKING.

THINK OF ME IN YOUR PRAYERS, MAMMA.

GIVE ME A KISS BEFORE I GO.

AND IF I DON'T COME BACK, REMEMBER SANTUZZA. SHE'LL NEED YOU.

A KISS, A KISS, ONE MORE KISS, MAMMA.

GOOD-BYE.

101

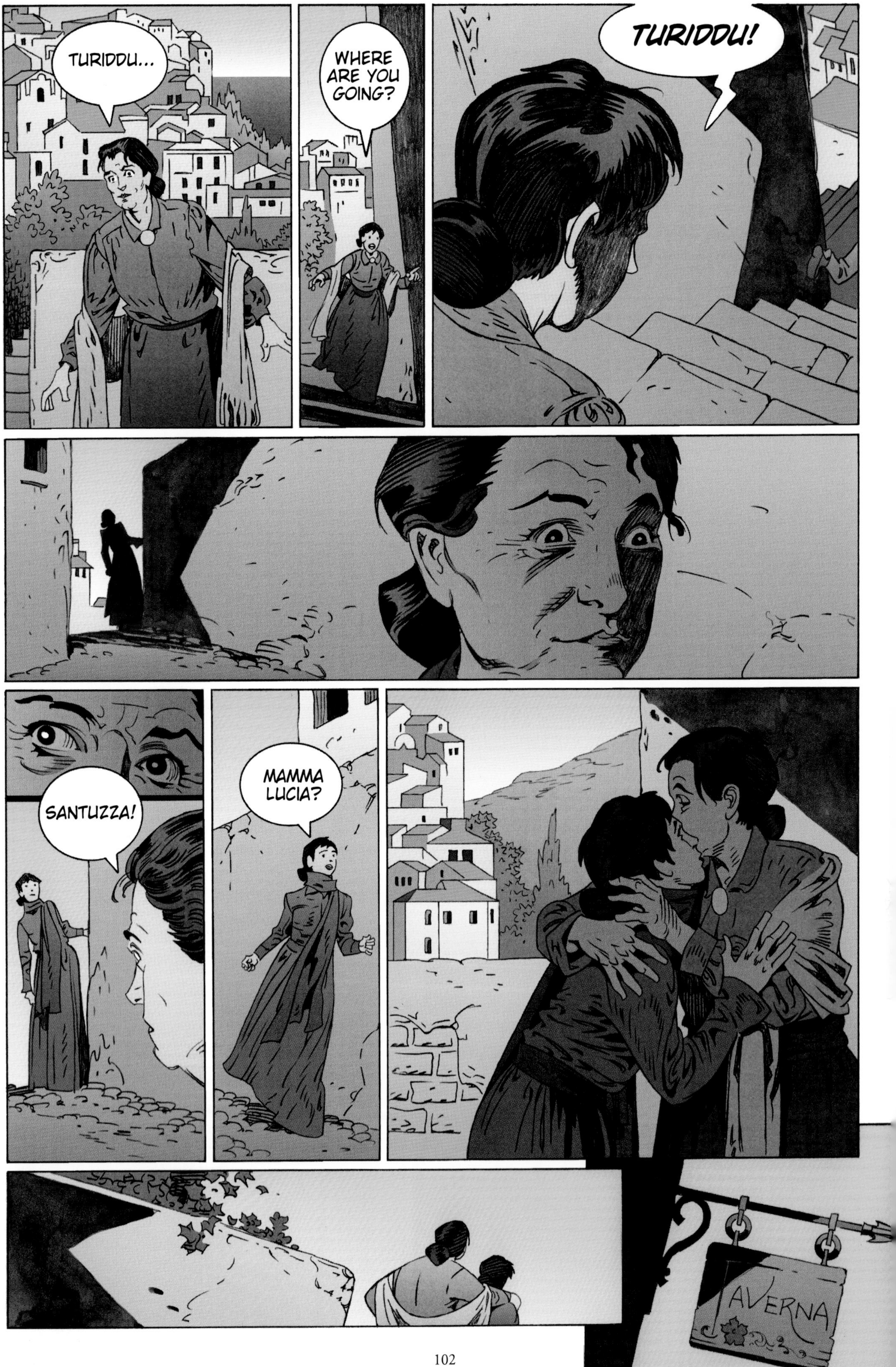
TURIDDU...
WHERE ARE YOU GOING?
TURIDDU!
SANTUZZA!
MAMMA LUCIA?
TAVERNA

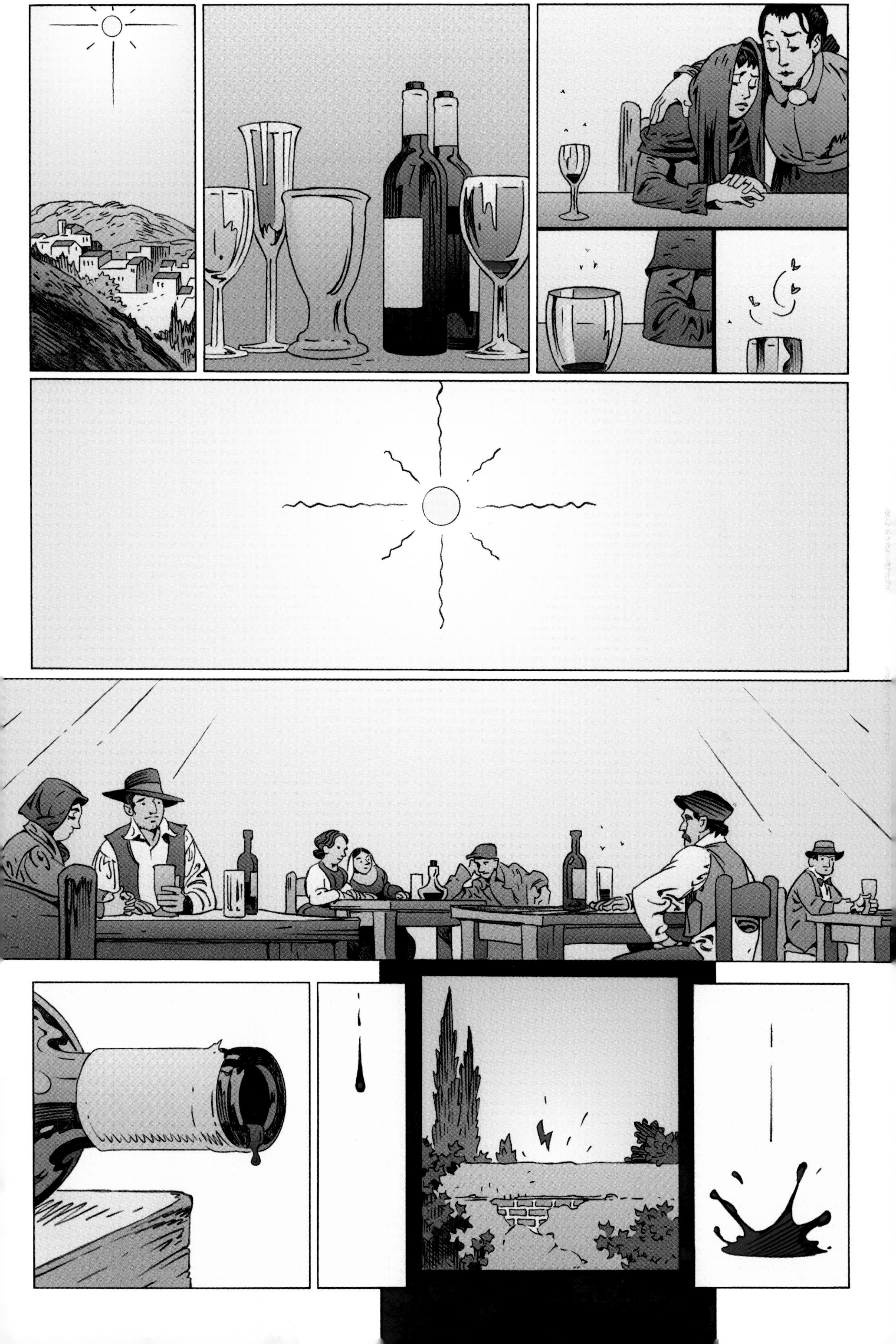

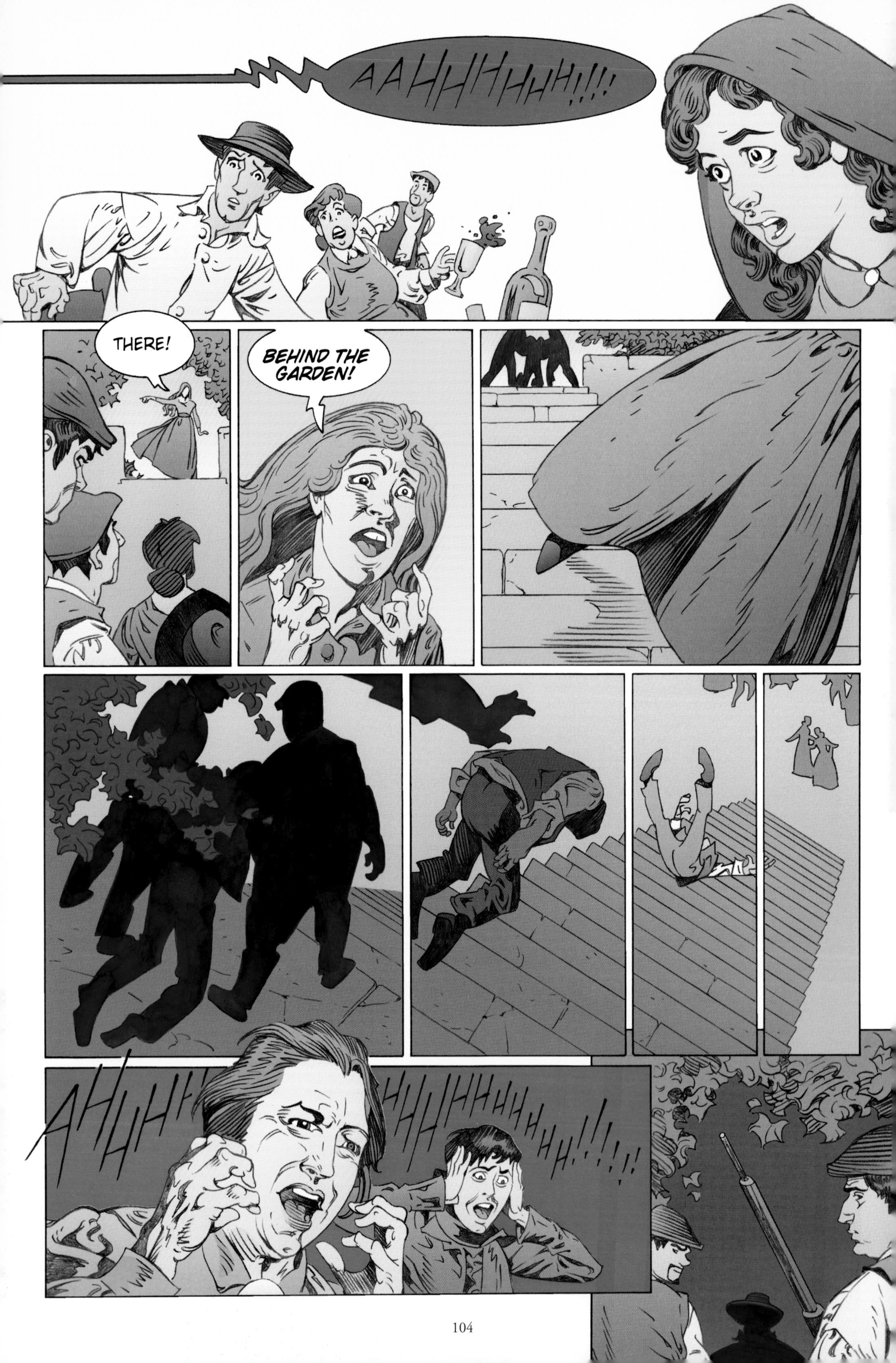
AAHHHHHHH!!!!
THERE!
BEHIND THE GARDEN!
AHHHHHHHHHHHHHHH!!!!!!

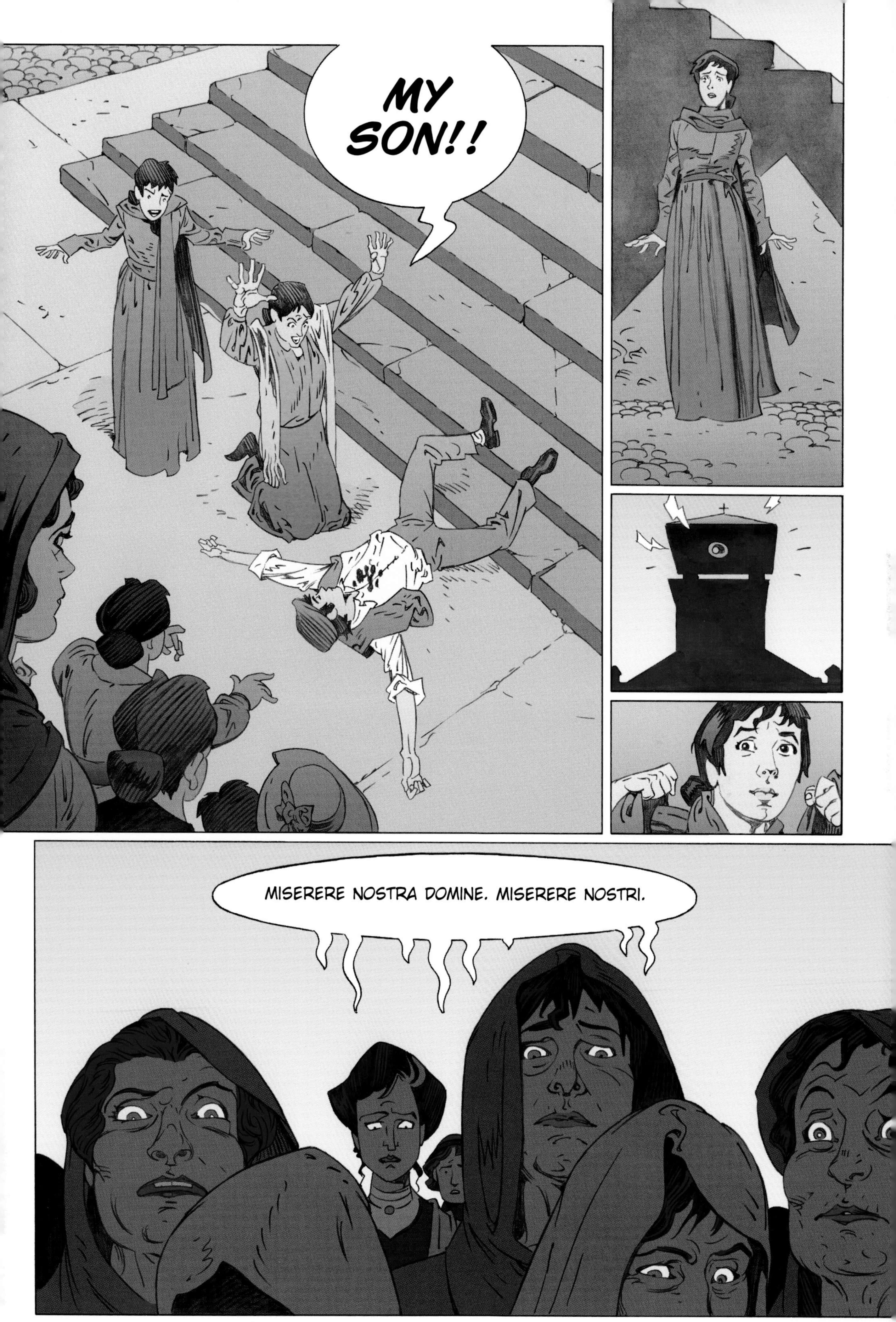
MY SON!!
MISERERE NOSTRA DOMINE. MISERERE NOSTRI.

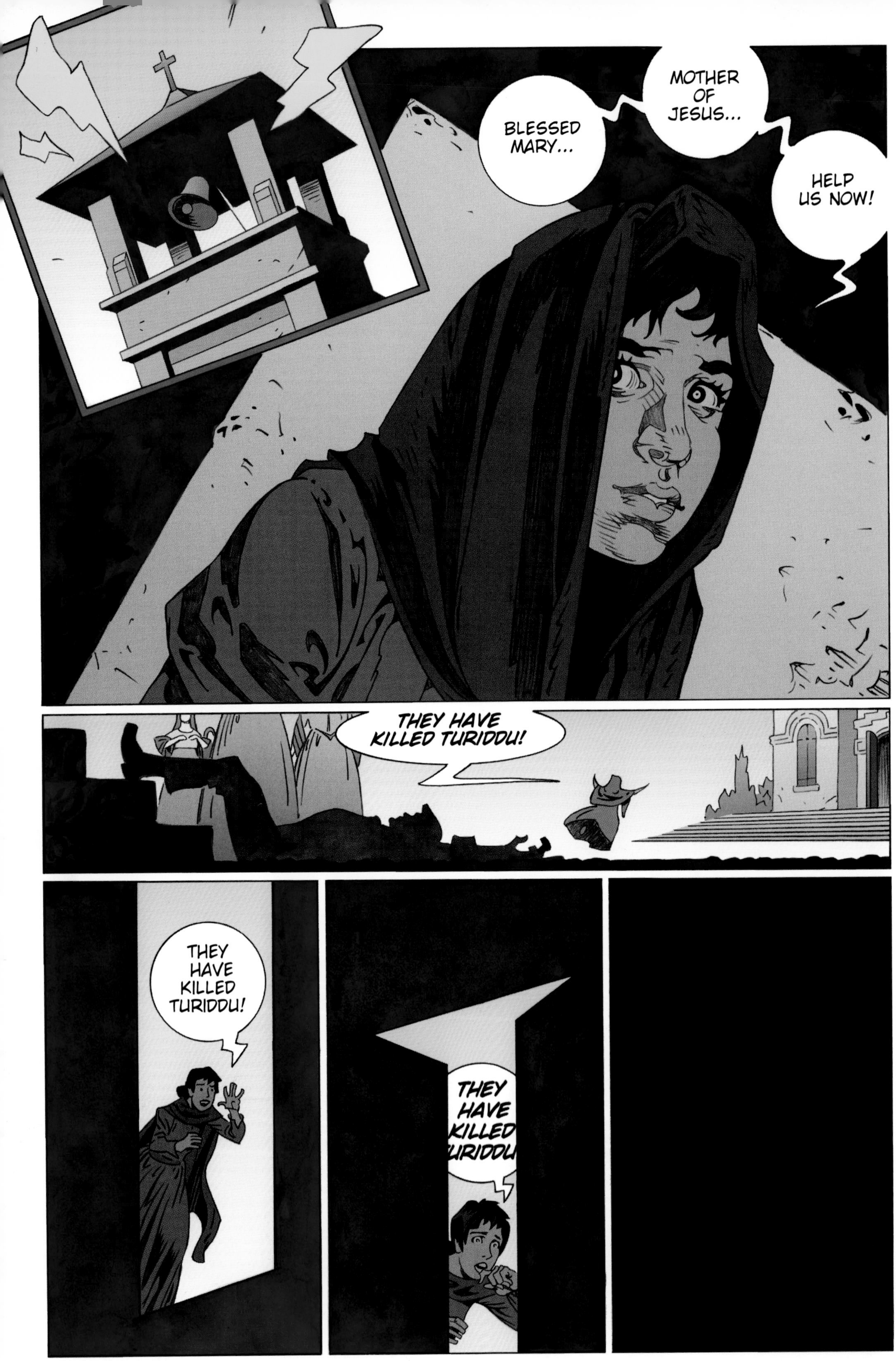
BLESSED MARY...
MOTHER OF JESUS...
HELP US NOW!
THEY HAVE KILLED TURIDDU!
THEY HAVE KILLED TURIDDU!
THEY HAVE KILLED TURIDDU

SALOME

INTRODUCTION

Oscar Wilde's play *Salomé* and Richard Strauss's operatic adaptation have long had a reputation of 'shocking depravity'. In its early years the opera was banned on numerous occasions. Frau Wittich, the dramatic soprano, who was the first Salomé, protested in rehearsal, 'I won't do it. I'm a decent woman.' The character of Salomé is, in fact, one of the great moral figures in all opera. Even John the Baptist (as conceived by Wilde) in his blind rigidity, his total lack of compassion, pales in contrast to the sixteen-year-old oriental princess. Raised in the most decadent of worlds, the virgin princess has retained her purity for sixteen years. She worships the chaste goddess of the moon and has remained untouched by the all-encompassing corruption of Herod's court. Salomé's first awareness of John the Baptist is that of a voice prophesying a great retribution, a cleansing of filth and corruption. It is her first encounter with a firmly held ethical standard. To Salomé, his voice, like the voice of God, is like a light in the wilderness. It is significant that Salomé hears John before she sees him. Her attraction then is not primarily physical, but spiritual (ethical) and, upon his emergence from the cistern, is made whole by physical attraction. Salomé is ready to give her virginity to the highest standard of virtue she has witnessed. Her mind-body integrity is complete.

The play's central conflict arises when Salomé, whose spirtual yearnings are expressed through her physical self, approaches the man to whom only the nonphysical is sacred.

And it is from there that the conflict intensifies in Salomé's mind, leading the story to its tragic conclusion.

P. Craig Russell

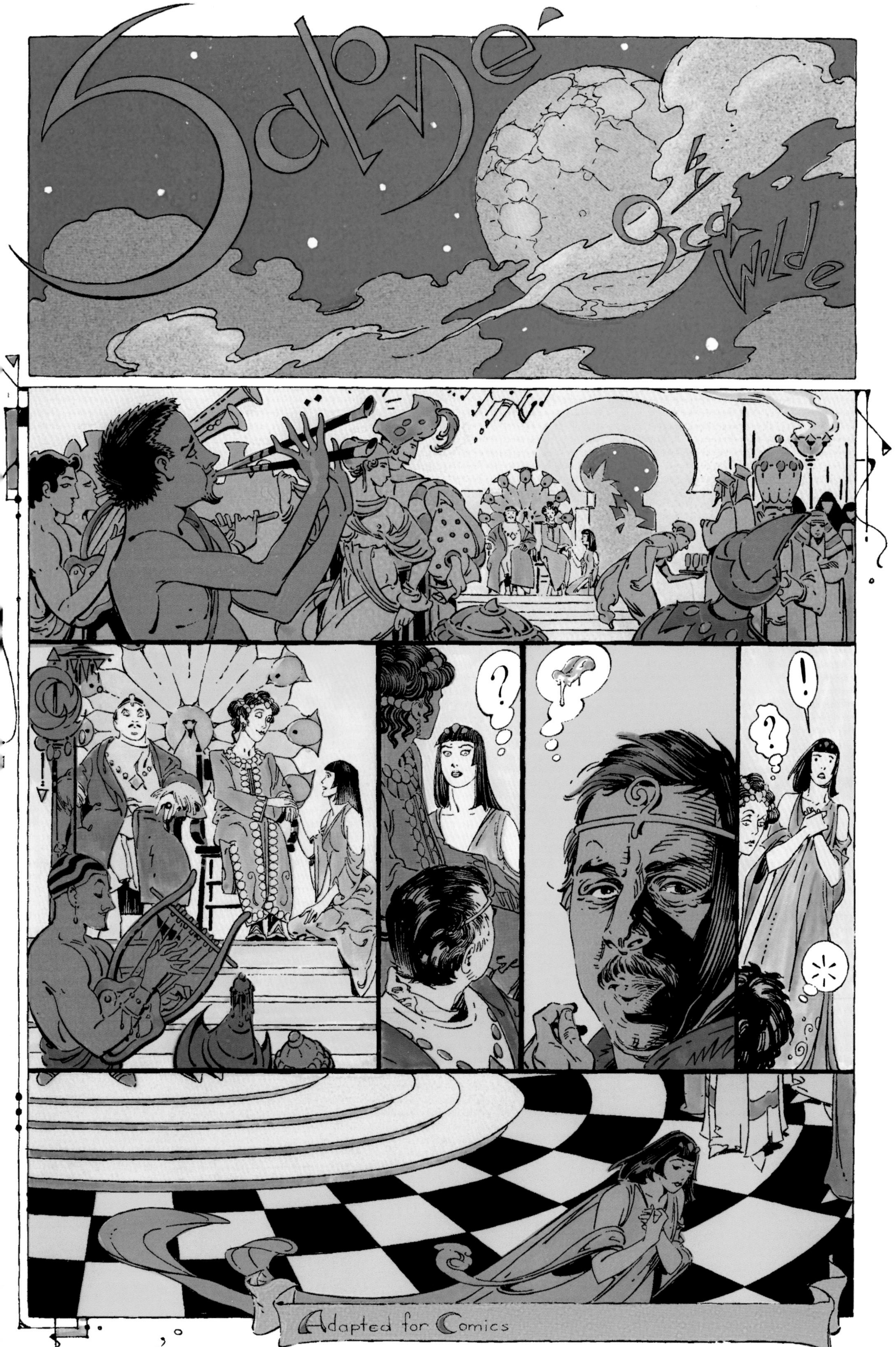
Salomé
by Oscar Wilde
?
!
?
Adapted for Comics

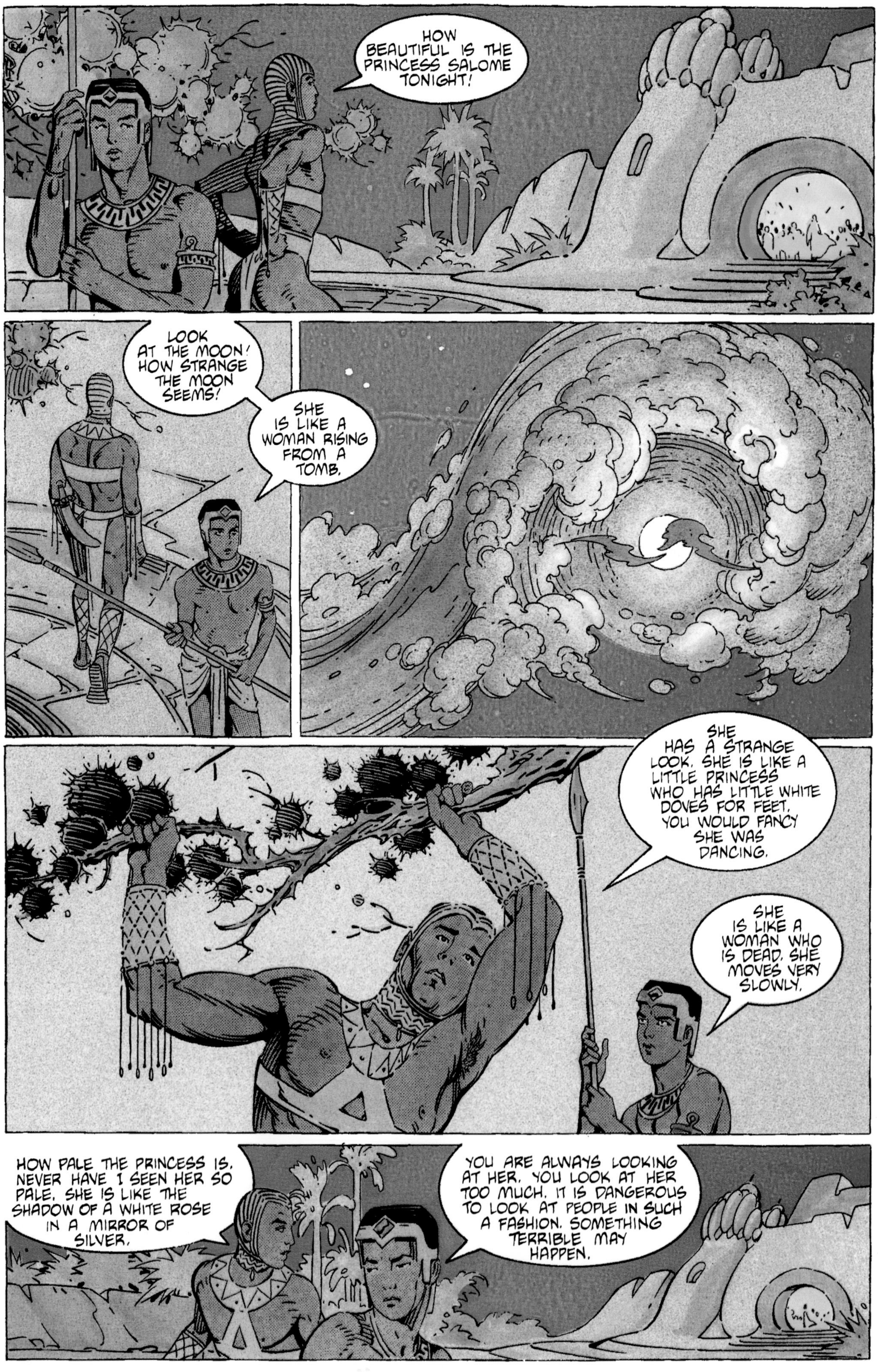
HOW BEAUTIFUL IS THE PRINCESS SALOME TONIGHT!
LOOK AT THE MOON! HOW STRANGE THE MOON SEEMS!
SHE IS LIKE A WOMAN RISING FROM A TOMB.
SHE HAS A STRANGE LOOK. SHE IS LIKE A LITTLE PRINCESS WHO HAS LITTLE WHITE DOVES FOR FEET. YOU WOULD FANCY SHE WAS DANCING.
SHE IS LIKE A WOMAN WHO IS DEAD. SHE MOVES VERY SLOWLY.
HOW PALE THE PRINCESS IS. NEVER HAVE I SEEN HER SO PALE. SHE IS LIKE THE SHADOW OF A WHITE ROSE IN A MIRROR OF SILVER.
YOU ARE ALWAYS LOOKING AT HER. YOU LOOK AT HER TOO MUCH. IT IS DANGEROUS TO LOOK AT PEOPLE IN SUCH A FASHION. SOMETHING TERRIBLE MAY HAPPEN.

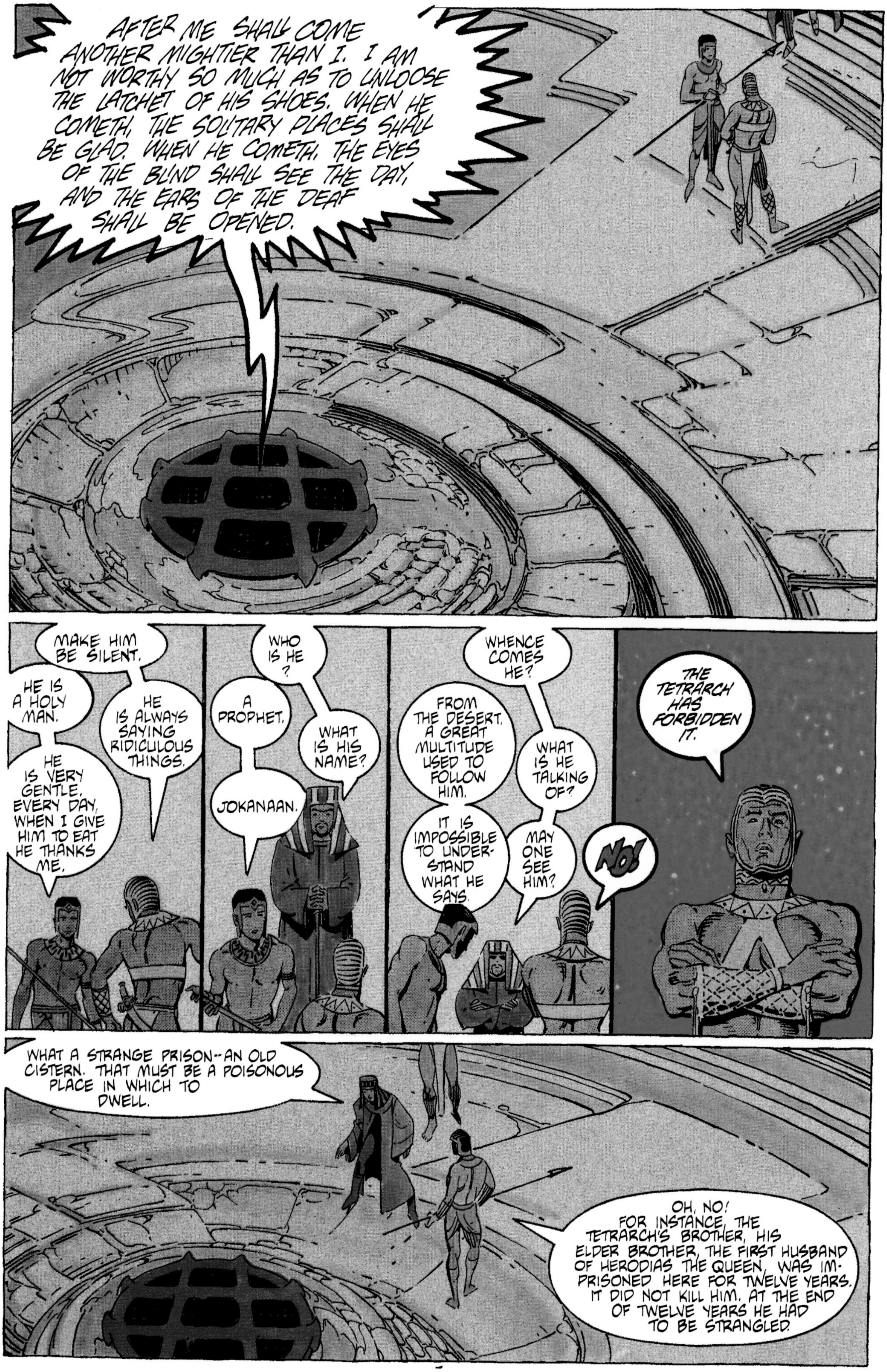
AFTER ME SHALL COME ANOTHER MIGHTIER THAN I. I AM NOT WORTHY SO MUCH AS TO UNLOOSE THE LATCHET OF HIS SHOES. WHEN HE COMETH, THE SOLITARY PLACES SHALL BE GLAD. WHEN HE COMETH, THE EYES OF THE BLIND SHALL SEE THE DAY, AND THE EARS OF THE DEAF SHALL BE OPENED.
MAKE HIM BE SILENT.
HE IS A HOLY MAN.
HE IS ALWAYS SAYING RIDICULOUS THINGS.
HE IS VERY GENTLE. EVERY DAY, WHEN I GIVE HIM TO EAT HE THANKS ME.
WHO IS HE ?
A PROPHET.
WHAT IS HIS NAME?
JOKANAAN.
WHENCE COMES HE?
FROM THE DESERT. A GREAT MULTITUDE USED TO FOLLOW HIM.
WHAT IS HE TALKING OF?
IT IS IMPOSSIBLE TO UNDER-STAND WHAT HE SAYS.
MAY ONE SEE HIM?
NO!
THE TETRARCH HAS FORBIDDEN IT.
WHAT A STRANGE PRISON--AN OLD CISTERN. THAT MUST BE A POISONOUS PLACE IN WHICH TO DWELL.
OH, NO! FOR INSTANCE, THE TETRARCH'S BROTHER, HIS ELDER BROTHER, THE FIRST HUSBAND OF HERODIAS THE QUEEN, WAS IM-PRISONED HERE FOR TWELVE YEARS. IT DID NOT KILL HIM. AT THE END OF TWELVE YEARS HE HAD TO BE STRANGLED.

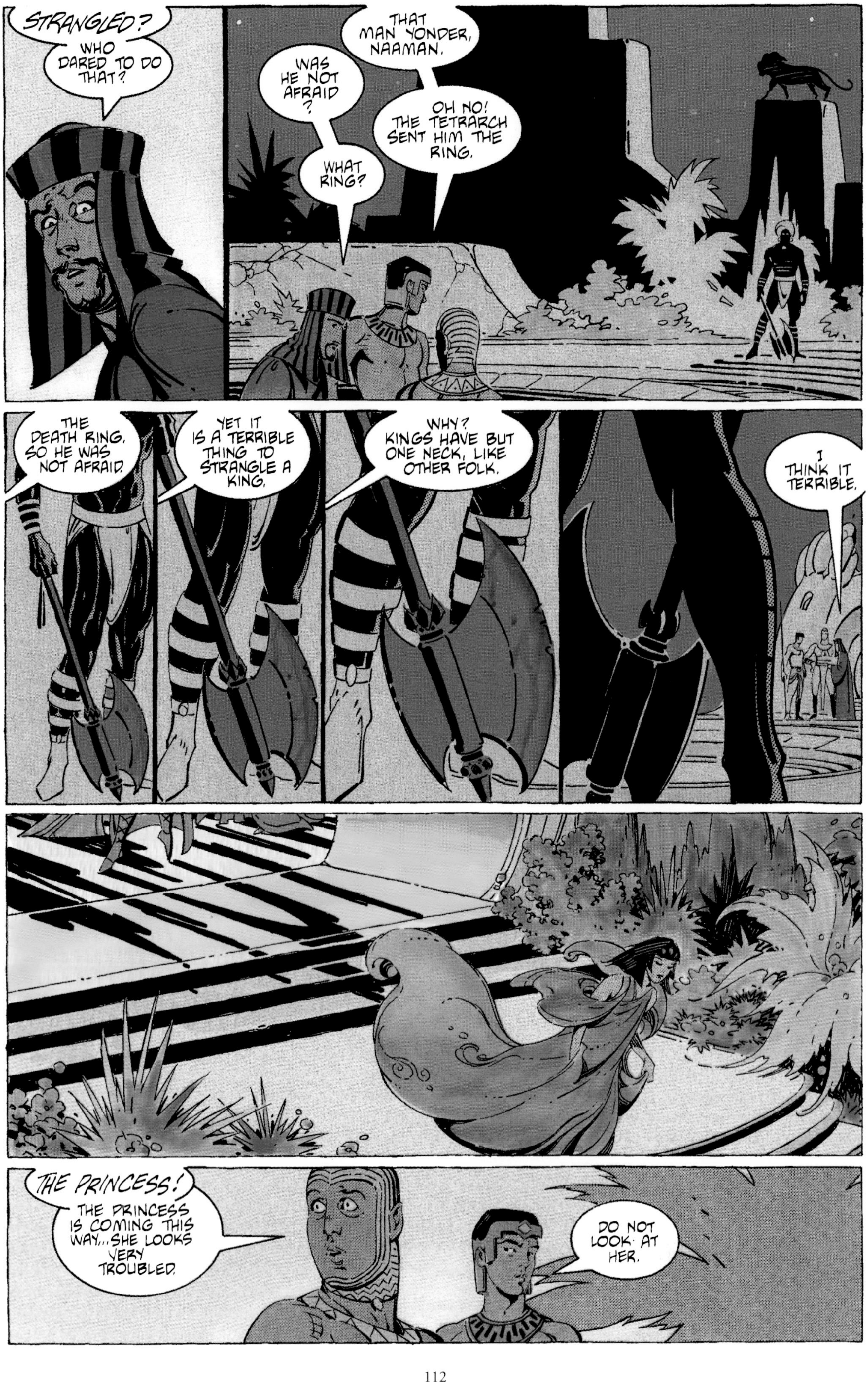
STRANGLED?
WHO DARED TO DO THAT?
WAS HE NOT AFRAID?
THAT MAN YONDER, NAAMAN.
OH NO! THE TETRARCH SENT HIM THE RING.
WHAT RING?
THE DEATH RING. SO HE WAS NOT AFRAID.
YET IT IS A TERRIBLE THING TO STRANGLE A KING.
WHY? KINGS HAVE BUT ONE NECK, LIKE OTHER FOLK.
I THINK IT TERRIBLE.
THE PRINCESS!
THE PRINCESS IS COMING THIS WAY... SHE LOOKS VERY TROUBLED.
DO NOT LOOK AT HER.

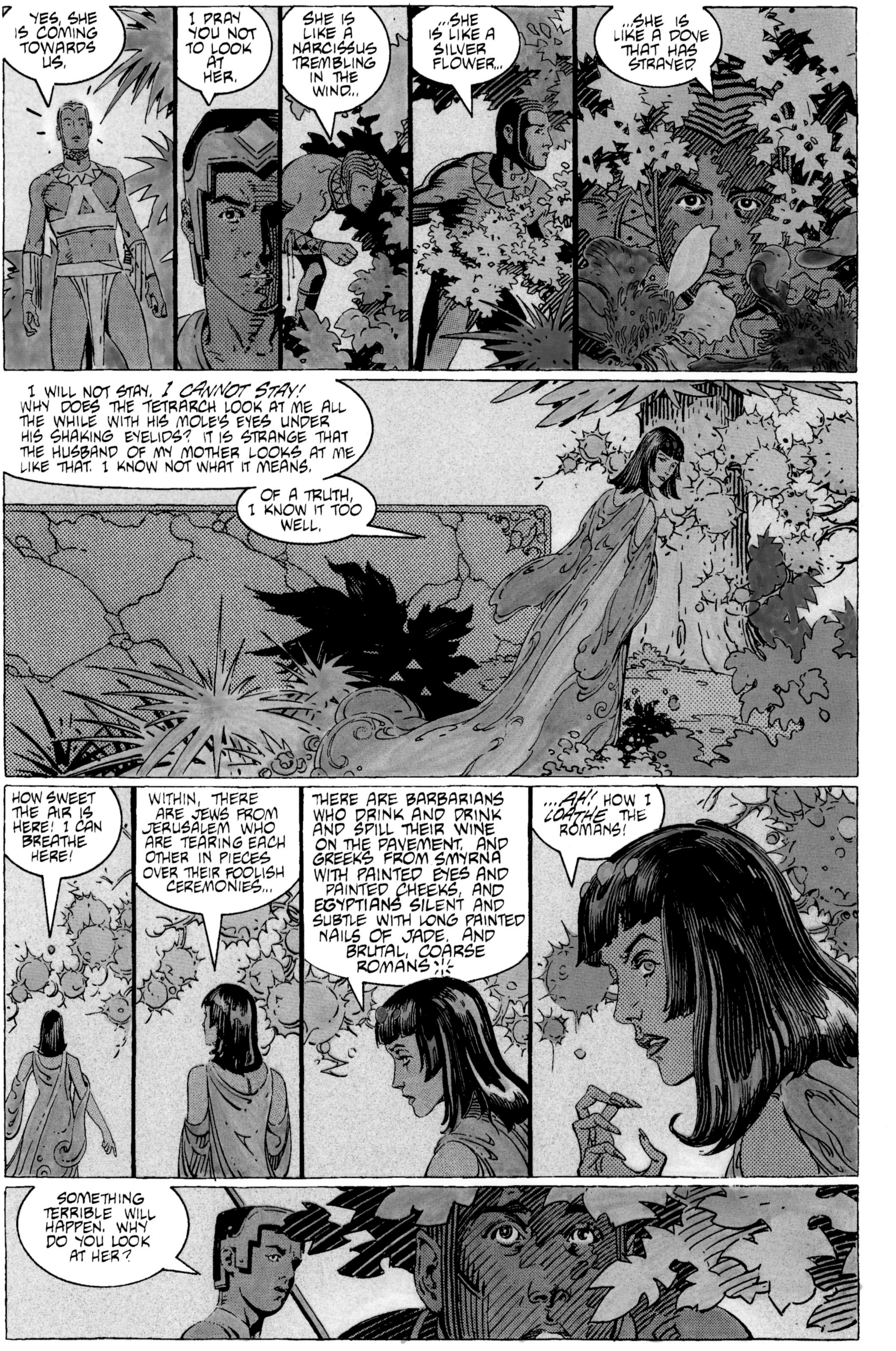
YES, SHE IS COMING TOWARDS US.
I PRAY YOU NOT TO LOOK AT HER.
SHE IS LIKE A NARCISSUS TREMBLING IN THE WIND...
...SHE IS LIKE A SILVER FLOWER...
...SHE IS LIKE A DOVE THAT HAS STRAYED.
I WILL NOT STAY. I CANNOT STAY! WHY DOES THE TETRARCH LOOK AT ME ALL THE WHILE WITH HIS MOLE'S EYES UNDER HIS SHAKING EYELIDS? IT IS STRANGE THAT THE HUSBAND OF MY MOTHER LOOKS AT ME LIKE THAT. I KNOW NOT WHAT IT MEANS.
OF A TRUTH, I KNOW IT TOO WELL.
HOW SWEET THE AIR IS HERE! I CAN BREATHE HERE!
WITHIN, THERE ARE JEWS FROM JERUSALEM WHO ARE TEARING EACH OTHER IN PIECES OVER THEIR FOOLISH CEREMONIES...
THERE ARE BARBARIANS WHO DRINK AND DRINK AND SPILL THEIR WINE ON THE PAVEMENT, AND GREEKS FROM SMYRNA WITH PAINTED EYES AND PAINTED CHEEKS, AND EGYPTIANS SILENT AND SUBTLE WITH LONG PAINTED NAILS OF JADE, AND BRUTAL, COARSE ROMANS...
...AH! HOW I LOATHE THE ROMANS!
SOMETHING TERRIBLE WILL HAPPEN. WHY DO YOU LOOK AT HER?

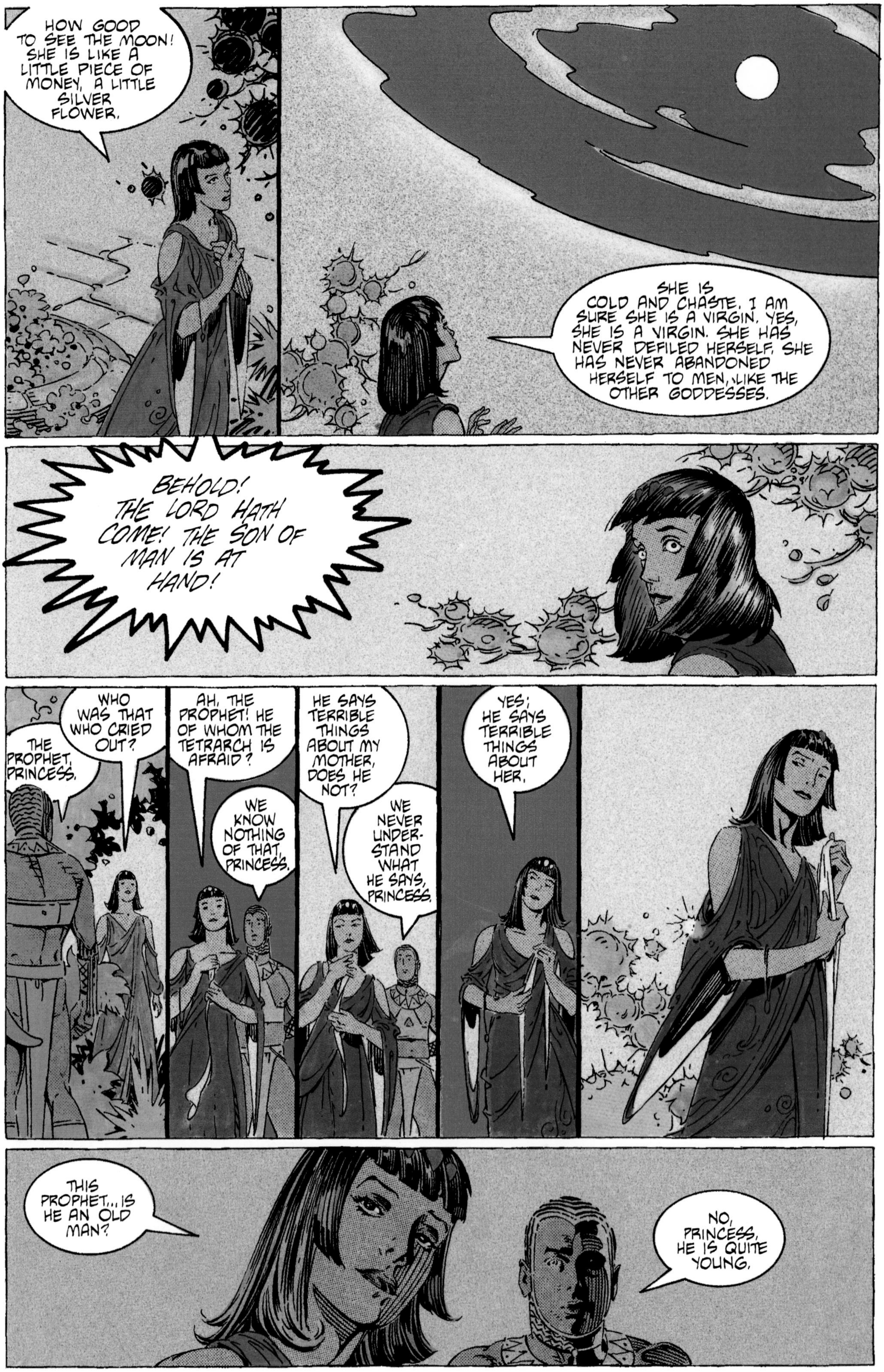
HOW GOOD TO SEE THE MOON! SHE IS LIKE A LITTLE PIECE OF MONEY, A LITTLE SILVER FLOWER.
SHE IS COLD AND CHASTE. I AM SURE SHE IS A VIRGIN. YES, SHE IS A VIRGIN. SHE HAS NEVER DEFILED HERSELF. SHE HAS NEVER ABANDONED HERSELF TO MEN, LIKE THE OTHER GODDESSES.
BEHOLD! THE LORD HATH COME! THE SON OF MAN IS AT HAND!
WHO WAS THAT WHO CRIED OUT?
THE PROPHET, PRINCESS.
AH, THE PROPHET! HE OF WHOM THE TETRARCH IS AFRAID?
WE KNOW NOTHING OF THAT, PRINCESS.
HE SAYS TERRIBLE THINGS ABOUT MY MOTHER, DOES HE NOT?
WE NEVER UNDER-STAND WHAT HE SAYS, PRINCESS.
YES; HE SAYS TERRIBLE THINGS ABOUT HER.
THIS PROPHET... IS HE AN OLD MAN?
NO, PRINCESS, HE IS QUITE YOUNG.

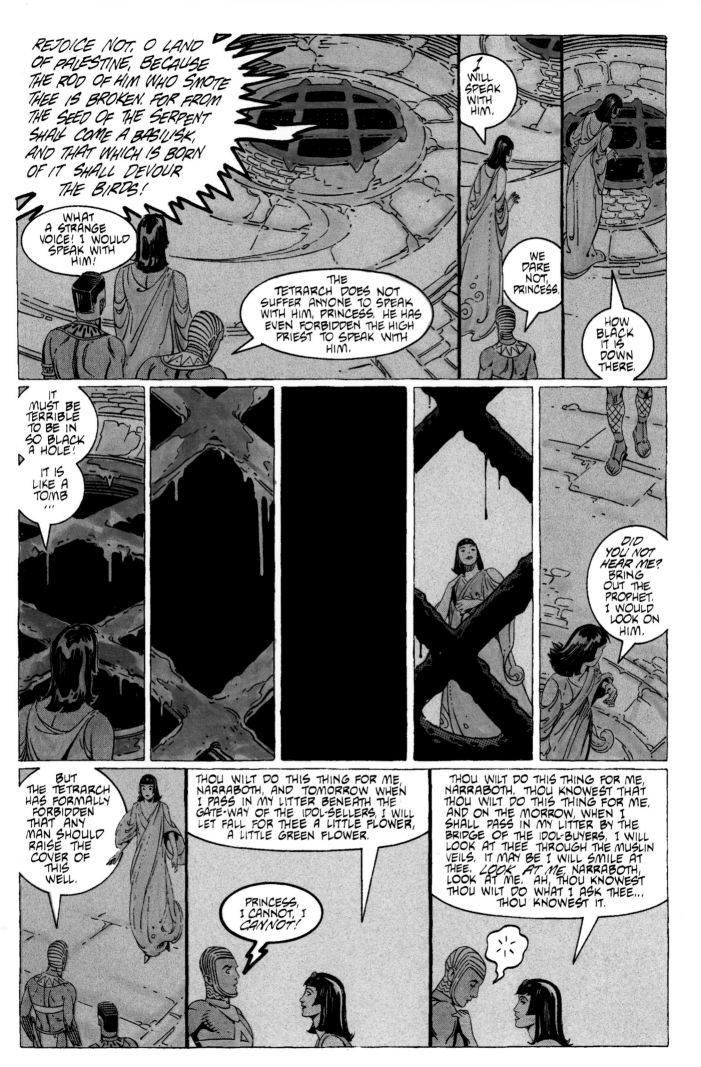

REJOICE NOT, O LAND OF PALESTINE, BECAUSE THE ROD OF HIM WHO SMOTE THEE IS BROKEN. FOR FROM THE SEED OF THE SERPENT SHALL COME A BASILISK, AND THAT WHICH IS BORN OF IT SHALL DEVOUR THE BIRDS!

WHAT A STRANGE VOICE! I WOULD SPEAK WITH HIM!

THE TETRARCH DOES NOT SUFFER ANYONE TO SPEAK WITH HIM, PRINCESS. HE HAS EVEN FORBIDDEN THE HIGH PRIEST TO SPEAK WITH HIM.

I WILL SPEAK WITH HIM.

WE DARE NOT, PRINCESS.

HOW BLACK IT IS DOWN THERE.

IT MUST BE TERRIBLE TO BE IN SO BLACK A HOLE!

IT IS LIKE A TOMB...

DID YOU NOT HEAR ME? BRING OUT THE PROPHET. I WOULD LOOK ON HIM.

BUT THE TETRARCH HAS FORMALLY FORBIDDEN THAT ANY MAN SHOULD RAISE THE COVER OF THIS WELL.

THOU WILT DO THIS THING FOR ME, NARRABOTH, AND TOMORROW WHEN I PASS IN MY LITTER BENEATH THE GATE-WAY OF THE IDOL-SELLERS, I WILL LET FALL FOR THEE A LITTLE FLOWER, A LITTLE GREEN FLOWER.

PRINCESS, I CANNOT, I CANNOT!

THOU WILT DO THIS THING FOR ME, NARRABOTH. THOU KNOWEST THAT THOU WILT DO THIS THING FOR ME, AND ON THE MORROW, WHEN I SHALL PASS IN MY LITTER BY THE BRIDGE OF THE IDOL-BUYERS, I WILL LOOK AT THEE THROUGH THE MUSLIN VEILS. IT MAY BE I WILL SMILE AT THEE. LOOK AT ME, NARRABOTH, LOOK AT ME. AH, THOU KNOWEST THOU WILT DO WHAT I ASK THEE... THOU KNOWEST IT.

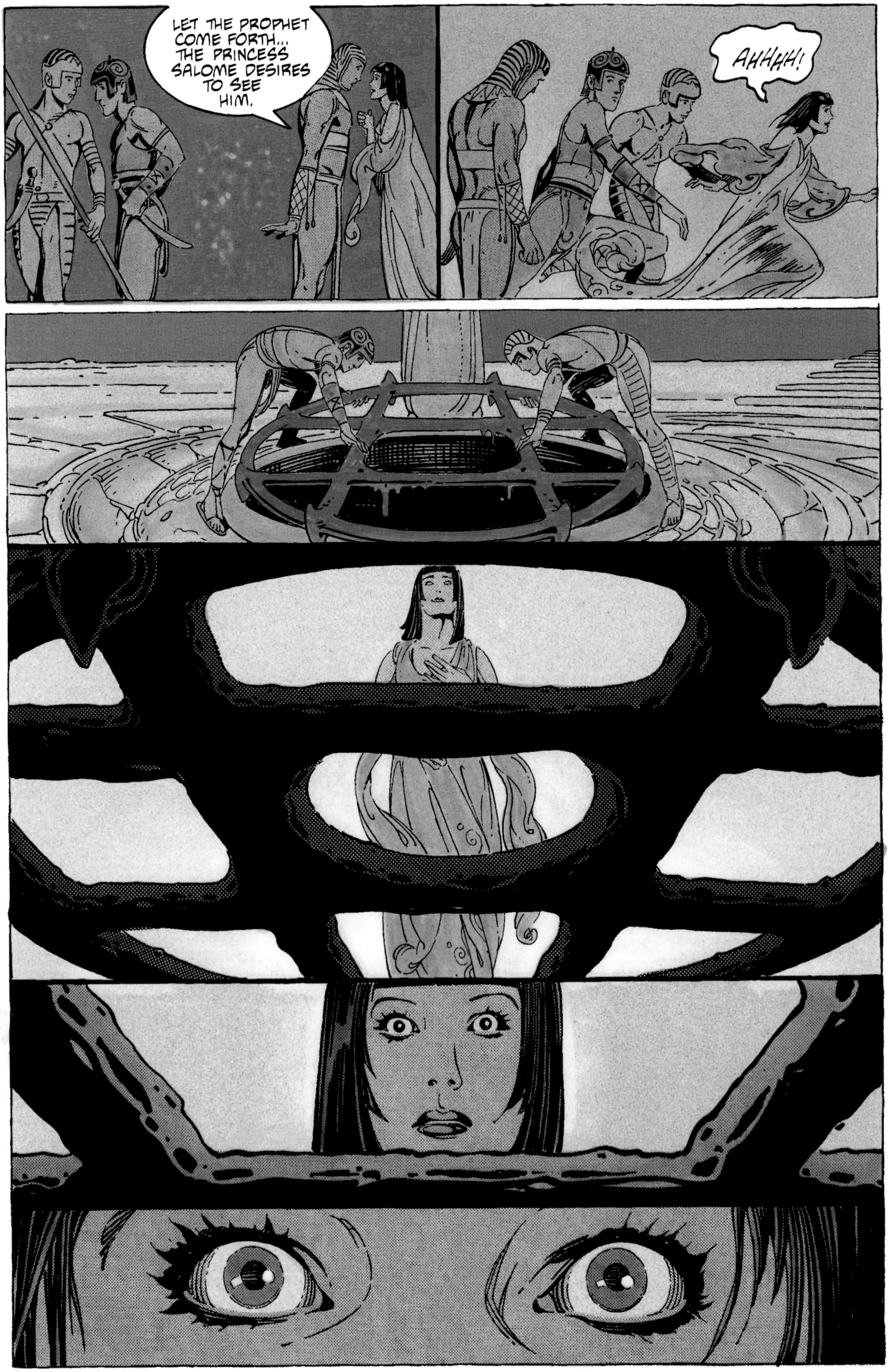
LET THE PROPHET COME FORTH... THE PRINCESS SALOME DESIRES TO SEE HIM.
AHHHH!

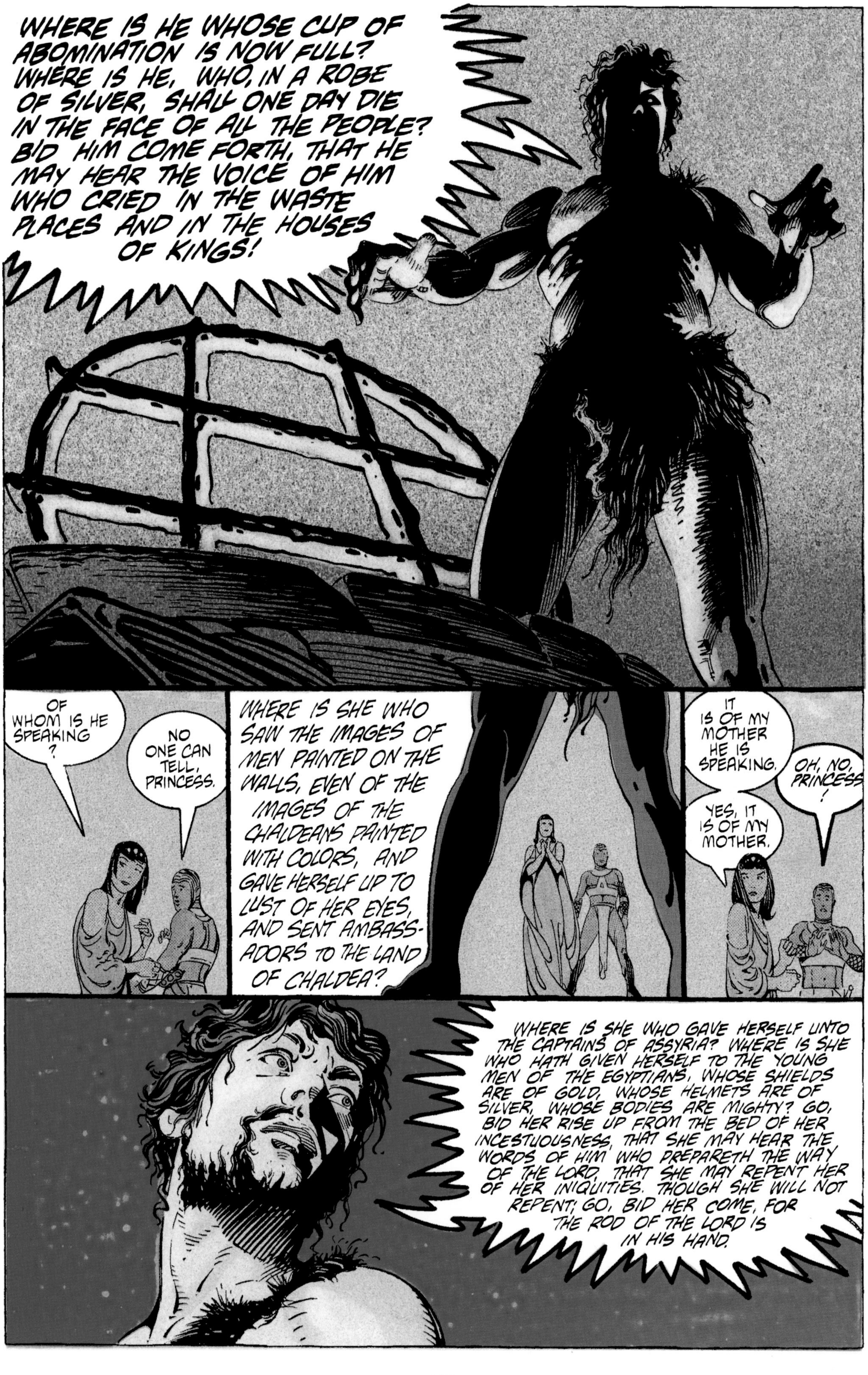
WHERE IS HE WHOSE CUP OF ABOMINATION IS NOW FULL? WHERE IS HE, WHO, IN A ROBE OF SILVER, SHALL ONE DAY DIE IN THE FACE OF ALL THE PEOPLE? BID HIM COME FORTH, THAT HE MAY HEAR THE VOICE OF HIM WHO CRIED IN THE WASTE PLACES AND IN THE HOUSES OF KINGS!
OF WHOM IS HE SPEAKING?
NO ONE CAN TELL, PRINCESS.
WHERE IS SHE WHO SAW THE IMAGES OF MEN PAINTED ON THE WALLS, EVEN OF THE IMAGES OF THE CHALDEANS PAINTED WITH COLORS, AND GAVE HERSELF UP TO LUST OF HER EYES, AND SENT AMBASSADORS TO THE LAND OF CHALDEA?
IT IS OF MY MOTHER HE IS SPEAKING.
OH, NO, PRINCESS!
YES, IT IS OF MY MOTHER.
WHERE IS SHE WHO GAVE HERSELF UNTO THE CAPTAINS OF ASSYRIA? WHERE IS SHE WHO HATH GIVEN HERSELF TO THE YOUNG MEN OF THE EGYPTIANS, WHOSE SHIELDS ARE OF GOLD, WHOSE HELMETS ARE OF SILVER, WHOSE BODIES ARE MIGHTY? GO, BID HER RISE UP FROM THE BED OF HER INCESTUOUSNESS, THAT SHE MAY HEAR THE WORDS OF HIM WHO PREPARETH THE WAY OF THE LORD, THAT SHE MAY REPENT HER OF HER INIQUITIES. THOUGH SHE WILL NOT REPENT; GO, BID HER COME, FOR THE ROD OF THE LORD IS IN HIS HAND.

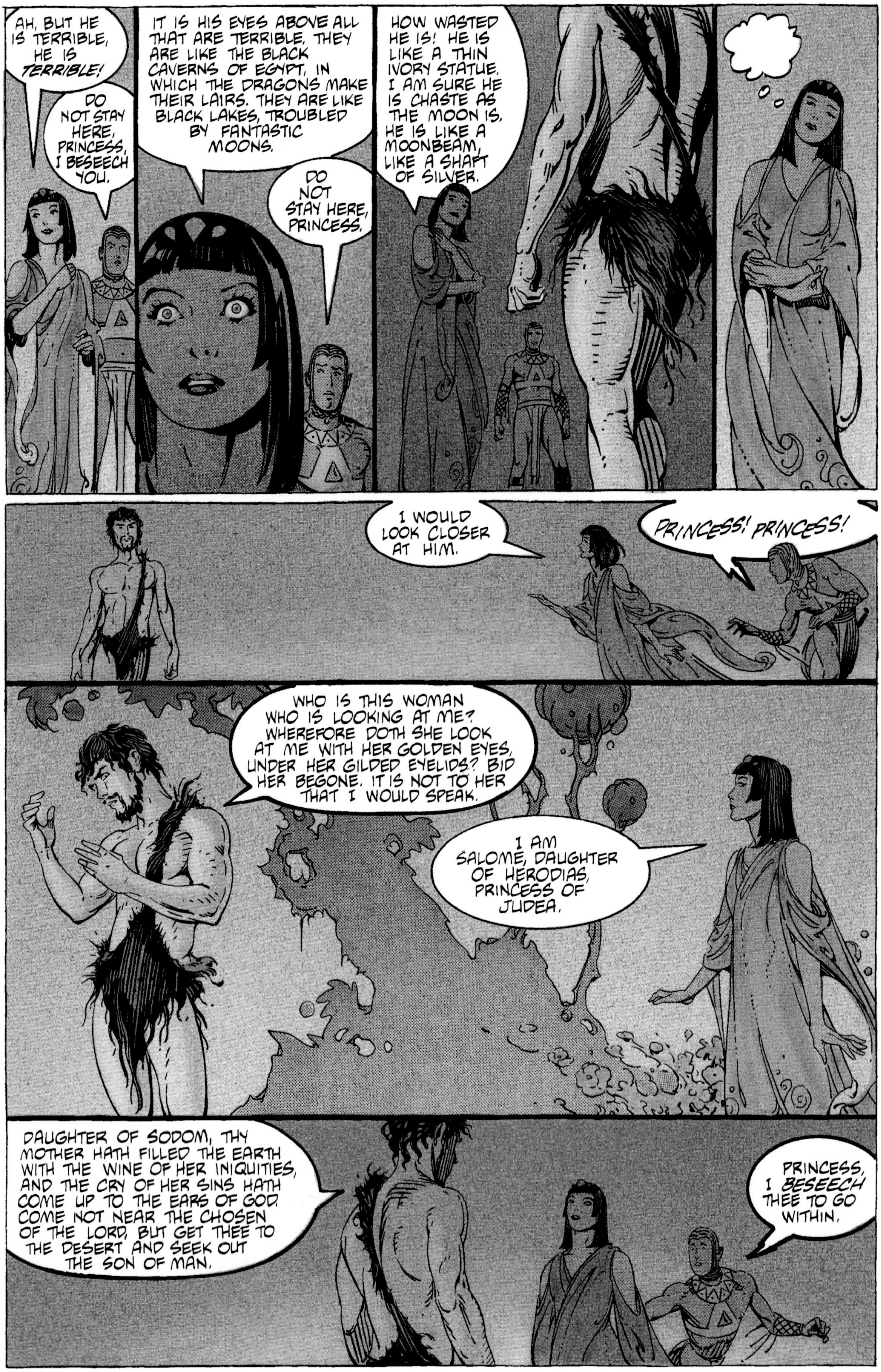
AH, BUT HE IS TERRIBLE, HE IS *TERRIBLE!*
DO NOT STAY HERE, PRINCESS, I BESEECH YOU.
IT IS HIS EYES ABOVE ALL THAT ARE TERRIBLE. THEY ARE LIKE THE BLACK CAVERNS OF EGYPT, IN WHICH THE DRAGONS MAKE THEIR LAIRS. THEY ARE LIKE BLACK LAKES, TROUBLED BY FANTASTIC MOONS.
DO NOT STAY HERE, PRINCESS.
HOW WASTED HE IS! HE IS LIKE A THIN IVORY STATUE. I AM SURE HE IS CHASTE AS THE MOON IS. HE IS LIKE A MOONBEAM, LIKE A SHAFT OF SILVER.
I WOULD LOOK CLOSER AT HIM.
PRINCESS! PRINCESS!
WHO IS THIS WOMAN WHO IS LOOKING AT ME? WHEREFORE DOTH SHE LOOK AT ME WITH HER GOLDEN EYES, UNDER HER GILDED EYELIDS? BID HER BEGONE. IT IS NOT TO HER THAT I WOULD SPEAK.
I AM SALOME, DAUGHTER OF HERODIAS, PRINCESS OF JUDEA.
DAUGHTER OF SODOM, THY MOTHER HATH FILLED THE EARTH WITH THE WINE OF HER INIQUITIES, AND THE CRY OF HER SINS HATH COME UP TO THE EARS OF GOD. COME NOT NEAR THE CHOSEN OF THE LORD, BUT GET THEE TO THE DESERT AND SEEK OUT THE SON OF MAN.
PRINCESS, I *BESEECH* THEE TO GO WITHIN.

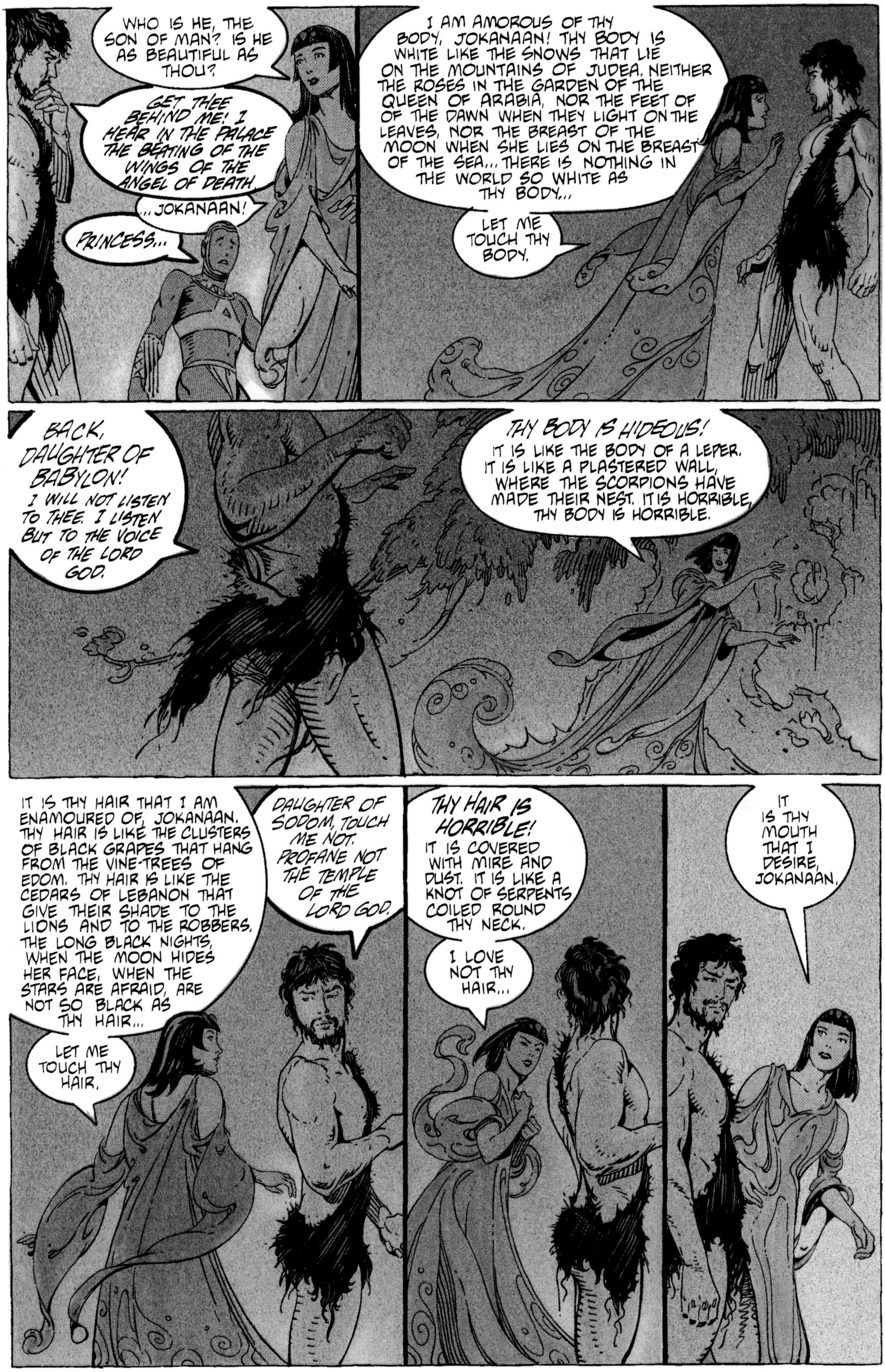
WHO IS HE, THE SON OF MAN? IS HE AS BEAUTIFUL AS THOU?
GET THEE BEHIND ME! I HEAR IN THE PALACE THE BEATING OF THE WINGS OF THE ANGEL OF DEATH.
...JOKANAAN!
PRINCESS...
I AM AMOROUS OF THY BODY, JOKANAAN! THY BODY IS WHITE LIKE THE SNOWS THAT LIE ON THE MOUNTAINS OF JUDEA. NEITHER THE ROSES IN THE GARDEN OF THE QUEEN OF ARABIA, NOR THE FEET OF OF THE DAWN WHEN THEY LIGHT ON THE LEAVES, NOR THE BREAST OF THE MOON WHEN SHE LIES ON THE BREAST OF THE SEA... THERE IS NOTHING IN THE WORLD SO WHITE AS THY BODY...
LET ME TOUCH THY BODY.
BACK, DAUGHTER OF BABYLON! I WILL NOT LISTEN TO THEE. I LISTEN BUT TO THE VOICE OF THE LORD GOD.
THY BODY IS HIDEOUS! IT IS LIKE THE BODY OF A LEPER. IT IS LIKE A PLASTERED WALL, WHERE THE SCORPIONS HAVE MADE THEIR NEST. IT IS HORRIBLE, THY BODY IS HORRIBLE.
IT IS THY HAIR THAT I AM ENAMOURED OF, JOKANAAN. THY HAIR IS LIKE THE CLUSTERS OF BLACK GRAPES THAT HANG FROM THE VINE-TREES OF EDOM. THY HAIR IS LIKE THE CEDARS OF LEBANON THAT GIVE THEIR SHADE TO THE LIONS AND TO THE ROBBERS. THE LONG BLACK NIGHTS, WHEN THE MOON HIDES HER FACE, WHEN THE STARS ARE AFRAID, ARE NOT SO BLACK AS THY HAIR...
LET ME TOUCH THY HAIR.
DAUGHTER OF SODOM, TOUCH ME NOT. PROFANE NOT THE TEMPLE OF THE LORD GOD.
THY HAIR IS HORRIBLE! IT IS COVERED WITH MIRE AND DUST. IT IS LIKE A KNOT OF SERPENTS COILED ROUND THY NECK.
I LOVE NOT THY HAIR...
IT IS THY MOUTH THAT I DESIRE, JOKANAAN.

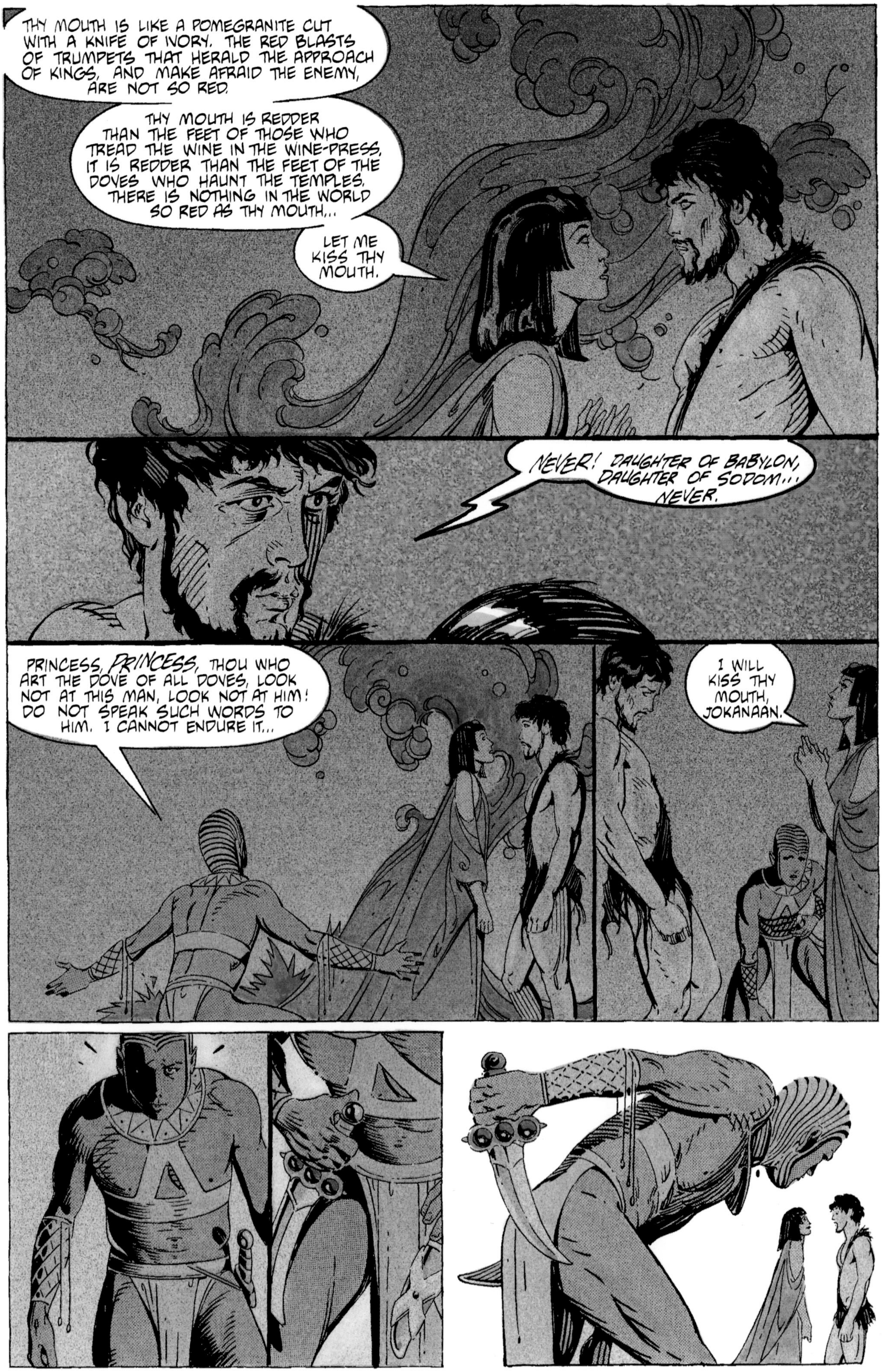
THY MOUTH IS LIKE A POMEGRANITE CUT WITH A KNIFE OF IVORY. THE RED BLASTS OF TRUMPETS THAT HERALD THE APPROACH OF KINGS, AND MAKE AFRAID THE ENEMY, ARE NOT SO RED.
THY MOUTH IS REDDER THAN THE FEET OF THOSE WHO TREAD THE WINE IN THE WINE-PRESS, IT IS REDDER THAN THE FEET OF THE DOVES WHO HAUNT THE TEMPLES. THERE IS NOTHING IN THE WORLD SO RED AS THY MOUTH,..
LET ME KISS THY MOUTH.
NEVER! DAUGHTER OF BABYLON, DAUGHTER OF SODOM... NEVER.
PRINCESS, PRINCESS, THOU WHO ART THE DOVE OF ALL DOVES, LOOK NOT AT THIS MAN, LOOK NOT AT HIM! DO NOT SPEAK SUCH WORDS TO HIM. I CANNOT ENDURE IT...
I WILL KISS THY MOUTH, JOKANAAN.

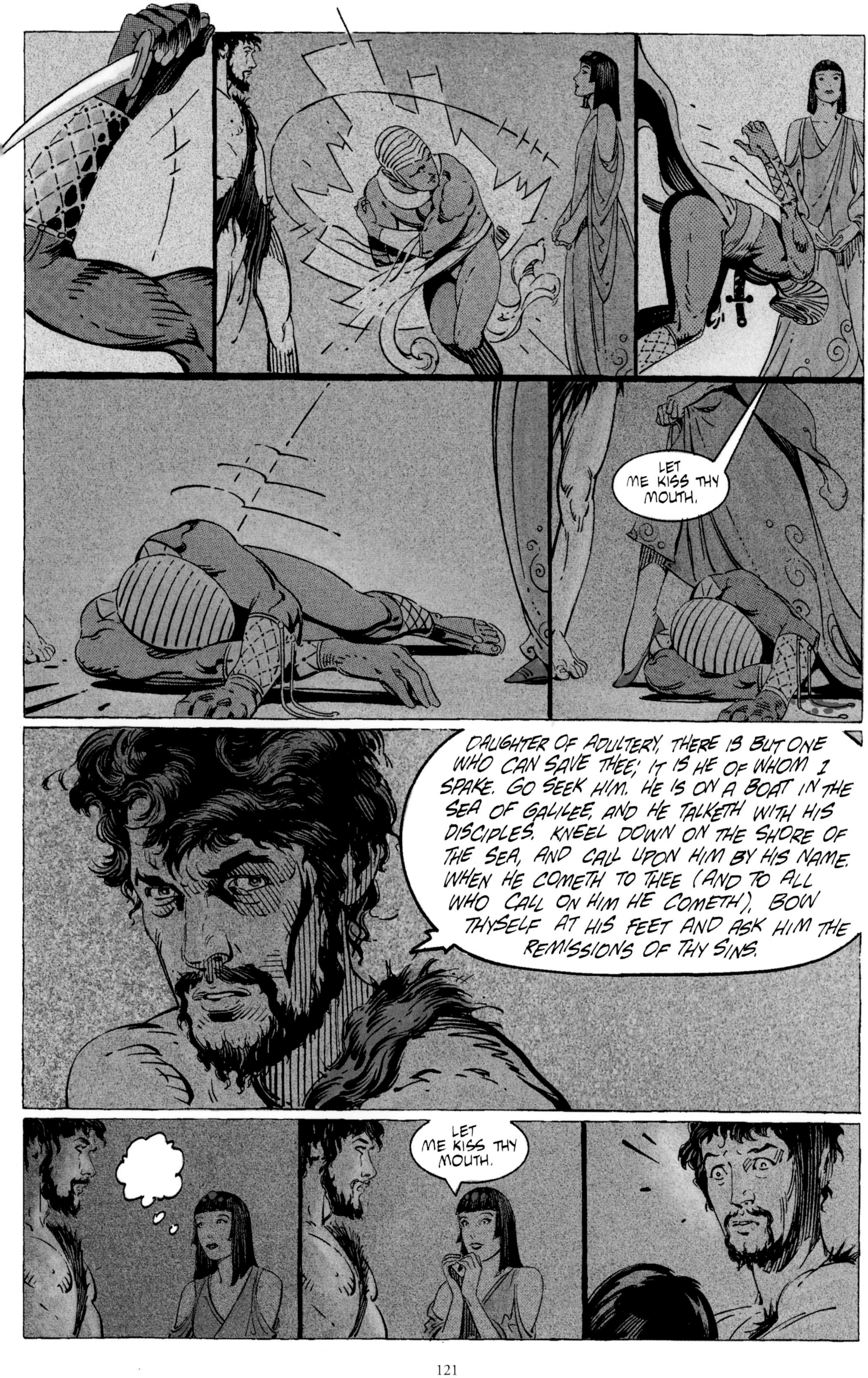
LET ME KISS THY MOUTH.
DAUGHTER OF ADULTERY, THERE IS BUT ONE WHO CAN SAVE THEE; IT IS HE OF WHOM I SPAKE. GO SEEK HIM. HE IS ON A BOAT IN THE SEA OF GALILEE, AND HE TALKETH WITH HIS DISCIPLES. KNEEL DOWN ON THE SHORE OF THE SEA, AND CALL UPON HIM BY HIS NAME. WHEN HE COMETH TO THEE (AND TO ALL WHO CALL ON HIM HE COMETH), BOW THYSELF AT HIS FEET AND ASK HIM THE REMISSIONS OF THY SINS.
LET ME KISS THY MOUTH.

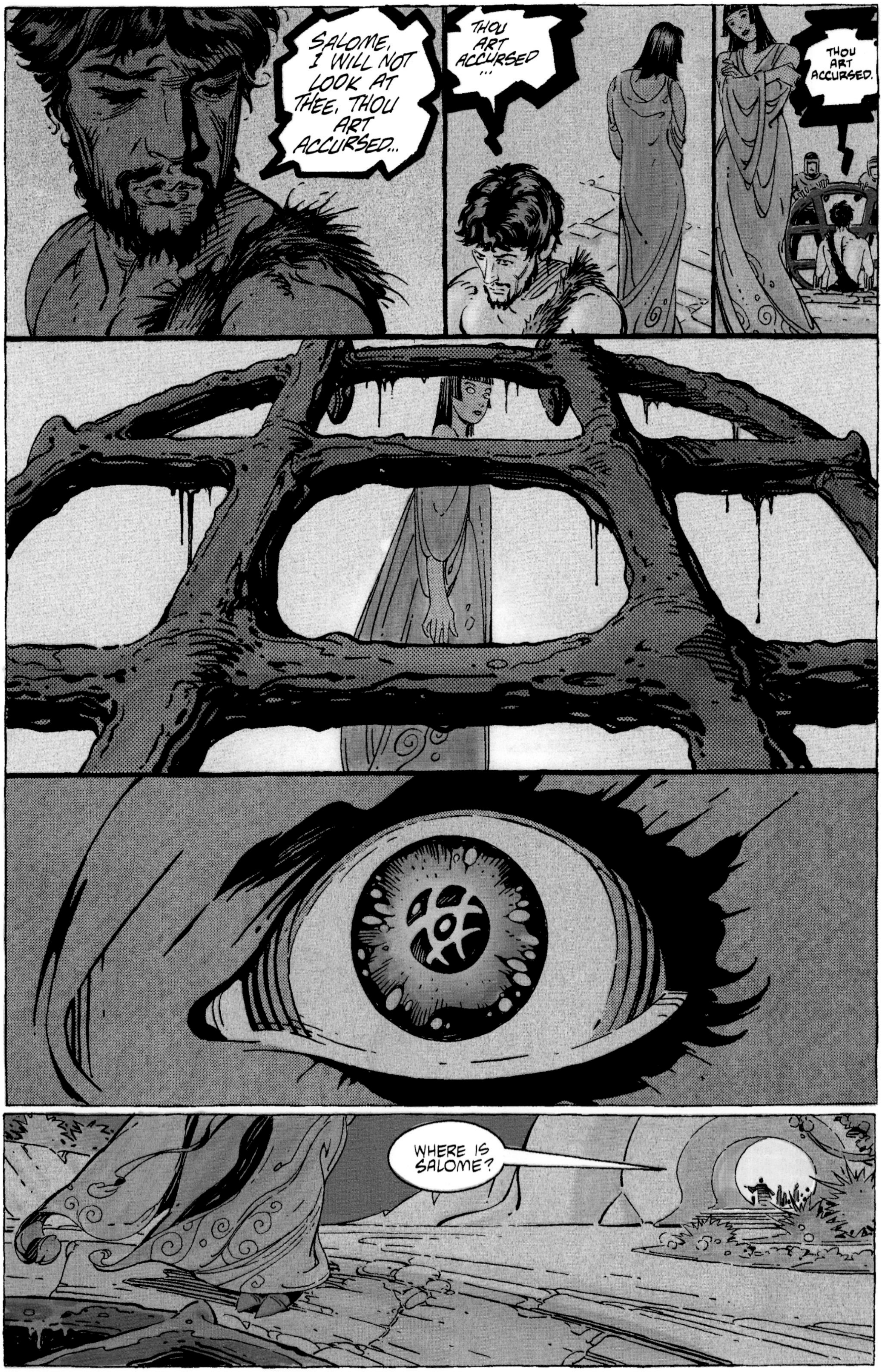
SALOME, I WILL NOT LOOK AT THEE, THOU ART ACCURSED...
THOU ART ACCURSED ...
THOU ART ACCURSED.
WHERE IS SALOME?

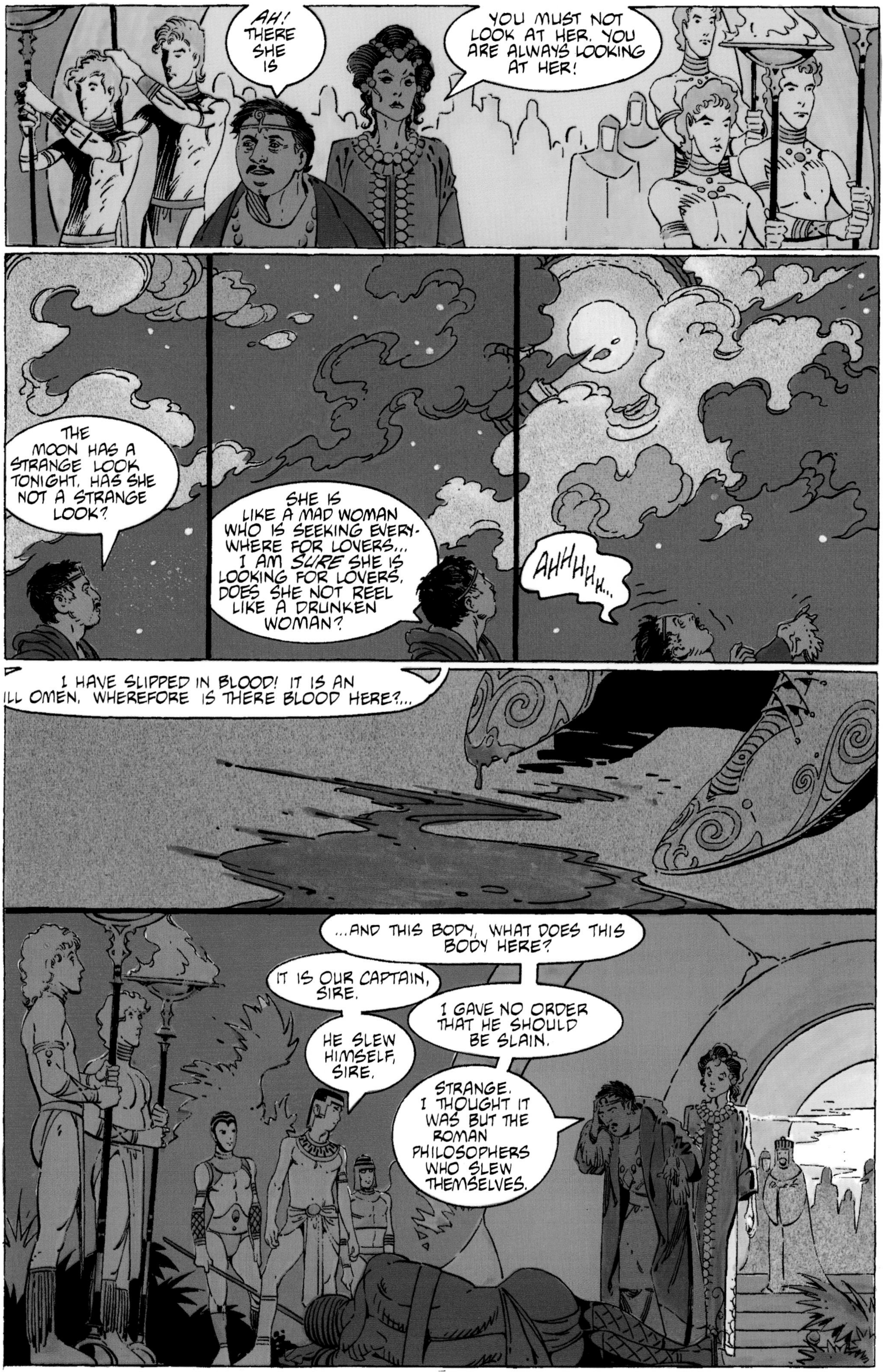
AH! THERE SHE IS
YOU MUST NOT LOOK AT HER. YOU ARE ALWAYS LOOKING AT HER!
THE MOON HAS A STRANGE LOOK TONIGHT. HAS SHE NOT A STRANGE LOOK?
SHE IS LIKE A MAD WOMAN WHO IS SEEKING EVERYWHERE FOR LOVERS... I AM SURE SHE IS LOOKING FOR LOVERS. DOES SHE NOT REEL LIKE A DRUNKEN WOMAN?
AHHHHH...
I HAVE SLIPPED IN BLOOD! IT IS AN ILL OMEN. WHEREFORE IS THERE BLOOD HERE?...
...AND THIS BODY, WHAT DOES THIS BODY HERE?
IT IS OUR CAPTAIN, SIRE.
I GAVE NO ORDER THAT HE SHOULD BE SLAIN.
HE SLEW HIMSELF, SIRE.
STRANGE. I THOUGHT IT WAS BUT THE ROMAN PHILOSOPHERS WHO SLEW THEMSELVES.

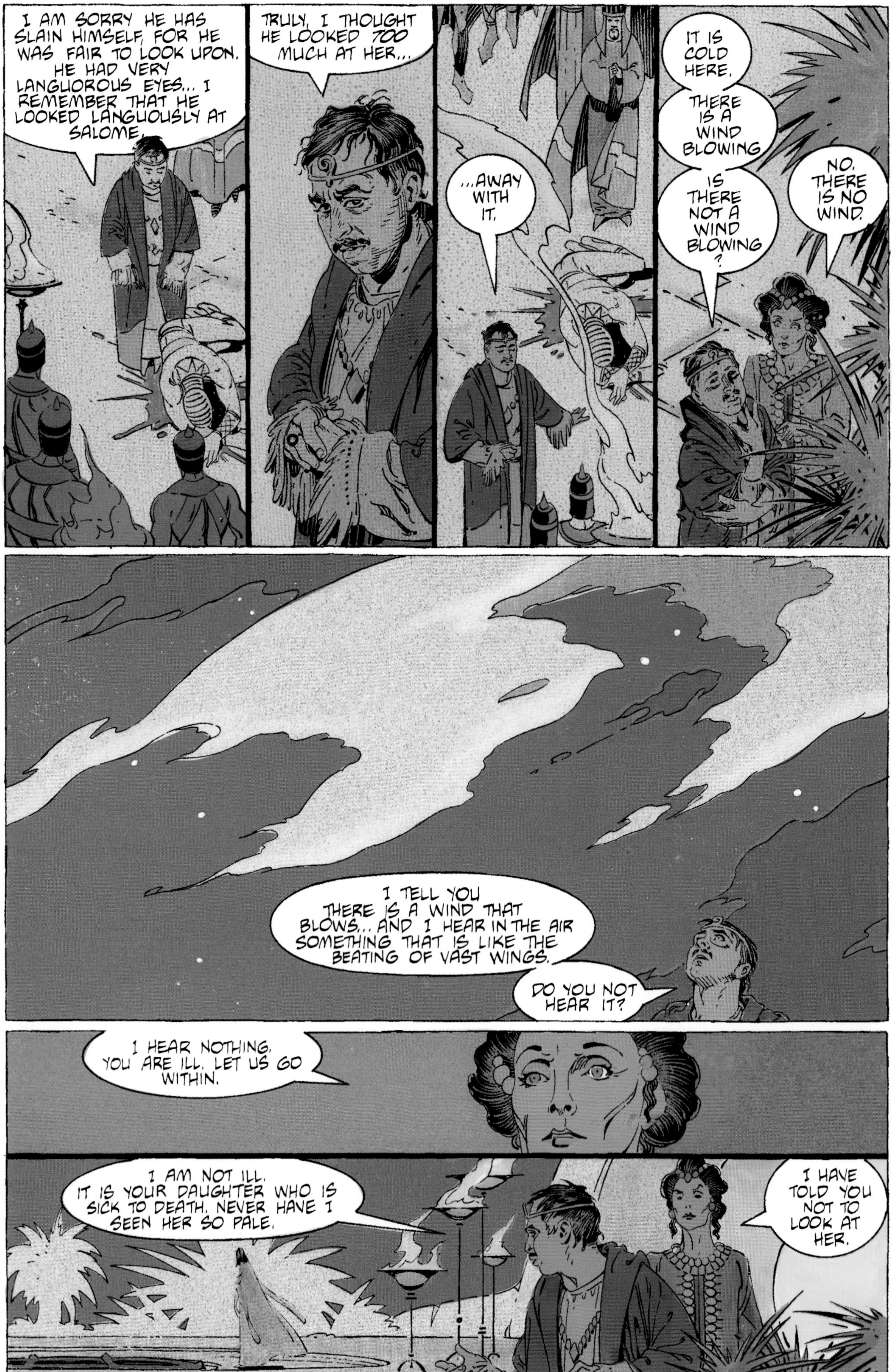
I AM SORRY HE HAS SLAIN HIMSELF, FOR HE WAS FAIR TO LOOK UPON. HE HAD VERY LANGUOROUS EYES... I REMEMBER THAT HE LOOKED LANGUOUSLY AT SALOME.
TRULY, I THOUGHT HE LOOKED TOO MUCH AT HER...
...AWAY WITH IT.
IT IS COLD HERE.
THERE IS A WIND BLOWING
IS THERE NOT A WIND BLOWING ?
NO. THERE IS NO WIND.
I TELL YOU THERE IS A WIND THAT BLOWS... AND I HEAR IN THE AIR SOMETHING THAT IS LIKE THE BEATING OF VAST WINGS.
DO YOU NOT HEAR IT?
I HEAR NOTHING. YOU ARE ILL. LET US GO WITHIN.
I AM NOT ILL. IT IS YOUR DAUGHTER WHO IS SICK TO DEATH. NEVER HAVE I SEEN HER SO PALE.
I HAVE TOLD YOU NOT TO LOOK AT HER.

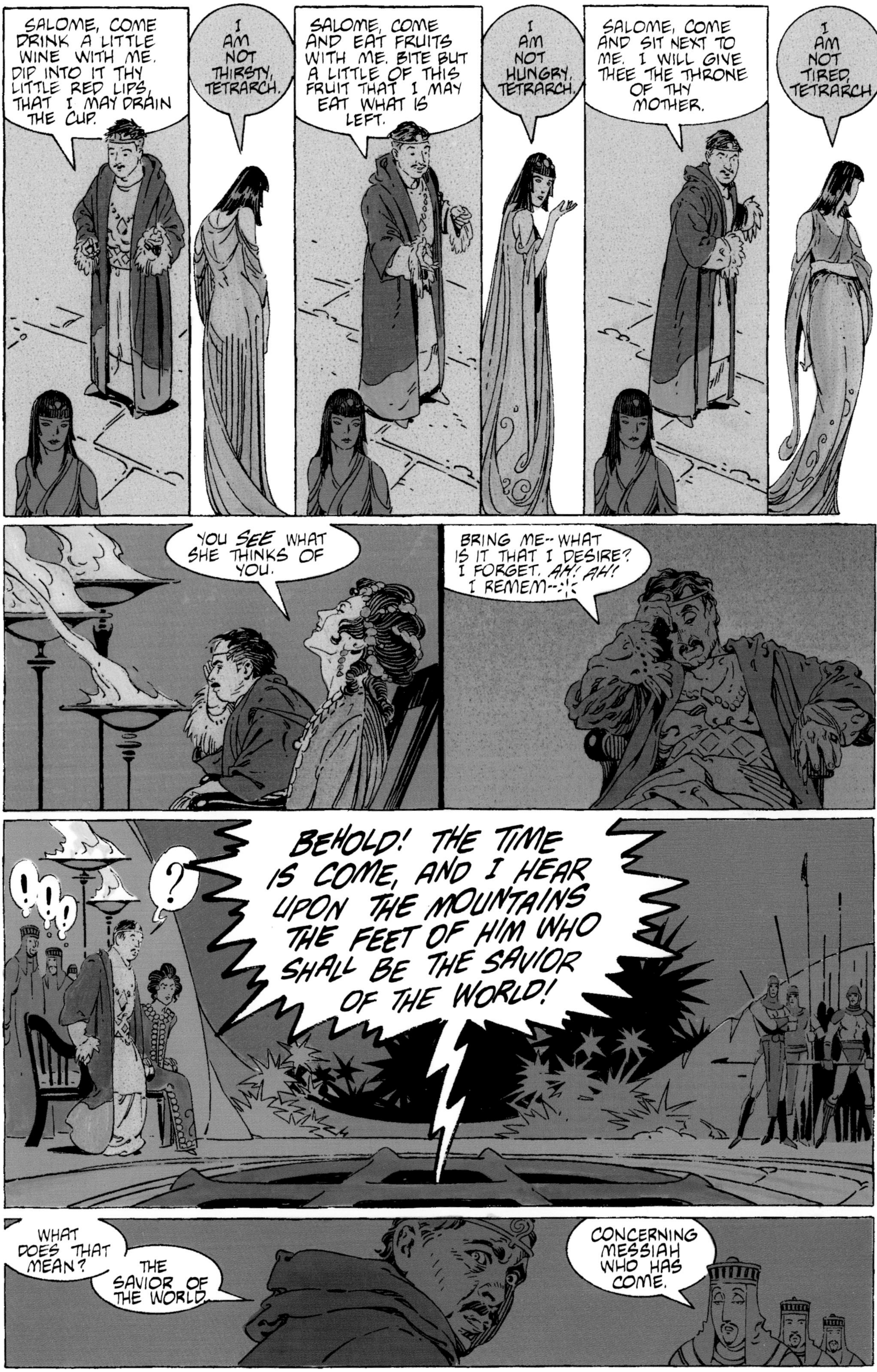
SALOME, COME DRINK A LITTLE WINE WITH ME. DIP INTO IT THY LITTLE RED LIPS, THAT I MAY DRAIN THE CUP.
I AM NOT THIRSTY, TETRARCH.
SALOME, COME AND EAT FRUITS WITH ME. BITE BUT A LITTLE OF THIS FRUIT THAT I MAY EAT WHAT IS LEFT.
I AM NOT HUNGRY, TETRARCH.
SALOME, COME AND SIT NEXT TO ME. I WILL GIVE THEE THE THRONE OF THY MOTHER.
I AM NOT TIRED, TETRARCH
YOU SEE WHAT SHE THINKS OF YOU.
BRING ME-- WHAT IS IT THAT I DESIRE? I FORGET. AH! AH! I REMEM--!
!!!
?
BEHOLD! THE TIME IS COME, AND I HEAR UPON THE MOUNTAINS THE FEET OF HIM WHO SHALL BE THE SAVIOR OF THE WORLD!
WHAT DOES THAT MEAN?
THE SAVIOR OF THE WORLD.
CONCERNING MESSIAH WHO HAS COME.

MESSIAH HATH *NOT* COME!

HE *HATH* COME, AND EVERYWHERE HE WORKETH MIRACLES. HE WAS SEEN ON A MOUNTAIN, TALKING WITH ANGELS, AND HE RAISED THE DAUGHTER OF JAIRUS FROM THE DEAD.

HO! HO! I DO NOT BELIEVE IN MIRACLES. I HAVE SEEN TOO MANY.

HE RAISES PEOPLE FROM THE DEAD?

I *FORBID* HIM TO DO *THAT!* IT WOULD BE *TERRIBLE* IF THE DEAD CAME BACK.

TRULY, MY LORD, IT WERE BETTER TO DELIVER HIM INTO OUR HANDS.

ENOUGH! I HAVE ALREADY GIVEN YOU MY ANSWER. I WILL NOT DELIVER HIM INTO YOUR HANDS. HE IS A HOLY MAN. HE IS A MAN WHO HAS SEEN GOD.

THAT CANNOT BE. THERE IS NO MAN WHO HATH SEEN GOD SINCE THE PROPHET ELIAS. GOD HIDETH HIMSELF.

VERILY, NO MAN KNOWETH IF ELIAS THE PROPHET DID INDEED SEE GOD.

GOD IS AT NO TIME HIDDEN.

HE SHOWETH HIMSELF IN EVERYTHING.

GOD IS IN WHAT IS EVIL, EVEN AS HE IS IN WHAT IS GOOD.

THOU SHOULDST NOT SAY THAT. IT IS A DOCTRINE THAT COMETH FROM THE GREEKS--AND THE GREEKS ARE GENTILES.

THEY ARE NOT EVEN CIRCUMCISED.

NO ONE CAN TELL HOW GOD WORKETH.

HIS WAYS ARE VERY DARK.

IT MAY BE THAT THE THINGS WE CALL EVIL ARE GOOD...

NAY...NAY THERE IS NO KNOWLEDGE OF ANYTHING.

GOD IS TERRIBLE BUT FOR MAN, HE HATH NEVER SEEN GOD.

NO MAN SINCE THE PROPHET ELIAS...

IS TOO

HE IS

IS NOT

I HAVE HEARD IT SAID THAT JOKANAAN *HIMSELF* IS THE PROPHET ELIAS...

I AM SURE HE IS THE PROPHET ELIAS...

THAT CANNOT BE. IT IS MORE THAN THREE HUNDRED YEARS...

NAY, BUT HE IS NOT THE PROPHET ELIAS!

SO YOU

WHO

ISN'T HE?

MAKE THEM BE SILENT. THEY WEARY ME.

AH! THE WANTON ONE! THE HARLOT! THUS SAITH THE LORD GOD!

COMMAND HIM TO BE SILENT! HE IS FOREVER VOMITING INSULTS AT ME!

LET THE PEOPLE TAKE STONES AND STONE HER...

NAY, BUT IT IS INFAMOUS.

...LET THE CAPTAINS OF THE HOSTS CRUSH HER BENEATH THEIR SHIELDS.

YOU HEAR WHAT HE SAYS AGAINST ME?

IT IS THUS THAT I SHALL WIPE OUT ALL WICKEDNESS FROM THE EARTH, AND THAT ALL WOMEN SHALL LEARN NOT TO IMITATE HER ABOMINATIONS!

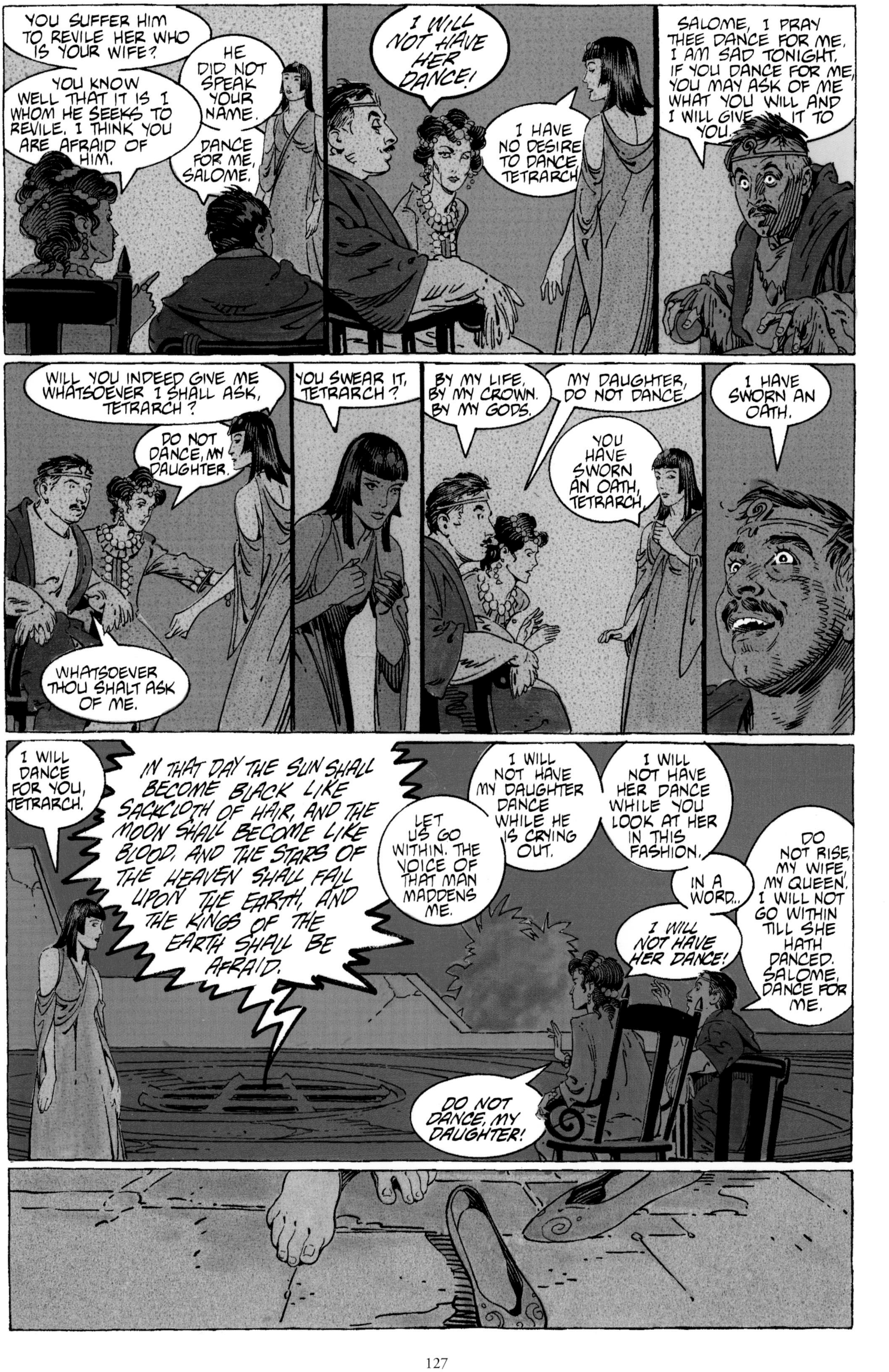
YOU SUFFER HIM TO REVILE HER WHO IS YOUR WIFE?
YOU KNOW WELL THAT IT IS I WHOM HE SEEKS TO REVILE. I THINK YOU ARE AFRAID OF HIM.
HE DID NOT SPEAK YOUR NAME.
DANCE FOR ME, SALOME.
I WILL NOT HAVE HER DANCE!
I HAVE NO DESIRE TO DANCE TETRARCH
SALOME, I PRAY THEE DANCE FOR ME, I AM SAD TONIGHT. IF YOU DANCE FOR ME, YOU MAY ASK OF ME WHAT YOU WILL AND I WILL GIVE IT TO YOU.
WILL YOU INDEED GIVE ME WHATSOEVER I SHALL ASK, TETRARCH?
DO NOT DANCE, MY DAUGHTER.
WHATSOEVER THOU SHALT ASK OF ME.
YOU SWEAR IT, TETRARCH?
BY MY LIFE, BY MY CROWN. BY MY GODS.
MY DAUGHTER, DO NOT DANCE.
YOU HAVE SWORN AN OATH, TETRARCH.
I HAVE SWORN AN OATH.
I WILL DANCE FOR YOU, TETRARCH.
IN THAT DAY THE SUN SHALL BECOME BLACK LIKE SACKCLOTH OF HAIR, AND THE MOON SHALL BECOME LIKE BLOOD, AND THE STARS OF THE HEAVEN SHALL FALL UPON THE EARTH, AND THE KINGS OF THE EARTH SHALL BE AFRAID.
LET US GO WITHIN. THE VOICE OF THAT MAN MADDENS ME.
I WILL NOT HAVE MY DAUGHTER DANCE WHILE HE IS CRYING OUT.
I WILL NOT HAVE HER DANCE WHILE YOU LOOK AT HER IN THIS FASHION.
IN A WORD...
I WILL NOT HAVE HER DANCE!
DO NOT RISE, MY WIFE, MY QUEEN, I WILL NOT GO WITHIN TILL SHE HATH DANCED. SALOME, DANCE FOR ME.
DO NOT DANCE, MY DAUGHTER!

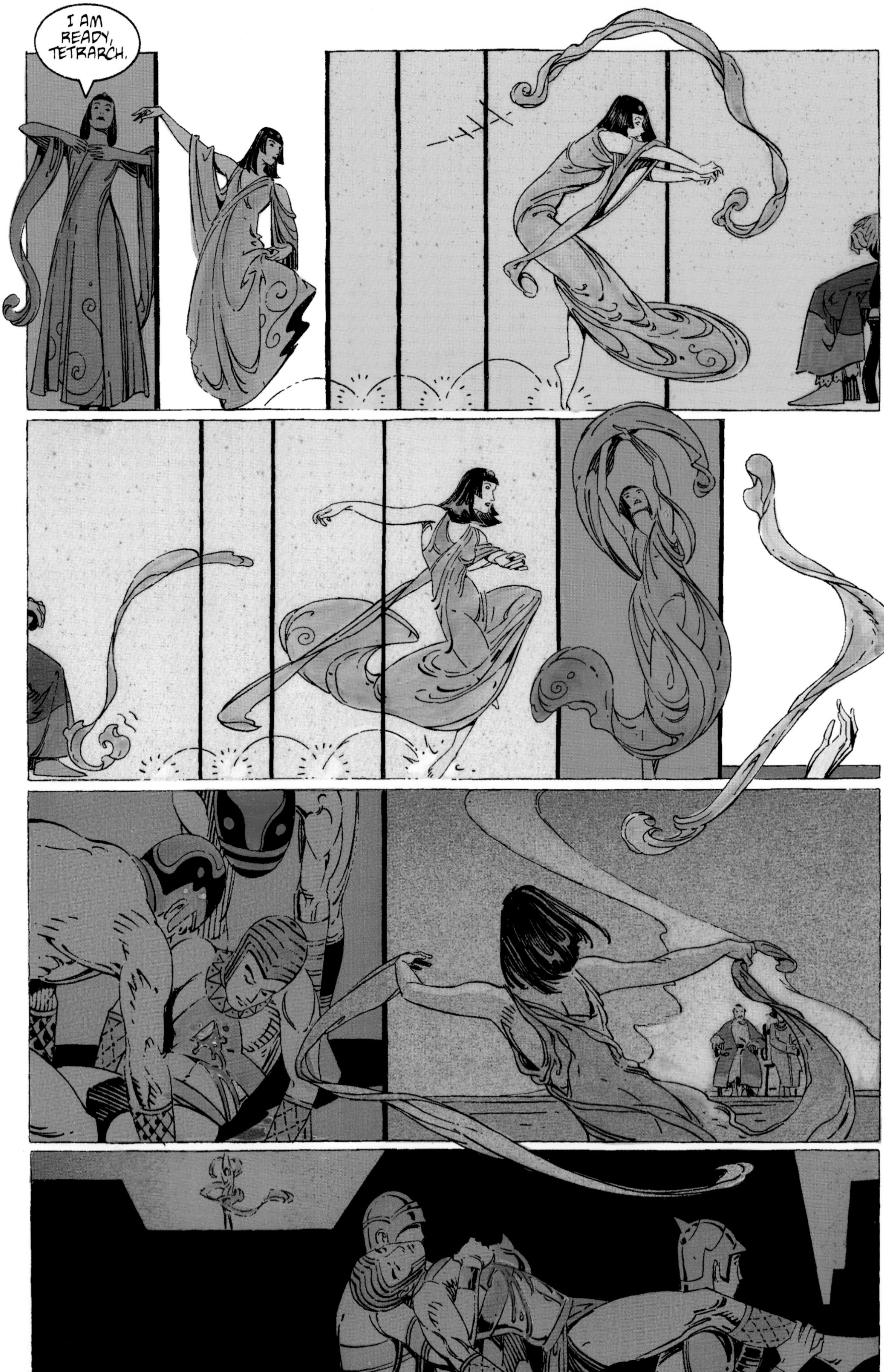
I AM READY, TETRARCH.

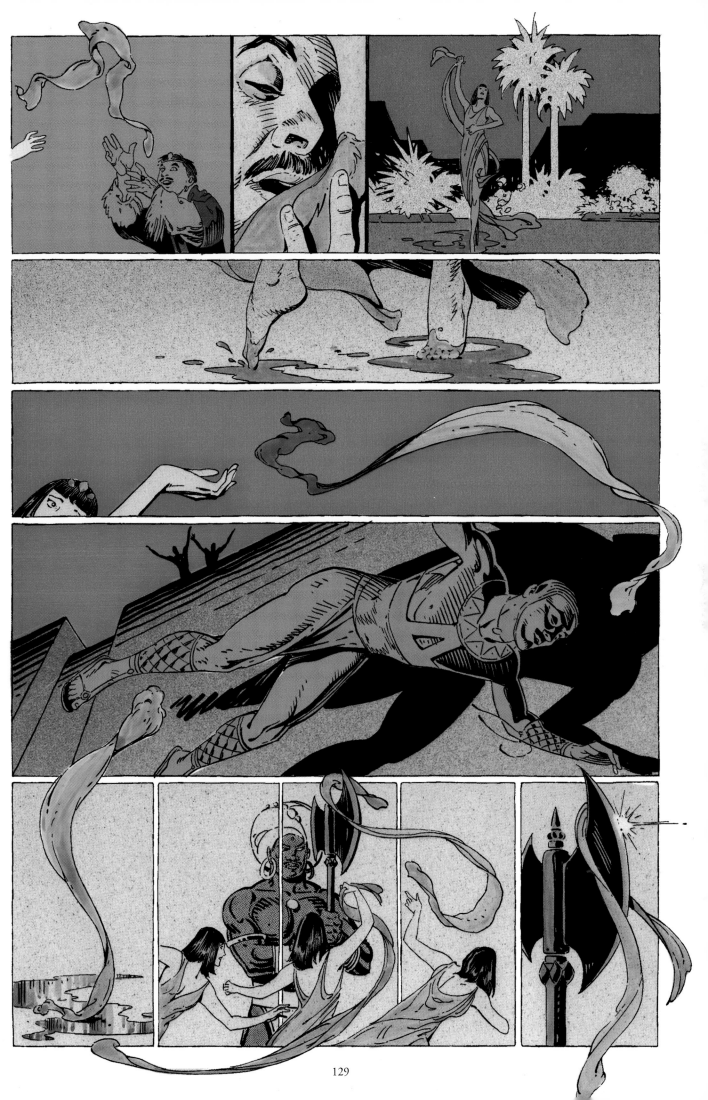

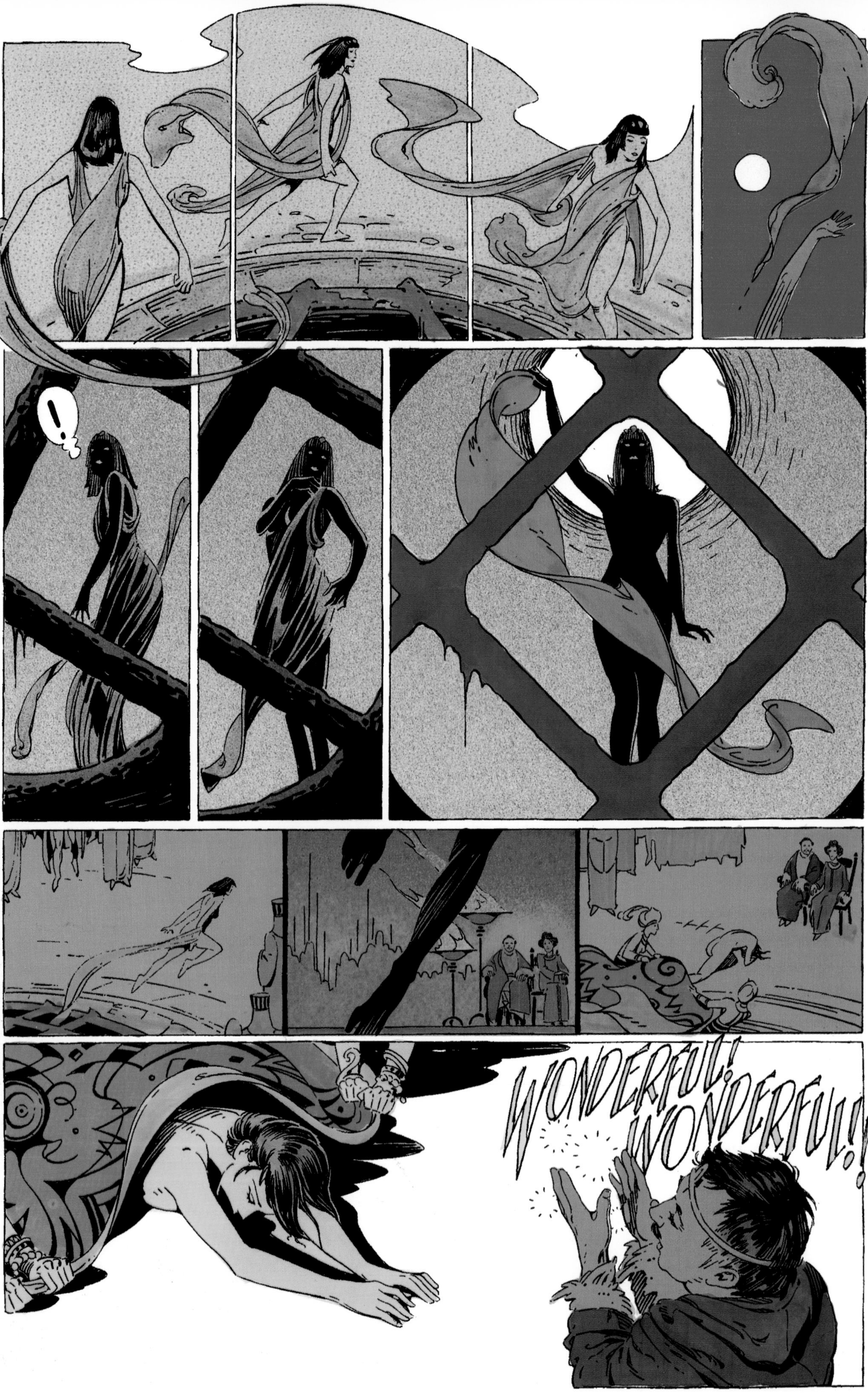
!
WONDERFUL! WONDERFUL!!

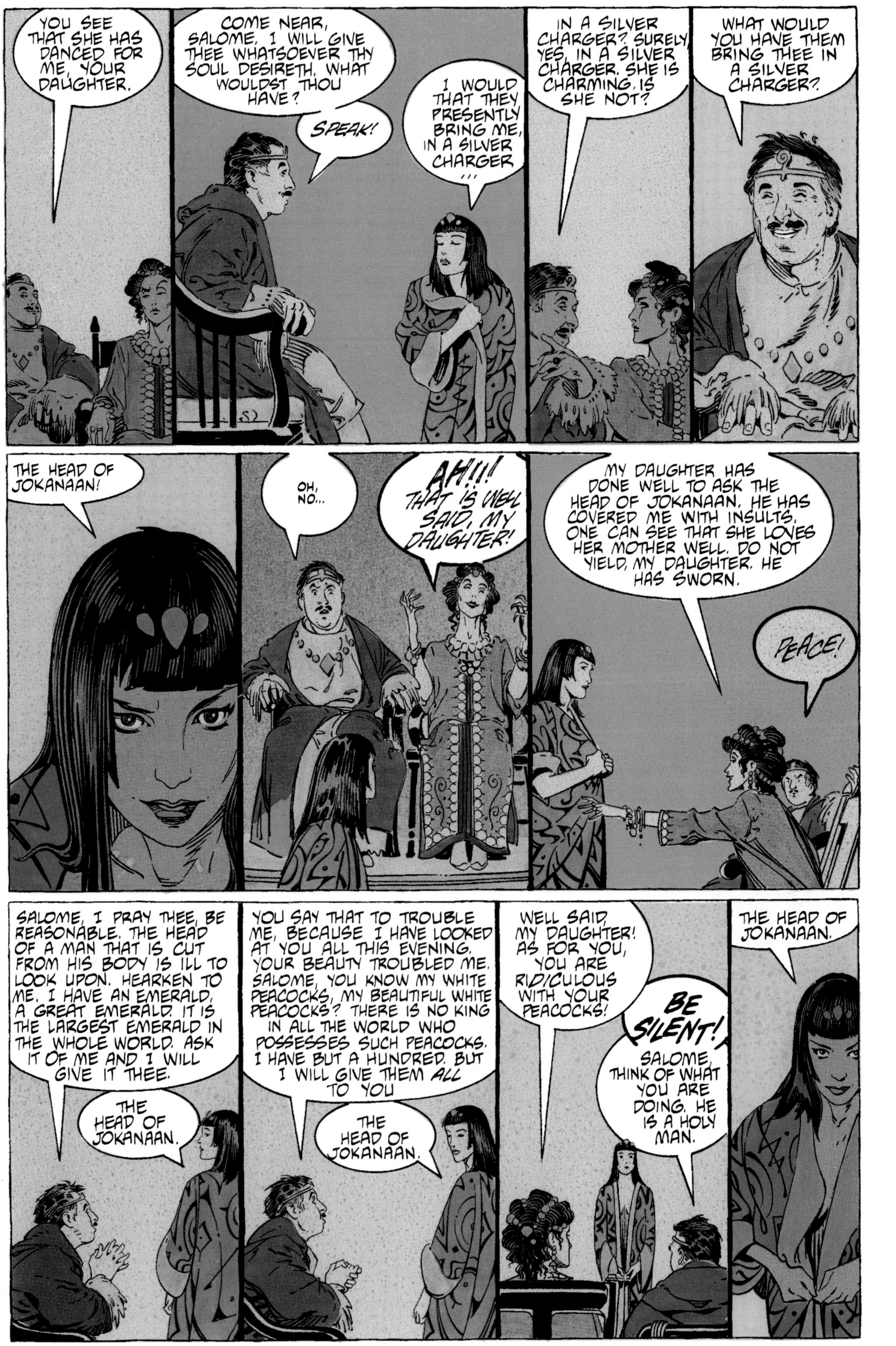
YOU SEE THAT SHE HAS DANCED FOR ME, YOUR DAUGHTER.
COME NEAR, SALOME. I WILL GIVE THEE WHATSOEVER THY SOUL DESIRETH. WHAT WOULDST THOU HAVE?
SPEAK!
I WOULD THAT THEY PRESENTLY BRING ME, IN A SILVER CHARGER ...
IN A SILVER CHARGER? SURELY, YES, IN A SILVER CHARGER. SHE IS CHARMING, IS SHE NOT?
WHAT WOULD YOU HAVE THEM BRING THEE IN A SILVER CHARGER?
THE HEAD OF JOKANAAN!
OH, NO...
AH!!! THAT IS WELL SAID, MY DAUGHTER!
MY DAUGHTER HAS DONE WELL TO ASK THE HEAD OF JOKANAAN. HE HAS COVERED ME WITH INSULTS. ONE CAN SEE THAT SHE LOVES HER MOTHER WELL. DO NOT YIELD, MY DAUGHTER. HE HAS SWORN.
PEACE!
SALOME, I PRAY THEE, BE REASONABLE. THE HEAD OF A MAN THAT IS CUT FROM HIS BODY IS ILL TO LOOK UPON. HEARKEN TO ME. I HAVE AN EMERALD, A GREAT EMERALD. IT IS THE LARGEST EMERALD IN THE WHOLE WORLD. ASK IT OF ME AND I WILL GIVE IT THEE.
THE HEAD OF JOKANAAN.
YOU SAY THAT TO TROUBLE ME, BECAUSE I HAVE LOOKED AT YOU ALL THIS EVENING. YOUR BEAUTY TROUBLED ME. SALOME, YOU KNOW MY WHITE PEACOCKS, MY BEAUTIFUL WHITE PEACOCKS? THERE IS NO KING IN ALL THE WORLD WHO POSSESSES SUCH PEACOCKS. I HAVE BUT A HUNDRED. BUT I WILL GIVE THEM ALL TO YOU
THE HEAD OF JOKANAAN.
WELL SAID, MY DAUGHTER! AS FOR YOU, YOU ARE RIDICULOUS WITH YOUR PEACOCKS!
BE SILENT!
SALOME, THINK OF WHAT YOU ARE DOING. HE IS A HOLY MAN.
THE HEAD OF JOKANAAN.

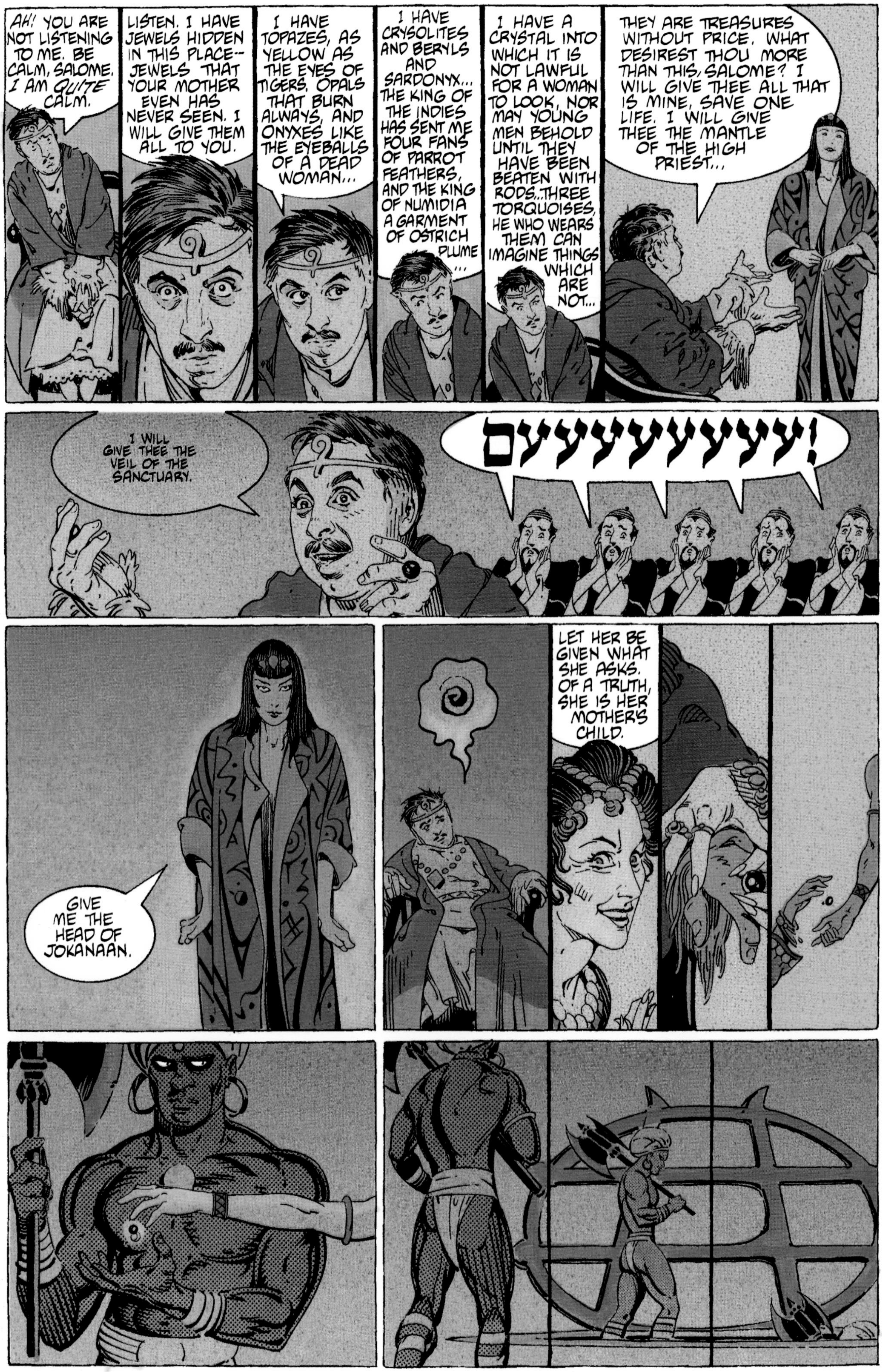
AH! YOU ARE NOT LISTENING TO ME. BE CALM, SALOME. I AM QUITE CALM.
LISTEN. I HAVE JEWELS HIDDEN IN THIS PLACE-- JEWELS THAT YOUR MOTHER EVEN HAS NEVER SEEN. I WILL GIVE THEM ALL TO YOU.
I HAVE TOPAZES, AS YELLOW AS THE EYES OF TIGERS, OPALS THAT BURN ALWAYS, AND ONYXES LIKE THE EYEBALLS OF A DEAD WOMAN...
I HAVE CRYSOLITES AND BERYLS AND SARDONYX... THE KING OF THE INDIES HAS SENT ME FOUR FANS OF PARROT FEATHERS, AND THE KING OF NUMIDIA A GARMENT OF OSTRICH PLUME...
I HAVE A CRYSTAL INTO WHICH IT IS NOT LAWFUL FOR A WOMAN TO LOOK, NOR MAY YOUNG MEN BEHOLD UNTIL THEY HAVE BEEN BEATEN WITH RODS... THREE TORQUOISES, HE WHO WEARS THEM CAN IMAGINE THINGS WHICH ARE NOT...
THEY ARE TREASURES WITHOUT PRICE. WHAT DESIREST THOU MORE THAN THIS, SALOME? I WILL GIVE THEE ALL THAT IS MINE, SAVE ONE LIFE. I WILL GIVE THEE THE MANTLE OF THE HIGH PRIEST...
I WILL GIVE THEE THE VEIL OF THE SANCTUARY.
OYYYYYYY!
GIVE ME THE HEAD OF JOKANAAN.
LET HER BE GIVEN WHAT SHE ASKS. OF A TRUTH, SHE IS HER MOTHER'S CHILD.

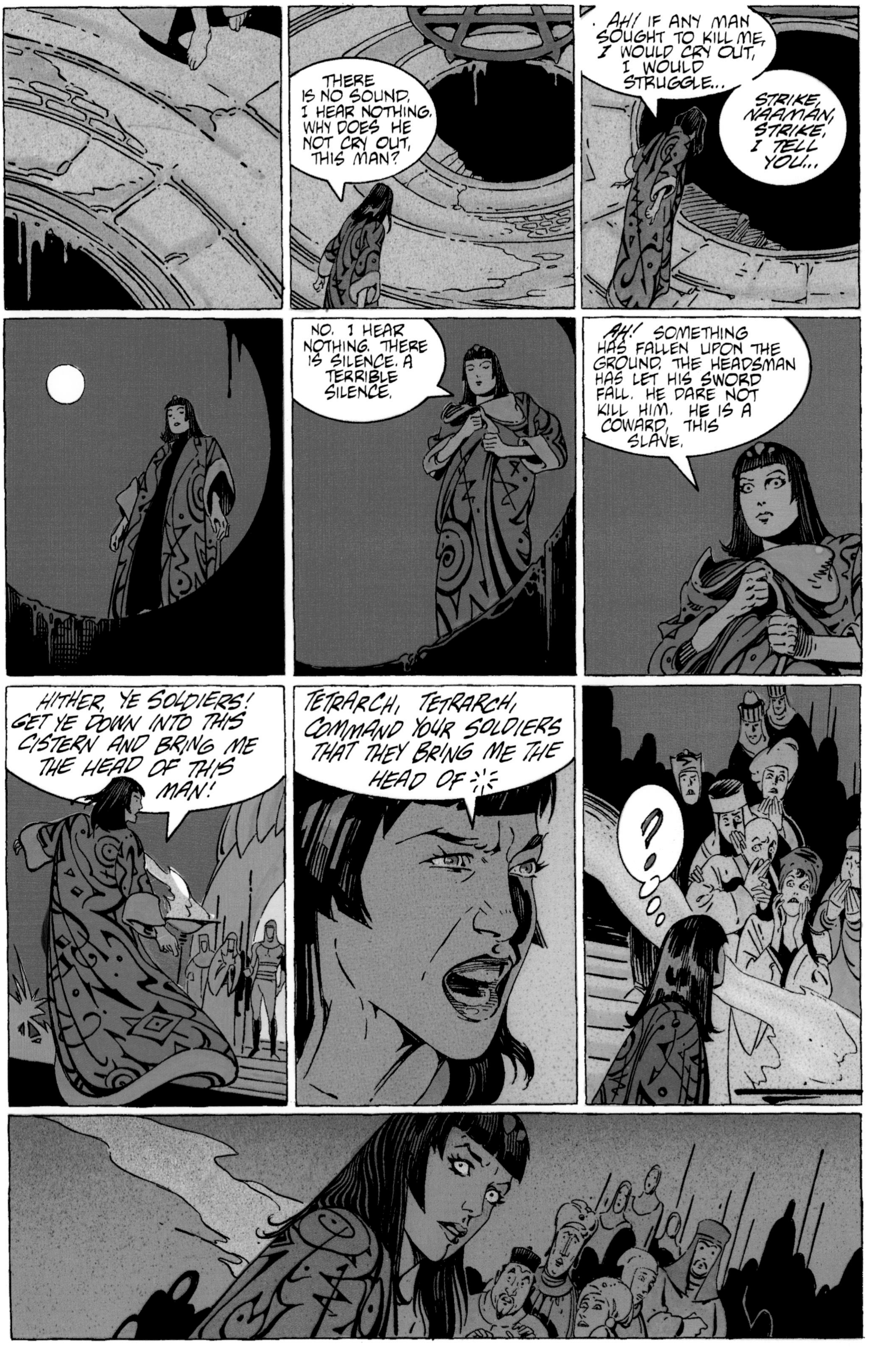
THERE IS NO SOUND, I HEAR NOTHING. WHY DOES HE NOT CRY OUT, THIS MAN?
AH! IF ANY MAN SOUGHT TO KILL ME, I WOULD CRY OUT, I WOULD STRUGGLE...
STRIKE, NAAMAN, STRIKE, I TELL YOU...
NO. I HEAR NOTHING. THERE IS SILENCE. A TERRIBLE SILENCE.
AH! SOMETHING HAS FALLEN UPON THE GROUND. THE HEADSMAN HAS LET HIS SWORD FALL. HE DARE NOT KILL HIM. HE IS A COWARD, THIS SLAVE.
HITHER, YE SOLDIERS! GET YE DOWN INTO THIS CISTERN AND BRING ME THE HEAD OF THIS MAN!
TETRARCH, TETRARCH, COMMAND YOUR SOLDIERS THAT THEY BRING ME THE HEAD OF
?

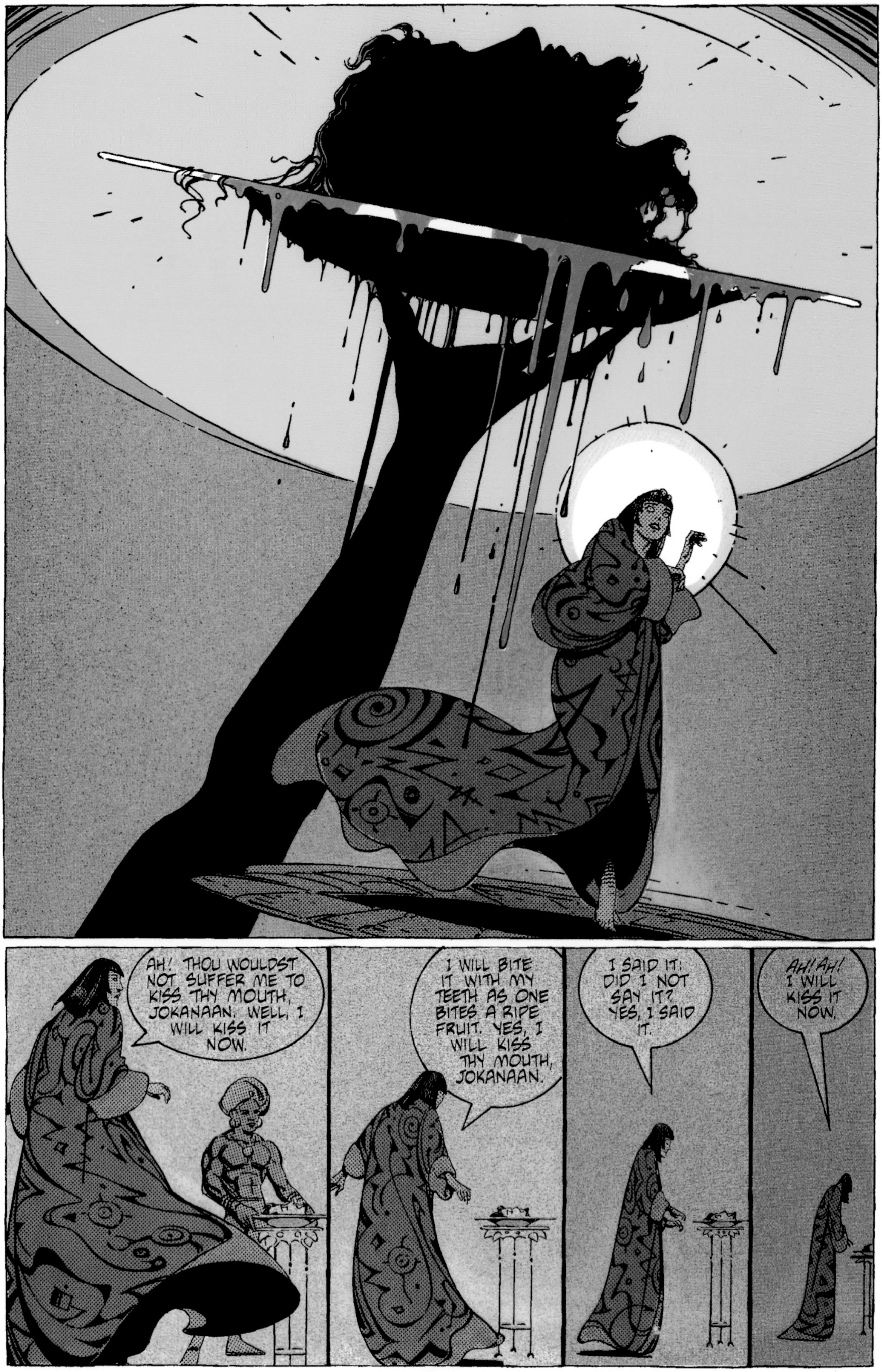
AH! THOU WOULDST NOT SUFFER ME TO KISS THY MOUTH, JOKANAAN. WELL, I WILL KISS IT NOW.
I WILL BITE IT WITH MY TEETH AS ONE BITES A RIPE FRUIT. YES, I WILL KISS THY MOUTH, JOKANAAN.
I SAID IT; DID I NOT SAY IT? YES, I SAID IT.
AH! AH! I WILL KISS IT NOW.

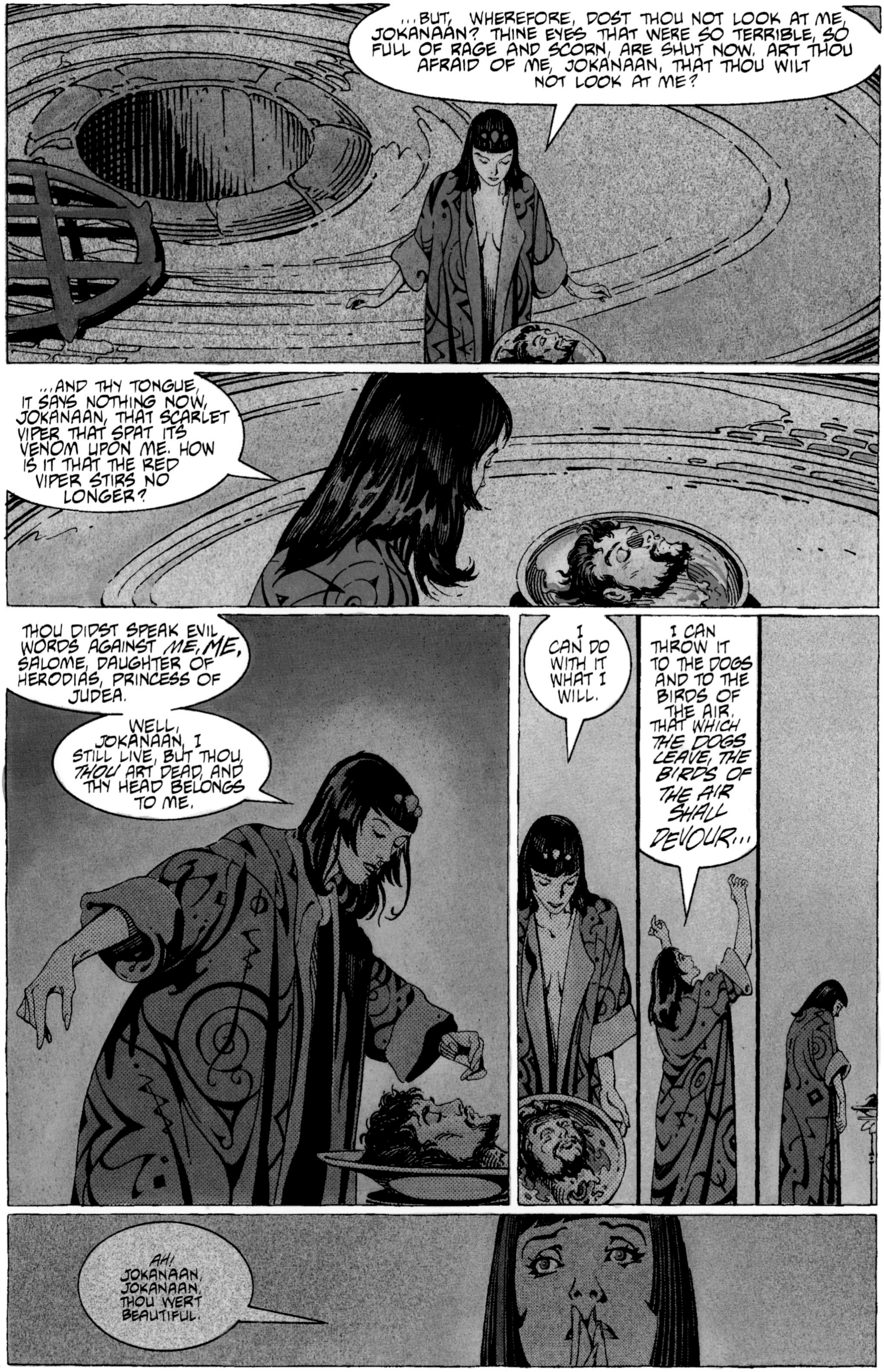
...BUT, WHEREFORE, DOST THOU NOT LOOK AT ME, JOKANAAN? THINE EYES THAT WERE SO TERRIBLE, SO FULL OF RAGE AND SCORN, ARE SHUT NOW. ART THOU AFRAID OF ME, JOKANAAN, THAT THOU WILT NOT LOOK AT ME?
...AND THY TONGUE, IT SAYS NOTHING NOW, JOKANAAN, THAT SCARLET VIPER THAT SPAT ITS VENOM UPON ME. HOW IS IT THAT THE RED VIPER STIRS NO LONGER?
THOU DIDST SPEAK EVIL WORDS AGAINST ME, ME, SALOME, DAUGHTER OF HERODIAS, PRINCESS OF JUDEA.
WELL, JOKANAAN, I STILL LIVE, BUT THOU, THOU ART DEAD, AND THY HEAD BELONGS TO ME.
I CAN DO WITH IT WHAT I WILL.
I CAN THROW IT TO THE DOGS AND TO THE BIRDS OF THE AIR. THAT WHICH THE DOGS LEAVE, THE BIRDS OF THE AIR SHALL DEVOUR...
AH! JOKANAAN, JOKANAAN, THOU WERT BEAUTIFUL.

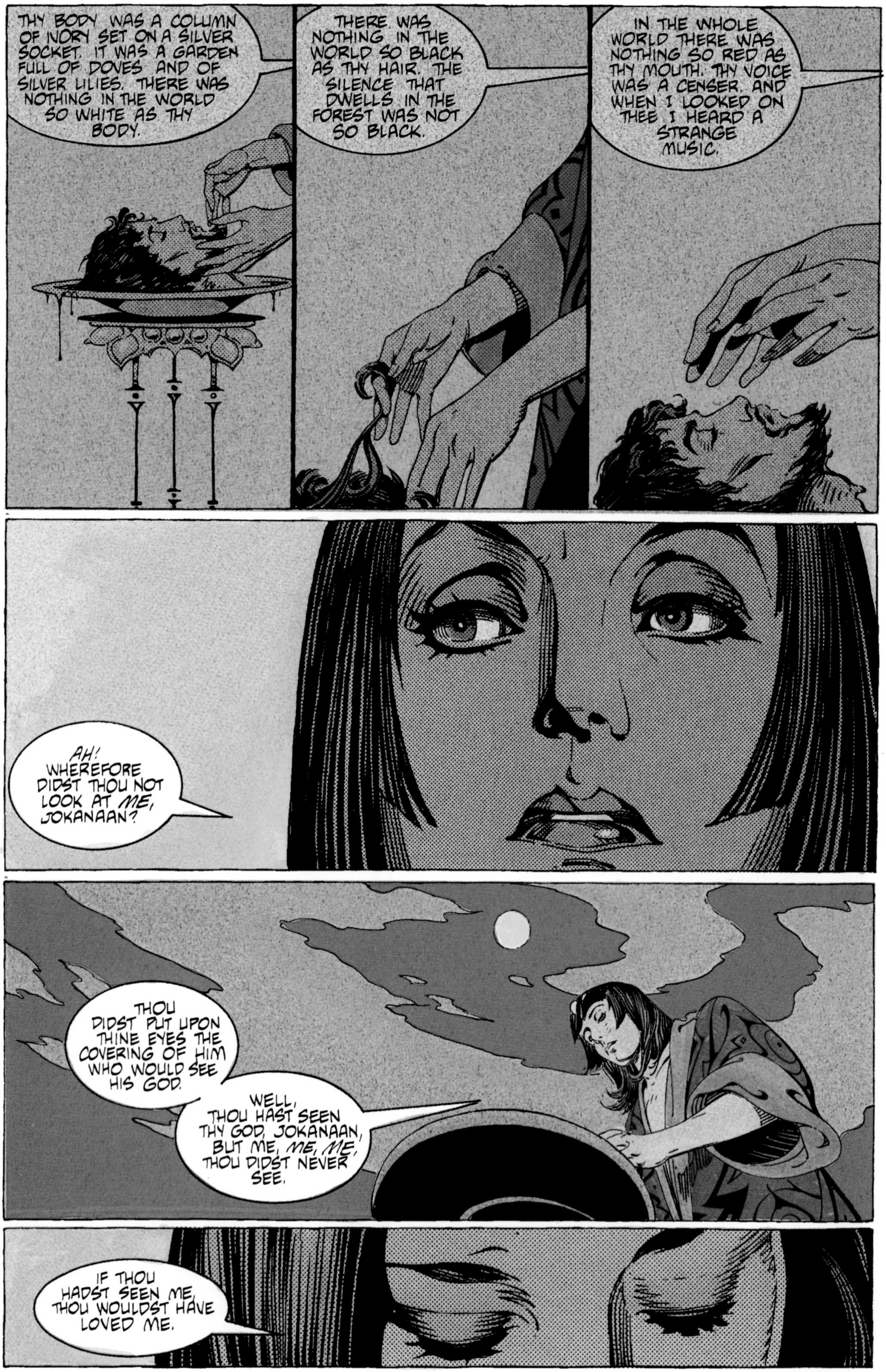
THY BODY WAS A COLUMN OF IVORY SET ON A SILVER SOCKET. IT WAS A GARDEN FULL OF DOVES AND OF SILVER LILIES. THERE WAS NOTHING IN THE WORLD SO WHITE AS THY BODY.
THERE WAS NOTHING IN THE WORLD SO BLACK AS THY HAIR. THE SILENCE THAT DWELLS IN THE FOREST WAS NOT SO BLACK.
IN THE WHOLE WORLD THERE WAS NOTHING SO RED AS THY MOUTH. THY VOICE WAS A CENSER. AND WHEN I LOOKED ON THEE I HEARD A STRANGE MUSIC.
AH! WHEREFORE DIDST THOU NOT LOOK AT ME, JOKANAAN?
THOU DIDST PUT UPON THINE EYES THE COVERING OF HIM WHO WOULD SEE HIS GOD.
WELL, THOU HAST SEEN THY GOD, JOKANAAN, BUT ME, ME, ME, THOU DIDST NEVER SEE.
IF THOU HADST SEEN ME, THOU WOULDST HAVE LOVED ME.

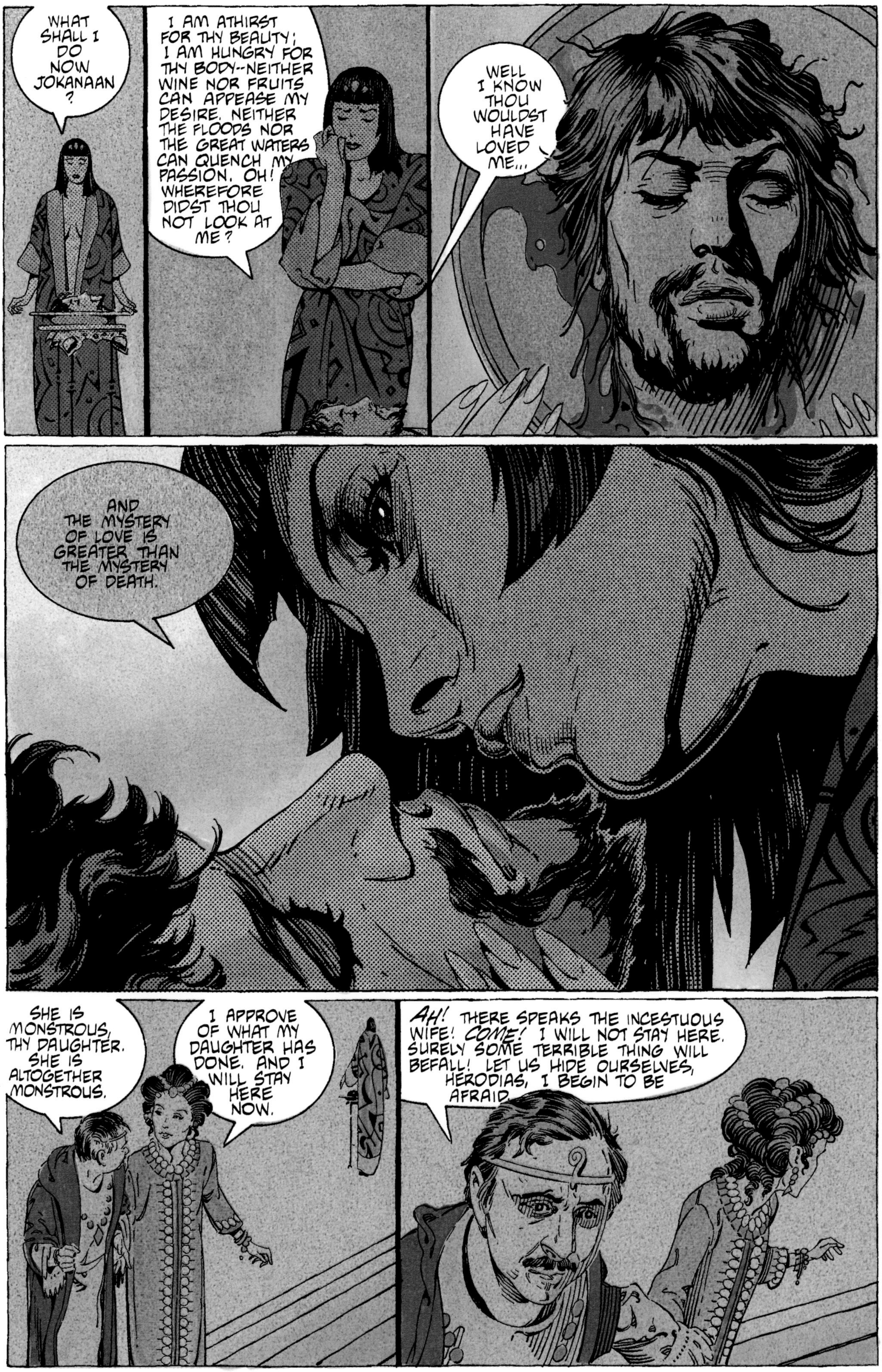

WHAT SHALL I DO NOW JOKANAAN?
I AM ATHIRST FOR THY BEAUTY; I AM HUNGRY FOR THY BODY--NEITHER WINE NOR FRUITS CAN APPEASE MY DESIRE. NEITHER THE FLOODS NOR THE GREAT WATERS CAN QUENCH MY PASSION. OH! WHEREFORE DIDST THOU NOT LOOK AT ME?
WELL I KNOW THOU WOULDST HAVE LOVED ME...
AND THE MYSTERY OF LOVE IS GREATER THAN THE MYSTERY OF DEATH.
SHE IS MONSTROUS, THY DAUGHTER. SHE IS ALTOGETHER MONSTROUS.
I APPROVE OF WHAT MY DAUGHTER HAS DONE. AND I WILL STAY HERE NOW.
AH! THERE SPEAKS THE INCESTUOUS WIFE! COME! I WILL NOT STAY HERE. SURELY SOME TERRIBLE THING WILL BEFALL! LET US HIDE OURSELVES, HERODIAS, I BEGIN TO BE AFRAID.

MANNESSAH, ISSACHAR, OZIAS, PUT OUT THE TORCHES. HIDE THE MOON! HIDE THE STARS! SOME TERRIBLE THING WILL BEFALL!

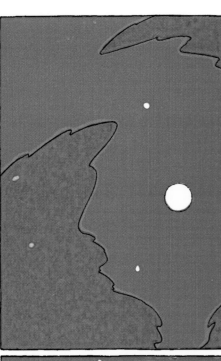

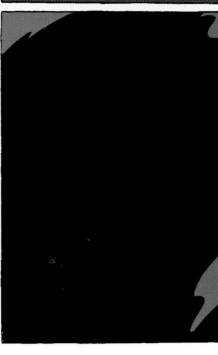

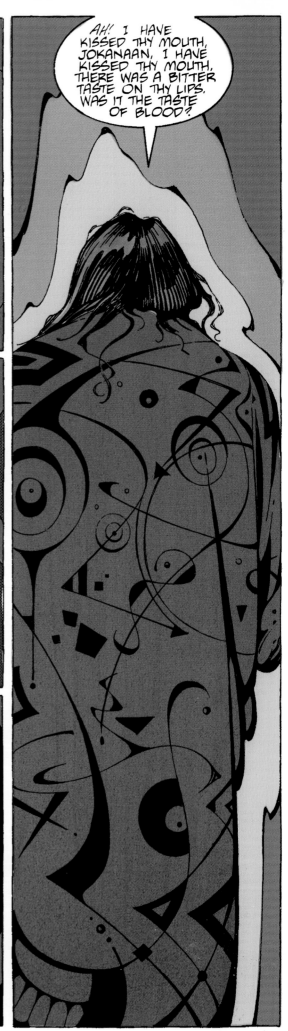

AH! I HAVE KISSED THY MOUTH, JOKANAAN, I HAVE KISSED THY MOUTH, THERE WAS A BITTER TASTE ON THY LIPS. WAS IT THE TASTE OF BLOOD?

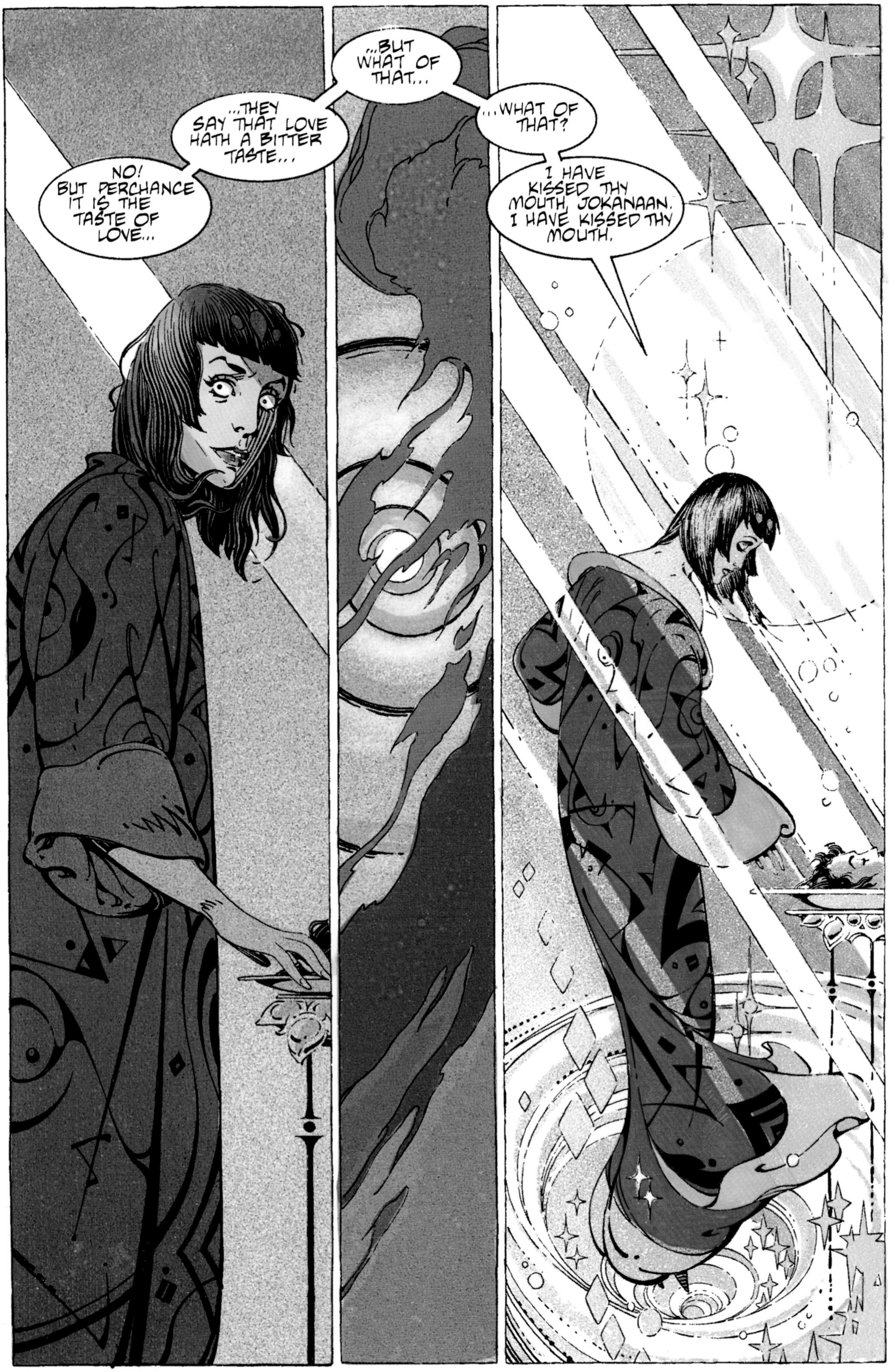
NO! BUT PERCHANCE IT IS THE TASTE OF LOVE...
...THEY SAY THAT LOVE HATH A BITTER TASTE...
...BUT WHAT OF THAT...
...WHAT OF THAT?
I HAVE KISSED THY MOUTH, JOKANAAN. I HAVE KISSED THY MOUTH.

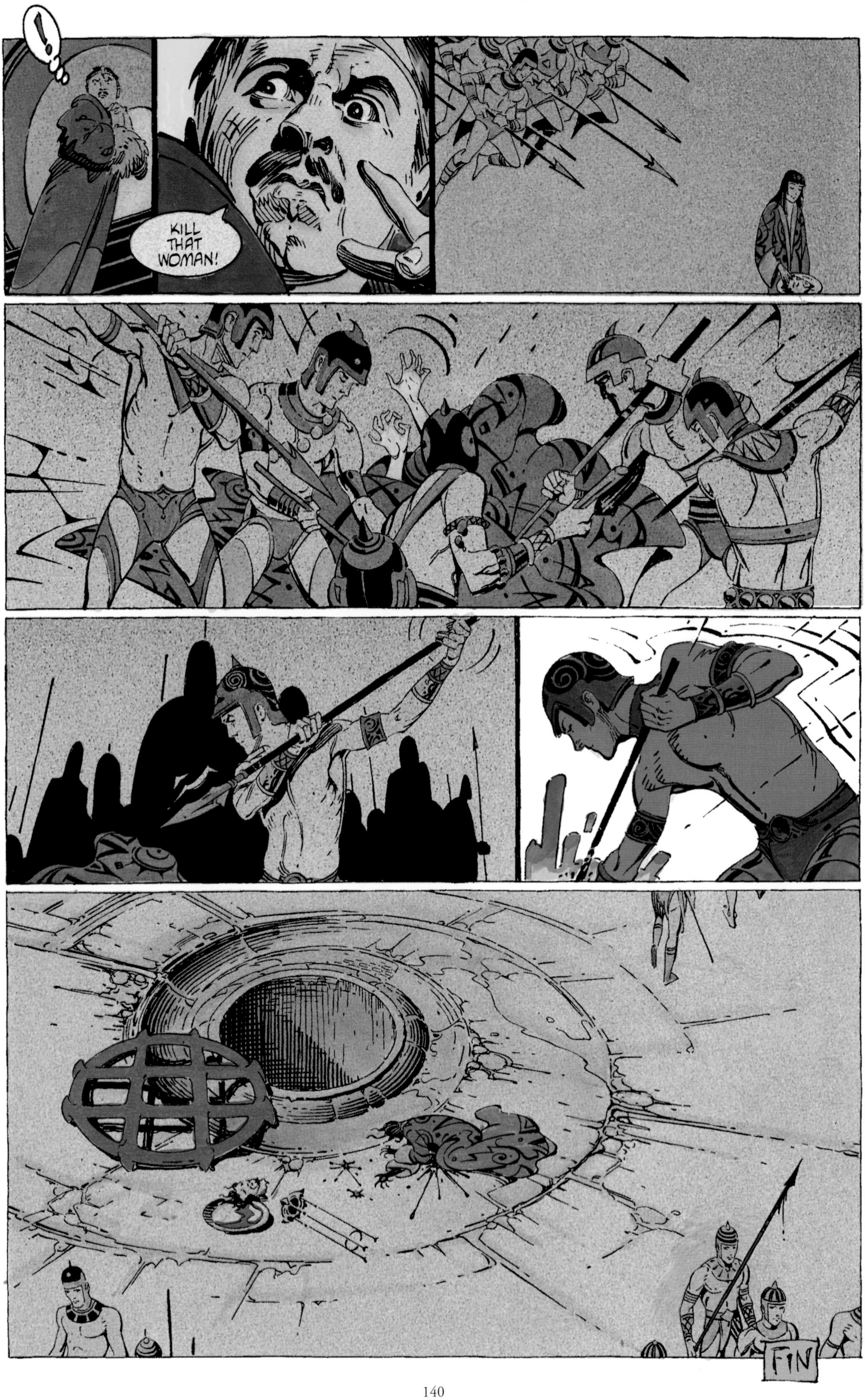
!
KILL THAT WOMAN!
FIN

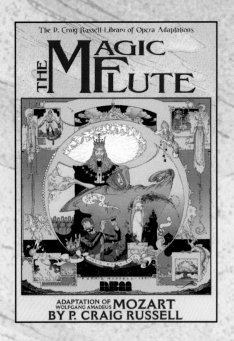

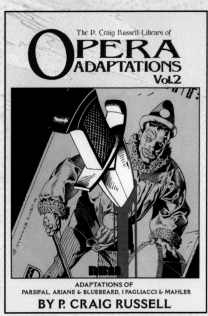

The P. Craig Russell Library of Opera Adaptations
THE MAGIC FLUTE
ADAPTATION OF WOLFGANG AMADEUS MOZART
BY P. CRAIG RUSSELL

The P. Craig Russell Library of
OPERA ADAPTATIONS
Vol.2
ADAPTATIONS OF
PARSIFAL, ARIANE & BLUEBEARD, I PAGLIACCI & MAHLER
BY P. CRAIG RUSSELL

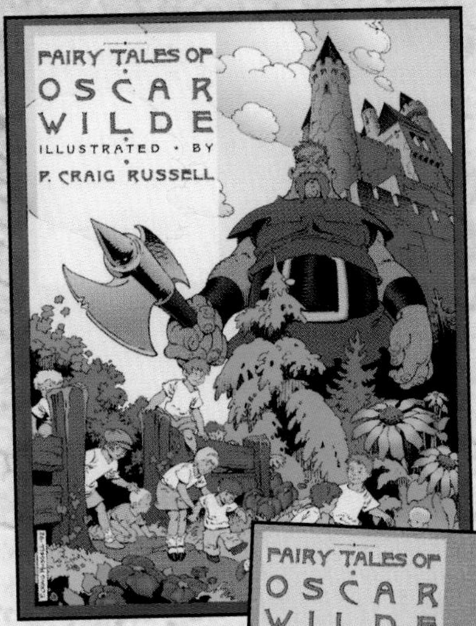
FAIRY TALES OF
OSCAR
WILDE
ILLUSTRATED • BY
P. CRAIG RUSSELL

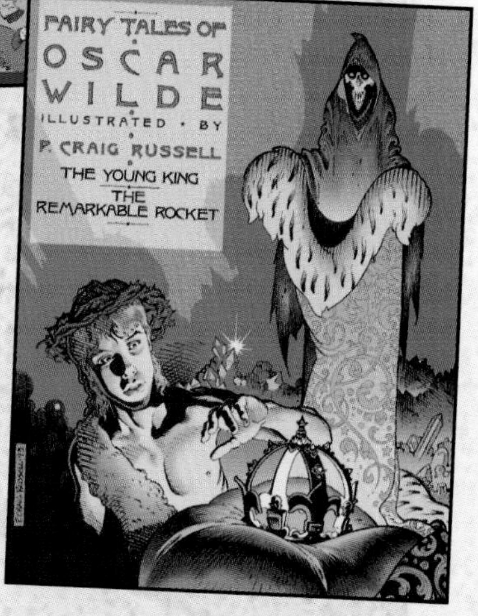
FAIRY TALES OF
OSCAR
WILDE
ILLUSTRATED • BY
P. CRAIG RUSSELL
THE YOUNG KING
THE
REMARKABLE ROCKET

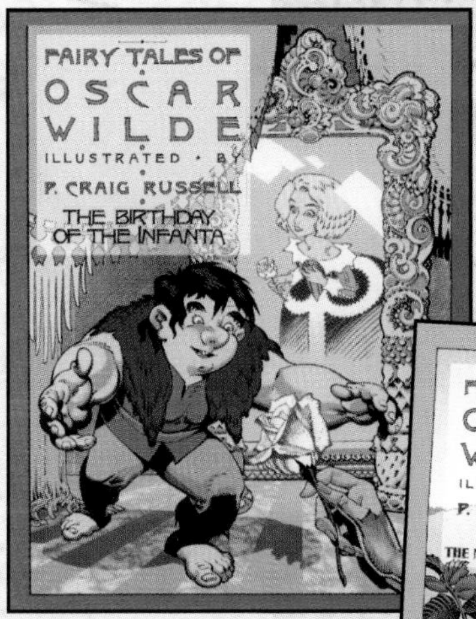
FAIRY TALES OF
OSCAR
WILDE
ILLUSTRATED • BY
P. CRAIG RUSSELL
THE BIRTHDAY
OF THE INFANTA

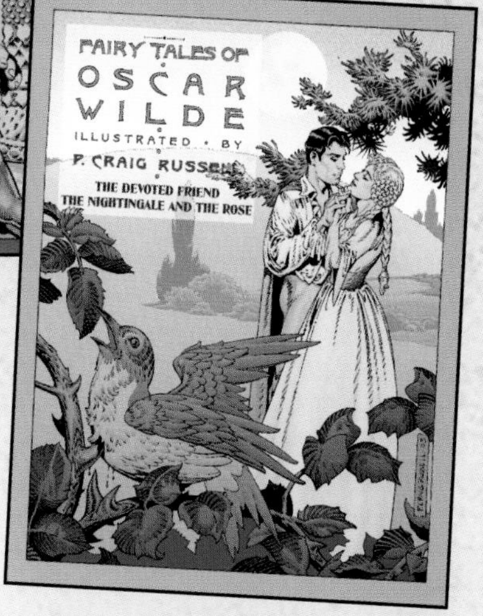
FAIRY TALES OF
OSCAR
WILDE
ILLUSTRATED • BY
P. CRAIG RUSSELL
THE DEVOTED FRIEND
THE NIGHTINGALE AND THE ROSE

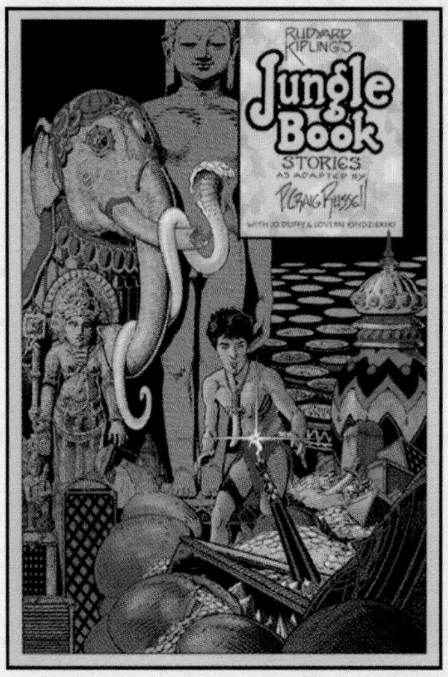
RUDYARD KIPLING'S
Jungle Book
STORIES
AS ADAPTED BY
P. CRAIG RUSSELL

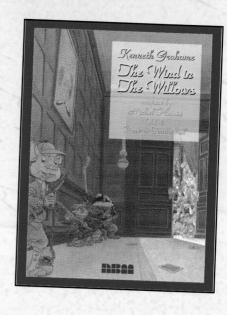

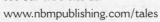

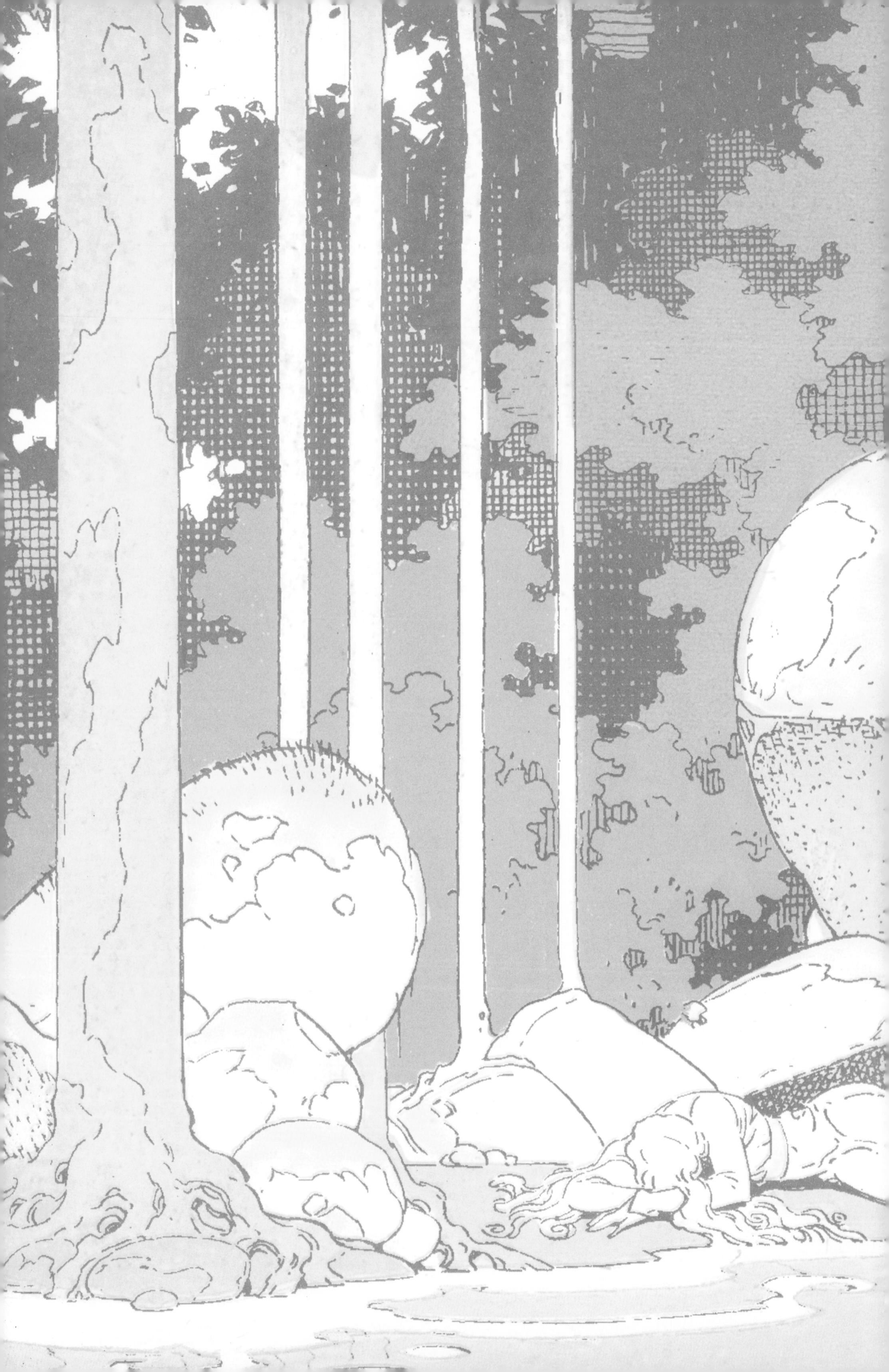